The Formation of the UAE

The Formation of the UAE

State-Building and Arab Nationalism in the Middle East

Kristi Barnwell

I.B. TAURIS
LONDON • NEW YORK • OXFORD • NEW DELHI • SYDNEY

I.B. TAURIS
Bloomsbury Publishing Plc, 50 Bedford Square, London, WC1B 3DP, UK
Bloomsbury Publishing Inc, 1359 Broadway, 12th Floor, New York, NY 10018, USA
Bloomsbury Publishing Ireland, 29 Earlsfort Terrace, Dublin 2, D02 AY28, Ireland

BLOOMSBURY, I.B. TAURIS and the I.B. Tauris logo
are trademarks of Bloomsbury Publishing Plc

First published in Great Britain 2024
This paperback edition published 2025

Copyright © Kristi Barnwell, 2024

Kristi Barnwell has asserted her rights under the Copyright,
Designs and Patents Act, 1988, to be identified as Author of this work.

For legal purposes the Acknowledgements on pp. vii–viii constitute
an extension of this copyright page.

Cover design: Adriana Brioso
Cover image © The National Archive and Library of the United Arab Emirates

All rights reserved. No part of this publication may be: i) reproduced or transmitted in any form, electronic or mechanical, including photocopying, recording or by means of any information storage or retrieval system without prior permission in writing from the publishers; or ii) used or reproduced in any way for the training, development or operation of artificial intelligence (AI) technologies, including generative AI technologies. The rights holders expressly reserve this publication from the text and data mining exception as per Article 4(3) of the Digital Single Market Directive (EU) 2019/790.

Bloomsbury Publishing Inc does not have any control over, or responsibility for, any third-party websites referred to or in this book. All internet addresses given in this book were correct at the time of going to press. The author and publisher regret any inconvenience caused if addresses have changed or sites have ceased to exist, but can accept no responsibility for any such changes.

A catalogue record for this book is available from the British Library.
Library of Congress Cataloging-in-Publication Data
Names: Barnwell, Kristi, author.
Title: The formation of the UAE : state-building and Arab nationalism in
the Middle East / Kristi Barnwell.
Other titles: Formation of the United Arab Emirates
Description: London ; New York : I. B. Tauris, 2024. |
Includes bibliographical references and index.
Identifiers: LCCN 2023036834 (print) | LCCN 2023036835 (ebook) |
ISBN 9781838605278 (hb) | ISBN 9780755654062 (paperback) |
ISBN 9781838605285 (ebook) | ISBN 9781838605292 (epdf) | ISBN 9781838605308
Subjects: LCSH: Arab nationalism–Middle East–History. |
United Arab Emirates–History. | Great Britain–Foreign relations–Persian Gulf Region. |
Persian Gulf Region–Foreign relations–Great Britain.
Classification: LCC DS247.T88 B37 2024 (print) | LCC DS247.T88 (ebook) |
DDC 320.540917/4927–dc23/eng/20230809
LC record available at https://lccn.loc.gov/2023036834
LC ebook record available at https://lccn.loc.gov/2023036835

ISBN: HB: 978-1-8386-0527-8
PB: 978-0-7556-5406-2
ePDF: 978-1-8386-0529-2
eBook: 978-1-8386-0528-5

Typeset by Newgen KnowledgeWorks Pvt. Ltd., Chennai, India

For product safety related questions contact productsafety@bloomsbury.com.

To find out more about our authors and books visit www.bloomsbury.com
and sign up for our newsletters.

Contents

List of illustrations	vi
Acknowledgements	vii
Introduction	1
1 Protected status	13
2 The interwar years	29
3 Building the foundations for a state	51
4 The dispute at Buraimi and the consequences of poverty	71
5 The Trucial States at the height of Arab nationalism, 1956–1967	103
6 Federation and withdrawal, 1968–1971	131
7 Security for the UAE	153
Conclusion: Departing from or returning to old patterns	175
Bibliography	181
Index	193

Illustrations

Maps
1.1	Map of the Gulf	14
3.1	Map of Bahrain	54
3.2	Map of internal boundaries of the Trucial States	69
4.1	Map of boundary claims between Qatar, Abu Dhabi and Saudi Arabia	79
7.1	Map of the Strait of Hormuz	169

Tables
1.1	Sheikhs Signatory to the General Maritime Treaty of 1820 and Their Territories Recognized by the British Government	19
2.1	Rulers of Abu Dhabi and Their End of Reign 1855–1928	31
2.2	Rulers and Status of Sharjah and Ras Al Khaimah, 1866–1951	32
3.1	Political Residents and Political Agents during the Formative Years of the Trucial Council	58
5.1	Population Growth in the Trucial Coast in the Mid-Twentieth Century	114

Acknowledgements

Historians understand that when writing one must make some decisions about what marks the beginning and ending of the subject of study. Shifting the opening and closing of a story by just a few years can reframe an argument entirely. I could begin my thanks with the sabbatical when I drew up my proposal, which would make it appear as though only a few short years (plus a pandemic) went into this book's production. The truth, however, is that this book has a much earlier origin story. In starting the history of this history further back, it will allow me to thank more people than may have ever realized just how integral to its writing they are.

I'd like to start with my appreciation for professors Mary C. Wilson and Wm. Roger Louis. As one of my undergraduate professors at University of Massachusetts Amherst, Mary inspired me to pursue Middle East history seriously. Her courses, reading recommendations, comments on my writing and support through my last years of college prepared me for my graduate studies – and introduced me to the histories of Gulf countries. When two years into my PhD program at Texas, I reviewed my options for my dissertation topics, it was Mary's assigned readings and discussions about the problems facing the Gulf countries which led me to propose the UAE as one of my topics. To WRL I owe a great deal of thanks for taking me on as an advisee, for encouraging me to pursue my research on the Gulf and for honoring me with the British Studies' Churchill Scholarship, which helped me complete archival work for my dissertation and thus the book that eventually grew out of it. Roger's writing tips (circle weak verbs in red; when your paragraph creeps past two-thirds of the page, hit 'return') and the intellectual rigor and camaraderie found in his seminars have all become deeply embedded in the way that I teach and write. Kamran Aghaie, who was the Director of the Middle East Studies Center while I was at the University of Texas at Austin, also warrants a note of appreciation. Kamran's courses expanded my knowledge of the region, and he frequently offered valuable practical advice for getting through the dissertation, applying for jobs and maintaining my morale in pursuit of my degree. Without the mentorship of these three scholars, this first-generation college student might never have navigated the difficult paths of academia.

A very special thank you goes to my dear colleague and friend Jane Bristol-Rhys. I met Jane while doing dissertation research in Abu Dhabi. Generous beyond measure, Jane invited me to stay with her, opened her personal library to me, and introduced me to other scholars of the Gulf. Since then, we've continued to meet every few years, in Al Ain, Manchester, Milwaukee, Dublin and London both to collaborate on presentations and to hold our own 'writing camps'. Her feedback has consistently enriched my scholarship and her friendship has helped me persist in my work.

Additional thanks are extended to friends who have helped in myriad ways. Thank you to Stefanie Wichhart for reading drafts chapter by chapter in the early stages and checking in during the later stages. To my University of Illinois, Springfield, colleagues, Heather Bailey, David Bertaina, Donna Bussell, Lan Dong, Tena Helton and Peter Shapinsky: thank you for your encouragement, your commiseration and for checking on my progress and taking an interest. To members of my writing groups, thank you for helping to hold me accountable as I reworked and revised. I would also like to thank several graduate assistants for their work at various stages in the research and preparation of this manuscript: Kiley Volker, Beth Kruse, Connor Krater and Courtney Hicks.

To my editors, I extend my appreciation for your interest, encouragement and patience. I owe additional thanks to my external reviewers for finding value in my work and for identifying areas for improvement.

Above all, I want to express my gratitude to my family. My husband read drafts, reminded me to take breaks and took on most of the housework when the semesters and writing deadlines weighed heavily on me. He has held down the fort while I travelled to visit archives. He has tolerated my complaints about writing, meetings and contract negotiations. Without him, I may never have finished this thing. Isaar, Gus and Duke: I have appreciated the farm-road walks, the snuggles and the dancing, wiggling excitement when I come home from work or travels. My life is truly wonderful because you four have been part of it.

Introduction

I made my first extended visit to the United Arab Emirates (UAE) in 2005. While staying in Abu Dhabi, I met up with some Jordanian friends who were living in Al Ain at the time. They wished to show me around, and during one visit, I expressed an interest in going to the Al Ain Museum to see how the local and national history was interpreted in the exhibits there. My friend laughed – the UAE wasn't old enough to have 'history', was it? I found myself sharing a similar exchange with an Egyptian scholar at a conference in Manchester, UK, joking again about the newness of the UAE. These casual anecdotes reflect an attitude within the greater Arab world that the UAE – a collection of tiny city-states that formed a modern nation state in only 1971 – are somehow less real, or less valid members of the Middle East.

Sheikh Zayed bin Sultan Al Nahyan opened the first *majlis* session in February 1972 with a speech that expressed an ambitious vision for the future of the UAE – and one which openly declared the UAE's place in the region and the world:

> [The UAE is] a part of the greater Arab homeland [*al-waṭan al-ʿaraby al-kabīr*], bound to it by ties of religion, language, history, and a shared destiny; and the people of the Union are one people and they are part of the Arab nation [*al-ʿāmah*], and Islam is the official religion of the Union; and Islamic *shariah* is the official source of law and the official language of the Union is Arabic.[1]

In so saying, Zayed placed the United Arab Emirates firmly within the region and the history of the greater Arab world. Historians since then have largely ignored the UAE, and indeed the Arab states of the Gulf more generally, when writing about the twentieth-century Arab world. Rather than presenting the examples

---

[1] 'Speech of His Highness Sheikh Zayid bin Sultan Al-Nahiyan, President of the State, at the opening of the first national *majlis* of the Union', (Arabic) in *al-Faraʾid min Aqwal Zayid* (Abu Dhabi: National Center for Documentation and Research, 2001), 15.

of the UAE and other Gulf countries within the broader story of developments in the Arab world, the Gulf countries, and the UAE specifically, are examined almost exclusively in the context of the rise of oil.[2]

The *imagining* of a modern Arab world into being began in the late nineteenth century in response to the centralizing efforts of the Ottoman Empire and the Egyptian government. They both recognized their military and economic declines relative to the European states, especially Britain, France and Russia. The Ottoman and Khedival rulers reordered their state systems to strengthen central governments at the expense of provincial notables. Surveys of this phenomenon largely ignore the effects of European encroachment in the Gulf and reverberations of Ottoman revitalization in the eighteenth and nineteenth centuries – and yet the Gulf experienced these phenomena, too.[3] And while the Trucial States were never part of a mandate system, their 'protected status', regulated through truces and treaties, established a variant of British political control. The British Political Resident administered and shaped the local political structures and influenced the succession and elimination of political leaders in the interwar period. During the 'Golden Age' of pan-Arab nationalism(s), in the 1950s and 1960s, when politicians from the so-called core Arab states expressed competing ideas of anti-imperialism and shared Arab identity, these ideas filtered outwards to the Trucial Coast as well.

In this book, I examine the history of the Trucial States and the events that led to their transformation into the United Arab Emirates. I do so with the explicit intent of recognizing the history of the Trucial Coast – so named because of the truces the British government brokered between them – as part of the informal extension of the British Empire in the Middle East, as well as a nation state oriented to and shaped by the politics and realities of the Arab world. While there is much to be said about the Trucial Coast as part of the Indian Ocean economic, political and cultural system before the twentieth century, in the post-war world the Trucial Coast increasingly oriented itself – and was viewed by British administrators in the region – as part of the nascent Arab world. As such, the story of the Trucial States must be considered against the backdrop of not only the re-visioning of Britain's global strategy but also as a single nation state creating itself from whole cloth. The transition of the Trucial States to the United Arab Emirates is the result of global, regional and local circumstances

---

[2] Throughout, I use 'the Gulf' to refer to the body of water which most historians and international organizations refer to as the Persian Gulf, but which some of the Arab states call the Arab Gulf.
[3] Frederick Anscombe, *The Ottoman Gulf: The Creation of Kuwait, Saudi Arabia, and Qatar* (New York: Columbia University Press, 1997).

that coalesced in the age of heightened awareness and (British) fear of anti-imperialist, anti-British Arab nationalist ideologies.

Transition from the Indian Ocean world to the Arab Middle East

This book bridges three broad bodies of scholarship as they apply to the Trucial Coast and Gulf. The expanding field of the Indian Ocean World seeks to situate the Arab coast of the Gulf in connection to the transnational world of trade and society. Fahad Bishara has made strong arguments for situating the Gulf in a trans-regional, maritime historiography.[4] The *longue durée* of the Gulf's coastal history relayed through the works of anthropologists illustrate strong trans-regional connections of the Gulf and the Indian Ocean world from pre-Islamic, late antiquity and medieval periods to modern times.[5] Bishara's own prolific work on maritime legal, economic and sociocultural networks in the Gulf illuminate the many ways in which people and goods circulated along the coasts of east Africa, south Asia, Persia and the Arab peninsula.[6] The dynamic maritime world of the Indian Ocean produced an interdependent culture which can be understood as a distinct society, particularly from the age of exploration through the nineteenth century. This body of literature includes important works on the circulation of people (both free and unfree) and cultural exchange and absorption, as well as works on merchants, merchant houses, pearling operations and the movement of cargo.[7]

---

[4] Fahad Bishara, 'The Many Voyages of *Fateh Al-Khayr*: Unfurling the Gulf in the Age of Oceanic History', *International Journal of Middle East Studies* 52, no. 3 (2020): 397–412.
[5] Dionisius Agius, *In the Wake of the Dhow: The Arabian Gulf and Oman* (Reading: Ithaca Press, 1999) and *Seafaring in the Arabian Gulf and Oman: The People of the Dhow* (New York: Routledge, 2005); D. T. Potts, 'The Archaeology and Early History of the Persian Gulf', in *The Persian Gulf in History*, ed. Lawrence G. Potter (New York: Palgrave Macmillan, 2009), 27–56 surveys developments and problems in studying and tracing the trans-regional nature of ancient Gulf society.
[6] Fahad Bishara, *A Sea of Debt: Law and Economic Life in the Western Indian Ocean, 1780-1950* (Cambridge: Cambridge University Press, 2017) and 'Circulation and Capitalism in a Maritime Bazaar: Notes from a Pearl Merchant's Chest', *Law and History Review* 40, no. 3 (2022): 491–3.
[7] On the movement of peoples, see especially Matthew S. Hopper, *Slaves of One Master: Globalization and Slavery in Arabia in the Age of Empire* (New Haven, CT: Yale University Press, 2015) and works edited by Gwyn Campbell: *Bondage and the Environment in the Indian Ocean World* (London: Palgrave Macmillan, 2018) and *Abolition and its Aftermath in the Indian Ocean, Africa and Asia* (London: Routledge, 2005). On economics and trade, see Laleh Khalili, *Sinews of War and Trade: Shipping and Capitalism in the Arabian Peninsula* (New York: Verso Books, 2020) and Martha Chaiklin, Philip Gooding, and Gwyn Campbell, eds, *Animal Trade Histories in the Indian Ocean World* (London: Palgrave Macmillan, 2020), for recent creative examples. For a more traditional example, see James Onley, 'Transnational Merchants in the Nineteenth-Century Gulf: The Case of the Safar Family', in *Transnational Connections and the Arab Gulf*, ed. Madawi al-Rasheed (London: Routledge, 2004), 37–56.

The second field focuses on the British Empire's role in the Gulf. Questions of how and why the Empire administered the Trucial Coast and other Arab states in the Gulf provide the subject matter of numerous works by historians and retired civil servants. James Onley's *The Arabian Frontier of the British Raj* argued for the expansion of our understanding of the British Empire in India to include the Arab littoral of the Gulf.[8] His work outlined the structures of the British administration in the nineteenth century as well as the economic ties between the Arab coast and Indian merchant houses under the East India Company and the Government of India. Nelida Fuccaro's *Histories of City and State in the Persian Gulf* examines in more specific detail the interaction of British power with the Al Khalifa of Bahrain, especially in the development of Manama as a seat of municipal and state power in Bahrain. Other scholars, with greater focus on the British metropole's perspective, have particularly explored Britain's role in the transformation of the Trucial Coast into nation states and the Gulf's place in Britain's retreat from east of Suez. J. B. Kelly's scholarship on the Arabian Peninsula serves as the primary point of departure for the field of British Empire in Arabia. As an advisor to the Foreign Office on boundaries, Kelly was well versed in the documents and policies contemporary to events considered in my own work. But Kelly was also deeply critical of the British withdrawal from East of Suez and its implications for the decline of British power and the future of Western civilization.[9] Since then, others have weighed in on the reasons behind the British Empire's withdrawal. Such works have debated whether the withdrawal was an anomaly in the decline of Britain's empire or a point of continuity in decolonization and global strategy.[10]

The third of these fields, and the one in which the Trucial Coast and United Arab Emirates are least integrated, is the rise of the modern Middle East and the forms of nationalism – especially the forms of pan-Arab nationalism which

---

[8] James Onley, *The Arabian Frontier of the British Raj: Merchants, Rulers, and the British in the Nineteenth Century Gulf* (Oxford: Oxford University Press, 2010).
[9] J. B. Kelly, *Arabia, the Gulf and the West* (New York: Weidenfeld & Nicholson, 1980) is the best example of his critique of British withdrawal from the Gulf, though essays from the recently published three-volume edited collection offer more insights into his perspective.
[10] For example, Simon Smith, *Britain's Revival and Fall in the Gulf: Kuwait, Bahrain, Qatar, and the Trucial States, 1950-71* (London: Routledge, 2004); Helene von Bismarck, *British Policy in the Persian Gulf, 1961-1968* (New York: Palgrave Macmillan, 2013); Shohei Sato, 'Britain's Decision to Withdraw from the Persian Gulf, 1964-68: A Pattern and a Puzzle', *Journal of Imperial and Commonwealth History* 37, no. 1 (2009): 99-117; William Roger Louis, 'The British Withdrawal from the Gulf, 1967-71', *Journal of Imperial and Commonwealth History* 31, no. 1 (2003): 83-108; and most recently, Tancred Bradshaw, *The End of Empire in the Gulf: From Trucial States to United Arab Emirates* (London: I. B. Tauris, 2019).

dominated the political landscape of the Arab world through the middle of the twentieth century. This field of scholarship recognizes the rise of the Arab Middle East in opposition to Western imperialism, especially as expressed through the mandate period (1919–46), into independence and the rise of Arab nationalisms, and particularly of pan-Arab nationalisms originating primarily in the Arab 'core states' of Greater Syria, Iraq and Egypt.

Albert Hourani's seminal work *Arabic Thought in the Liberal Age* delineated the many ways in which political and cultural movements were informed by and adapted from European examples of nationalism during the nineteenth century. The centralizing efforts of the Ottoman Empire limited the autonomy Arab notables in the provinces had enjoyed historically. They began agitating for greater independence and espoused ideas of Arab identity and history distinct from those of Ottomanism, Turkish nationalism and Islamic nationalisms.[11] The interwar period severed the provinces from the Ottoman Empire, and the national identities that formed in the war's wake took diverse forms, often with strong anti-imperialist sentiments.[12]

The predominant forms of nationalism in the region from independence through the 1960s can be viewed under a broad umbrella of pan-Arab ideology which emphasized Arab language and culture, opposition to Western imperialism and the rejection of Israel in 1948. Malcolm Kerr and other scholars have characterized the 1950s and 1960s as a period of fierce anti-imperialist pan-Arabism, with Arab rulers competing for recognition as the foremost advocate for the Arab world.[13] Baathism and Nasserism were the most widely recognized expressions of pan-Arabism regionally and internationally. In the British records used in this study, Arab nationalism and Nasserist ideology are used

---

[11] William Cleveland, *The Making of an Arab Nationalist: Ottomanism and Arabism in the Life and Thought of Sati' al-Husri* (Princeton, NJ: Princeton University Press, 1972); Albert Hourani, 'Ottoman Reform and the Politics of Notables', in *Beginnings of Modernization in the Middle East: The Nineteenth Century*, ed. William R. Polk and Richard L. Chambers (Chicago: University of Chicago Press, 1968), 41–68; Philip S. Khoury, *Urban Notables and Arab Nationalism, the Politics of Damascus, 1860–1920* (Cambridge: Cambridge University Press, 1983).

[12] George Antonius, *The Arab Awakening* (London: J. B. Lippincott, 1938); Bassam Tibi, *Arab Nationalism: A Critical Enquiry*, ed. and trans. Marion Farouk-Sluglett and Peter Sluglett, 2nd edn (London: Palgrave Macmillan, 1990), originally published in German in 1971; Hanna Batatu, *The Old Social Classes and the Revolutionary Movements of Iraq: A Study of Iraq's Old Landed and Commercial Classes and of Its Communists, Ba'thists and Free Officers* (Princeton, NJ: Princeton University Press, 1978); James Gelvin, *Divided Loyalties: Nationalism and Mass Politics in Syria at the Close of Empire* (Berkeley: University of California Press, 1999); Salim Tamari and Ihsan Turjman, *Year of the Locust: A Soldier's Diary and the Erasure of Palestine's Ottoman Past* (Berkeley: University of California Press, 2011).

[13] Malcolm H. Kerr, *The Arab Cold War: Gamal 'Abd al-Nasir and His Rivals, 1958–1970*, 3rd edn (London: Oxford University Press, 1971); Malik Mufti, *Sovereign Creations: Pan-Arabism and Political Order in Syria and Iraq* (Ithaca: Cornell University Press, 1996).

as nearly synonymous.[14] The Arab-Israeli war in 1967 and Israel's defeat of the Arab armies marked the effective end of Arab nationalism as the predominant ideology, giving way to state-based nationalisms and Islamist movements which eclipsed Arabism and Nasserism in the 1970s.[15]

This outline of the basic narrative of modern nationalism and identity in the Arab world admittedly glosses over a wide variety of interventions and variations on the themes which complicate the frameworks by which scholars consider the Middle East and the Arab world today. In doing so, I do not dismiss or ignore the works which have demonstrated that pan-Arabism was not the only significant form of identity or ideology. Arab nationalism(s) encompassed regional and state-based variants which adapted or resisted the generally accepted tenets of pan-Arabism.[16] Even within overtly pan-Arab nationalist movements, there were meaningful distinctions, and these movements could and did change over time in response to changing regional and global circumstances.

The overview of the narrative is useful, however, as a backdrop to this work. Some works on the Gulf have recognized the role of Arab nationalism in the development of the Trucial States. Frederick Anscomb's *Ottoman Gulf* demonstrated the reach of the Ottoman Tanzimat into the Gulf as far south as Qatar, which then drew British involvement deeper into the Trucial States. Rosemarie Said-Zahlan's *Origins of the United Arab Emirates* (1978) remains one of the most important works on the Trucial States. In it, she made pointed connections to Sheikh Shakhbut of Abu Dhabi's interest in the affairs of Palestine under British mandatory rule, as well as the broader ideological influence of Arab politics in the reform movements in Bahrain and Dubai. She continued in this vein with her *Palestine and the Gulf States*. Abdullah O. Taryam's contribution continued the work that Said-Zahlan did in her first work, as has Aqil Kazim's

---

[14] John F. Devlin, 'The Baath Party: Rise and Metamorphosis', *American Historical Review* 96, no. 5 (1991): 1396–407, provides an excellent overview of the key works on the origins and evolution of the Baath Party through 1991. On Nasserism, see also, Joel Gordon, *Nasser's Blessed Movement: Egypt's Free Officers and the July Revolution* (Oxford: Oxford University Press, 1992); Reem Abou-el-Fadl, 'Early Pan-Arabism in Egypt's July Revolution: The Free Officers' Political Formation and Policymaking, 1946–54', *Nations and Nationalism* 21, no. 2 (2015): 289–308. See also Israel Gershoni, Sara Pursley and Beth Baron, 'Relocating Arab Nationalism', Special Issue, *International Journal of Middle East Studies* 43, no. 2 (2011), especially the 'Preface' by Peter Wein, 203–4.

[15] Fouad Ajami, 'The End of Pan-Arabism', in *Pan-Arabism and Arab Nationalism: The Continuing Debate*, ed. Tawfic E. Farah (New York: Routledge, 1987), 96–114 and Hassan Nafaa, 'Arab Nationalism: A Response to Ajami's Thesis on the "End of Pan-Arabism"', in *Pan-Arabism and Arab Nationalism: The Continuing Debate*, ed. Tawfic E. Farah (New York: Routledge, 1987), 133–51.

[16] This is not meant to be an exhaustive list, but some examples include Sherene Seikaly, *Men of Capital: Scarcity and Economy in Mandate Palestine* (Palo Alto: Stanford University Press, 2015); Orit Bashkin, *The Other Iraq: Pluralism and Culture in Hashemite Iraq* (Palo Alto: Stanford University Press, 2009); Betty S. Anderson, *Nationalist Voices in Jordan: The Street and the State* (Austin: University of Texas Press, 2005).

United Arab Emirates A.D. 600 to the Present. Both of these works incorporate greater acknowledgement of the role of Arab nationalism as a backdrop to the development of the Trucial States.

My own work contributes to the foundations laid by the scholars in all three fields, layering them together to create a fuller understanding of this period in the UAE's history. In telling the story of the Trucial States' transformation into the United Arab Emirates, I intentionally weave the broader historical framework of the modern Arab world through this narrative. The expansion of Ottoman power into the Gulf in the nineteenth century and the subsequent intensification of British involvement in the Trucial Coast coincide with British involvement in the provinces of the Ottoman Empire late in the Ottoman period into the interwar era. From this period onwards the Trucial Coast begins to see itself and be seen by British policymakers as part of the Arab world more than the Indian Ocean world. The administrative shift of the Trucial States from Britain's India Office to its Foreign Office played a significant role in this reorientation. As such, the political movements and machinations in the core Arab states took on greater consequence in the shaping of the Trucial States from the 1950s onwards.[17]

Reading with and against the British archival grain

This work is the product of many years of research across several countries and through a multitude of archives and libraries. Archived documents on the nineteenth and early-twentieth-century records from the Trucial States' perspective for the period under consideration in this work are largely unavailable to researchers. Because the Trucial Coast was under the administration of the Political Residency, however, there is extensive documentation from British sources. The majority of source materials for the period under study comes from British archival sources. The greatest amount of material was collected from The National Archive at Kew over several trips and many hours in the reading room there. I reviewed additional materials for this project at the British Library;

---

[17] I presented these ideas in an early form in 2018: 'Positioning the Trucial States/UAE in the World of Arab Nationalism(s)', *Fifth World Congress for Middle Eastern Studies*. Seville. 16–20 July 2018. This general outline of Middle East historiography is echoed in Omnia El Shakry, ed. *Understanding and Teaching The Modern Middle East* (Madison: University of Wisconsin Press, 2020). Other scholars have recently taken similar approaches to mine in reconciling Gulf states' histories with pan-Arab and Arab nationalist movements. For example, Talal al-Rashoud, 'From Muscat to the Maghreb: Pan-Arab Networks, Anti-colonial Groups, and Kuwait's Arab Scholarships (1953–1961)', *Arabian Humanities* 12 (2019), doi: https://doi.org/10.4000/cy.5004.

the Special Collections at the University of Exeter, which houses some of the papers of Sir William Luce; and the Richard Holmes Collection at the Middle East Centre Archive (MEC) housed at St. Antony's College at Oxford University. Still more research was completed at the Lyndon B. Johnson Presidential Library and the Library of Congress. The National Library and Archives in Abu Dhabi (formerly the Center for Documentation and Research) also augmented my research with its collections of speeches and memoirs.

More archival records have become available as published and digitized materials. The Archive Editions for the *Records of the Emirates* (*ROE*) and the *Buraimi Dispute* are invaluable sources of information and commentary. Some of these sources and others are now available through Qatar Digital Library (QDL) and Arabian Gulf Digital Archive (AGDA). I accessed these from the British Library and The National Archives in Kew, or from the National Library and Archives in Abu Dhabi, and virtually from my living room through the Qatar Digital Library or the Arabian Gulf Digital Archive.

These materials are almost all in English, produced by British administrators and filtered through British administrators' notions of what was worth noting for meeting British goals and expectations in the Gulf. This is both a blessing and a curse for those researching the Trucial Coast in the twentieth century. On the one hand, there is a surfeit of detailed documentation to provide historians with years of research opportunities from numerous angles, all relatively easy to access in a variety of formats. On the other hand, the record is indeed almost entirely British made and derived for British purposes and projecting an official perspective. Trucial rulers, merchants, advisors and, even occasionally, the average emirati or rogue gun smuggler may make an appearance in the documents and provide insights from the non-British perspective – but even these are filtered through an administrator's summary, translated through intermediaries from *khaleeji* Arabic into English.[18]

The current state of archives in the Emirates presents an obstacle to most scholars who wish to balance the British perspective with the views of the leaders of the Trucial Coast. The Trucial Coast did not enjoy a robust print culture even as late as the 1970s, leaving us with few local periodicals; those which did exist were sporadic and short lived for the crucial period. They are not contained in the digital archives available today, and were not housed in the Abu Dhabi National Archive at the time I was there. The ongoing work of local archives and research centres will undoubtedly produce broader source materials with

---

[18] Arabic for 'of or belonging to the Gulf', but loosely translated as 'Gulfie'.

time, but for now, the records documenting the history of the Trucial States are primarily British records.

This does not mean the story of the Trucial States and the formation of the United Arab Emirates is a British story. I have made efforts to bring in Arab and Emirati perspectives to enhance this work wherever possible. Published memoirs serve to offer up local memories of local figures who lived through the transformation of the Trucial States into the UAE and I have attempted to use these carefully to enrich the narrative and offer alternative perspectives on significant events. These are not sufficient to balance the record in and of themselves, but such works have proved useful, nonetheless. Where possible, I have consulted secondary literature by scholars from the region, including works published in Arabic.

Throughout the research, I have endeavoured to read critically both *along the archival grain* and *against it* with an eye to understanding the tensions between local rulers and British administrators as their combined efforts shaped the realities of state formation on the ground. The idea of reading *against* the grain is a widely understood idea for historians but it is worth revisiting consciously and deliberately with my application of it in this book. When Walter Benjamin exhorted historians to 'brush history against the grain', he encouraged us to question the dominant reading of history by those in power.[19] Only in so doing can we uncover the stories of those not in power. James Axtell connected this idea of finding substance in the negative space of 'official' records of the powerful in his essay on 'Ethnohistory'.[20] In it, he argues that ethnohistory provides approaches to understanding interactions on frontiers and borders where multiple cultures come into contact and reveal information through their interactions. His work has so thoroughly permeated the works of historians today that the idea is often referenced as common knowledge. It remains relevant, however, in a variety of works.[21]

The British archives themselves readily invite readers to accept the dominant narrative. Foreign Office officials attempt to make sense of the Arab Gulf as it fits into the British Empire's official narrative. In talking with one another across

---

[19] See 'Thesis VII', in Walter Benjamin, *Illuminations*, ed. Hannah Arendt (New York: Schocken Books, 1968), 256–7.
[20] James Axtell, 'Ethnohistory: An Historian's Viewpoint, *Ethnohistory* 26, no. 1 (1979): 1–13.
[21] For example, James C. Scott, *The Art of Not Being Governed: An Anarchist History of Upland Southeast Asia* (New Haven, CT: Yale University Press, 2010); James C. Scott, *Against the Grain: A Deep History of the Earliest States* (New Haven, CT: Yale University Press, 2017); and Stefan Eklöf Amirell, *Pirates of Empire: Colonisation and Maritime Violence in Southeast Asia* (Cambridge: Cambridge University Press, 2019).

time and government offices, British policymakers in Sharjah and in London conformed to the broad ideas about the Trucial States and their place in Britain's global strategy. If we take the archives at face value, we would be led to believe that the rulers of the Trucial States were primitive, backward, wily, wise and mischievous. In reading *against the grain* of the British record, the historian questions British assumptions about the attitudes and motivations of the local rulers through the extensive discursive comments Political Residents and other agents of British administration made in their official documents. This can be seen most clearly in Chapter 3. What British policymakers describe as essential characteristics of the rulers' natures can alternatively be read as moments of tension and resistance by rulers who often resented being directed to serve British goals at the expense of their own reputations in their respective emirates.

Reading *along* the archival grain adds an additional layer of analysis. The archive, as Stoler has argued, reveals the anxieties and tensions of those producing it.[22] The ebb and flow of the documentary record, the numbers of pages produced and the urgency with which telegrams are exchanged, give the historian an understanding of the fears that drive the decision-making process. In understanding the flow, organization and points of repetition within the archive, we learn more about the inner workings of the colonial/imperial system and the patterns it defaults to. This methodological approach should not be confused with accepting the dominant narrative of the archive. Rather, it is a form of resistant reading that allows the historian to observe patterns of behaviour across offices and decades. It supplements the knowledge gleaned from reading *against* the grain and supplies additional information in what drives policymakers' decisions.

Throughout this work, I endeavour to combine the two approaches to develop a deeper understanding of the history of the Trucial States and their transformation into the United Arab Emirates. The archives reveal a deep anxiety on the part of British policymakers over their status as the predominant power in the Gulf driving many of the decisions they make with regard to the Trucial States. Across the first half of the twentieth century, the archives reveal a Foreign Office fearful of Saudi incursions, Arab nationalism and anti-imperialism, and the economic collapse at home should Britain lose influence over the oil states. Meanwhile, the Trucial rulers strive to maintain traditional markers of legitimacy within their own populations even as the structures of tribal politics

---

[22] Ann Laura Stoler, *Along the Archival Grain: Epistemic Anxieties and Colonial Common Sense* (Princeton, NJ: Princeton University Press, 2010).

are forced to adapt the new political structures of the modern nation state. In the interplay of reading both *with* and *against* the grain of the archive, these tensions are revealed more fully.

Chapter structure

Chapter 1 introduces the Gulf's social and political structures before and at the time of Europe's growing interest in the Indian Ocean trade. Local and European powers competed into the nineteenth century to dominate the sea lanes and coastal trade. In the nineteenth century, however, the British Empire succeeded in edging out all other European empires and established Britain as the dominant military and trading power, establishing the trucial system that would come to shape the future development of the Arab coast of the Gulf.

Chapters 2 and 3 consider the increasing impact of Britain's presence in the Gulf and on the Trucial Coast. In the interwar period, the Trucial Coast would be drawn further into the sphere of Arab politics as the British Empire reckoned with its changing relationship to India and the rest of its empire. Britain's control of the Iraq mandate and withdrawal from India reoriented internal British bureaucracy in Whitehall, and effectively drew the Trucial rulers into the broader imaginary of the Arab world as understood by the British advisors and officials conducting the foreign policy of the Trucial Coast. This was accomplished first through the technological innovations of the air routes and growing interest in oil exploration, and then through building the administrative precursors to the modern nation state, most significantly the drawing and controlling of movement across borders.

The 1950s and 1960s would prove pivotal for the Trucial States and their future as a nation state in the Arab world. Saudi Arabia revived its ambition to dominate the Arabian Peninsula in earnest in the late 1940s. In 1952, the Saudis occupied frontier territory at the Buraimi Oasis situated between Abu Dhabi and Oman with the goal of drawing local leaders and their populations into the Saudi orbit with the promise of economic development. This provides the setting for Chapter 4. The conflict over the future of Buraimi highlighted two major concerns that would drive future Trucial Coast policies under British advice. First, it highlighted the extreme poverty of the Trucial States and the degree to which Britain's long presence had failed to provide meaningful relief from that reality. Second, the conflict brought the Trucial States to the notice of the broader Arab world, which I take up in Chapter 5. Anti-imperialist Arab nationalist movements swept through the Middle East in the latter part of the 1950s and 1960s. The underdevelopment of the Trucial Coast through British neglect and differing priorities of the local rulers and British officials remained a constant concern for British policymakers in the Gulf who anticipated the arrival of anti-British Arab nationalism in the Gulf. The spectre of Arab nationalism on the periphery of the Middle East drove British policy decisions in the Gulf and created new tensions among the local rulers themselves and especially in terms of their relationship to Britain.

Chapters 6 and 7 examine Britain's decision to withdraw from its empire east of Suez and preparations for the Trucial States after Britain's withdrawal. Chapter 6 examines the background to Britain's unexpected announcement in 1968, as well as the efforts by the local rulers to establish a viable future for themselves without the overt protection of the British military. The three years between Harold Wilson's declaration and Britain's withdrawal comprised negotiations over the establishment of a future state that might, or might not, include Bahrain and Qatar, as well as inter-emirate competition for power and autonomy within a future federated state. The resulting federation of seven emirates and the creation of two independent nations outside of the United Arab Emirates was very much a product of the pre-state structures created under British administration since the interwar period. One of the most significant obstacles to federal cooperation and British withdrawal, security, is the subject of Chapter 7. This chapter considers the regional and local security priorities of the Trucial States. British withdrawal created a vacuum the United States was unwilling to fill. Local regional forces, Iran and Saudi Arabia, were both potential threats to the new federation's sovereignty, but were also the only military powers in the region capable of offering deterrence to any future invading force. The 'twin pillar' strategy would prove short lived but also created an opportunity for the transition from British military protection to the eventual takeover of Gulf security under the American military. At one level, the debates over security between the emirates reflected anxieties among the rulers over their ability to sustain individual autonomy in their emirates within a federation where Abu Dhabi would be the wealthiest and largest emirate. At a deeper level, the debates illustrated the inherent tensions of decolonization. Britain sought to ensure its influence on the Trucial Coast after withdrawal even as the rulers sought to forge their own path as independent, sovereign rulers of an Arab nation state.

1

Protected status

The United Arab Emirates today comprises the seven federated states, or emirates: Abu Dhabi, Dubai, Sharjah, Ajman, Fujairah, Umm Al Quwain and Ras Al Khaimah. The UAE is located on the eastern side of the Arabian Peninsula, east of Saudi Arabia and north of the Sultanate of Oman. Much of the country's 30,000 square miles is made up of desert and salt flats in the east, though the terrain is varied by the presence of the Hajar mountain range that extends from Oman into the southern region of Abu Dhabi and along the eastern coast near Ras Al Khaimah and Fujairah. Small strips of fertile agricultural land are situated on the Batinah Coast south of Sharjah, and oases dot the country in varying sizes, allowing for inland date farms fed by irrigation systems and underground spring. In addition to the mainland, the Emirates include numerous small islands in the Persian Gulf, including Das Island off the north coast of Abu Dhabi (see Map 1.1).

The location of the United Arab Emirates on the Persian Gulf has made the emirates a centre of trade and migration from the Arabian Peninsula, South Asia and Iran. The population of the Emirates today is estimated at approximate 9.3 million, though only a small percentage (between 10 per cent and 15 per cent) are Emirati citizens.[1] The local Emirati population is largely Arab, originating from the tribes that have historically inhabited the region, though many also claim Persian, South Asian and African ancestry due to the long history of regional trade, migration and intermarriage.

For centuries, the eastern coast of the Arabian Peninsula maintained deep and extensive ties to the Persian coast of the Gulf, and the trade networks in eastern Africa and India, forming a kind of maritime world system.[2] Port cities

---

[1] https://u.ae/en/about-the-uae/fact-sheet (accessed 24 October 2023).
[2] R. J. Barendse, 'Trade and State in the Arabian Seas: A Survey from the Fifteenth to the Eighteenth Century', *Journal of World History*, 11, no. 2 (2000): 173–225. Barendse builds on the work of Janet Abu-Lughod, *Before European Hegemony: The World System, AD 1250-1350* (London: Oxford University Press, 1989) but notes that the 'world system' of the Arabian Seas was more diffuse in nature than a more centralized, hierarchical 'system' would suggest.

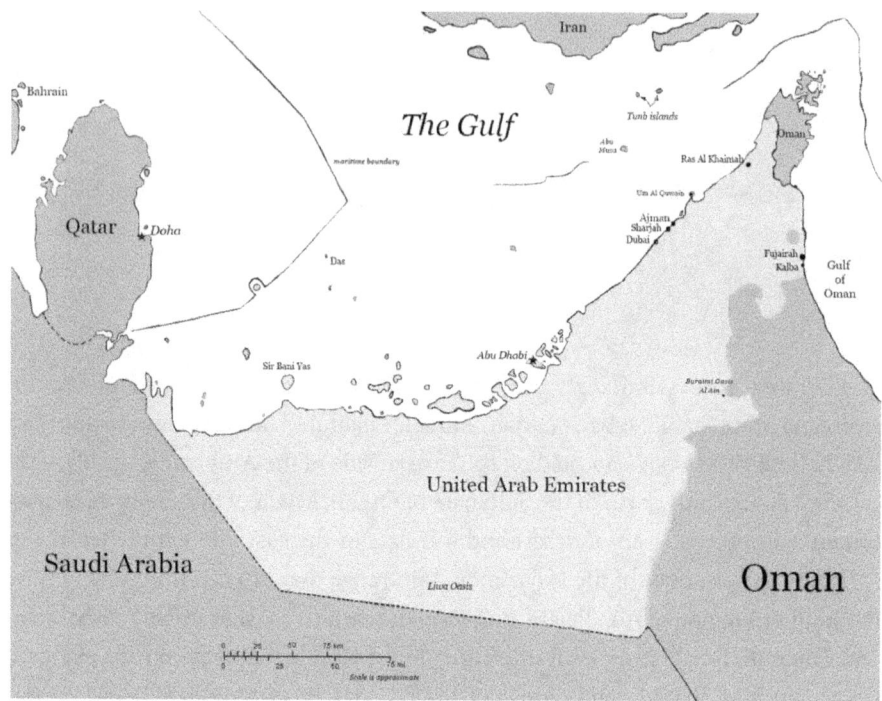

Map 1.1 Map of the Gulf.

up and down both coasts represented nodes of cultural and economic exchange spanning Basra to Muscat, Kuwait to Bandar Abbas. Merchant families of the Persian coast established businesses – and families – in multiple ports, tracing cross-water networks that intersected with the dynamic rise and fall of political influences in the area. The 'Arab-Persian hybrid' Safar family maintained businesses in six or more port cities in the late-eighteenth and early-nineteenth centuries.[3] The Omani Empire of Muscat and Zanzibar was built on the extensive cultural, political, religious and legal ties that bound the Omani Coast to Basra, Mozambique and Khozikode (Calicut) and locations in between.[4] Until the twentieth century, the inhabitants of the Arabian coast of the Gulf looked to the east and south more than to the west and north.

These connections lasted through multiple centuries of invasions from Persia and Europe. The Portuguese, Ottomans, Dutch, Safavids, Qajars, French and

---

[3] James Onley, 'Transnational Merchant Families in the Nineteenth- and Twentieth-Century Gulf', in *The Gulf Family: Kinship Policies and Modernity*, ed. Alanoud Alsharekh (London: Saqi Books, 2007), 37–56.
[4] Bishara, *Sea of Debt*.

British each attempted to establish and control economic and political links in the region. Each wave of infiltration shifted the economic and cultural centres up and down the coasts of the Arabian Peninsula and Persia and across the Gulf. As the foci of political power relocated, so too did the coffee, pearl, textile and spice merchants. Until the twentieth century, the main orientation of the Trucial States as part of the Gulf cultural world was tied to India and the Indian Ocean trade. While there were attempts to establish greater Ottoman control, for example, it was not until the twentieth century, and particularly post First World War, that the Trucial Coast increasingly oriented itself towards the political and cultural orientations of the Arab core states.

This chapter will look at the rise of European empires' presence in the Gulf and the ultimate rise of British hegemony in the nineteenth century. In the twentieth century, shifts in cultural and economic attitudes and the political orientation within the Trucial States began – the air route and communication lines would further support the ties between the Trucial States and India, but the rise of political movements in Palestine, radio communication and migrant workforces to oil fields in Bahrain, Kuwait and Saudi Arabia would draw the Trucial States more and more into the political, economic and cultural spheres of the Middle East.

The Gulf and European expansion

The age of European exploration brought a sustained European presence to the Gulf in the sixteenth century. The Portuguese were the first of the European mercantile empires to find a foothold in the trade and politics of the region, and their forays into the Gulf would leave a legacy not only in the form of abandoned fortresses but also as the first of a series of European empires that sought to leave a mark in the Gulf. From 1507 until 1622, Portugal's position in the Gulf depended on its control over trade and customs coming in and out of the Straits of Hormuz, which it sustained through fortresses at key locations, particularly at Hormuz. Occasionally, the Portuguese attempted to extend power as far north as Bahrain just off the Arabian coast. Even with a slowly growing military presence, however, Portugal could not consolidate direct control over the myriad political and economic powers that emerged in the region. The Safavid Empire, established in 1501, began to spread its power from inland Persia to the coast and then across the Gulf, conquering Bahrain in 1602. The Omanis by the latter half of the sixteenth century also expanded their naval power in the Gulf and Indian

Ocean, creating greater competition. In 1622, the Portuguese found themselves forced from Hormuz to Muscat at the hands of Safavid Shah, Abbas I (r.1588–1629). Only two decades later the Portuguese abandoned Muscat for the small island of Kung and never established a lasting foothold in the Gulf again.

Dutch, French and British mercantile companies made the next significant foray into the Gulf from Europe. The English East India Company (EIC) arrived first. The EIC received its charter from the English government in 1600. Twenty-two years later, the EIC established its commercial site in the lower Gulf at Bandar Abbas near the Straits of Hormuz. The Dutch East India Company (VOC) formed in 1602, and, in 1623, also opened a trading post in Bandar Abbas. The French followed suit in 1665 with their own *Compagnie Française des Indes Orientales* trading house at Bandar Abbas. Despite their ability to establish trading posts at various locations through the Gulf, none of the European powers succeeded in dominating Gulf trade effectively until the nineteenth century.

The EIC eclipsed its European rivals in the Indian and Persian Gulf trade, and the eighteenth century witnessed the withdrawal of the Dutch and French companies from the field. Portuguese trade collapsed in the mid-seventeenth century as the British and Dutch cooperated to squeeze out competitors. Dutch fortunes began to decline in subsequent years. By 1798, only the British and French remained active in the European contest for domination in the Indian Ocean. This coincided with the decline of the empires along the Persian Gulf. Merchants' successes in the subcontinent had increased wealth among provincial leaders who exercised greater autonomy from the central Mughal government. Along the Persian Gulf coasts, this pattern was repeated. The Ottoman government held only nominal control over the province of Basra, while the Safavid dynasty that had ruled over Persia crumbled in the mid-eighteenth century. Amid these changes, Britain's rising sea power and its political and economic influence allowed its merchants to take advantage of local rivalries and ultimately dominate the waters of the Persian Gulf.[5]

Trade patterns in the Indian Ocean and Gulf reflected the shifting political dynamics. Basra, in southern Iraq, had grown significantly as a business and commercial centre in the seventeenth and early eighteenth centuries. The Portuguese had strangled trade routes through the Red Sea, causing trade to be rerouted increasingly through the Gulf and Basra.[6] The EIC's original

---

[5] C. A. Bayly, *Imperial Meridian: The British Empire and the World 1780–1830* (New York: Longman, 1989).
[6] Rudi Matthee, 'Boom and Bust: The Port of Basra in the Sixteenth and Seventeenth Centuries', in *The Persian Gulf in History*, ed. Lawrence G. Potter (London: Macmillan, 2009), 105–28.

headquarters at Bandar Abbas also lost some of its strategic value. Poor port conditions and political and maritime instability on the Omani coast contributed to the desirability of a new trading site farther north.

In a series of moves in the second half of the eighteenth century, the locus of British trade and political power followed the move northward. The EIC had established a factory in Basra in 1723. In 1763, the EIC's political agency in the Gulf shifted from Bandar Abbas to Bushehr.[7] Two years later, the Bombay Marine force of the EIC relocated to the Gulf, marrying EIC commercial power with military might.[8] The political agency was then upgraded to a Gulf Residency Office in 1778.[9] This move signalled the growing importance of trade through the Gulf and allowed the EIC to exercise even greater political influence through a diplomatic and bureaucratic presence. The EIC's positions in the north and its connections to Bandar Abbas and routes south to India brought them into increasing contact with Arab merchants, and their ships from Bahrain, Qatar and the Omani coast. The move ultimately set the stage for the conflicts that would establish British primacy in the Gulf.

Several populations along the northern Omani coast developed trade networks in the lower Gulf in the latter half of the eighteenth century, which participated in and competed with the very markets that the British EIC sought to control. Pearl diving had been a perennial activity in the waters off Bahrain extending south and east on the Gulf. By the middle of the eighteenth century, more tribes and merchants began to group around cities along the coast, taking advantage of the pearling season and the year-round trade in other goods. The Bani Yas tribe increased its presence in Abu Dhabi town in 1761 following the discovery of sweet water there. The Bani Yas would become the most significant group of tribes in the eighteenth century in the interior of the Trucial Coast and would maintain its power through the nineteenth century to the current day. Today's ruling families of Abu Dhabi and Dubai descend from the larger Bani Yas federation. The Al Nahyan (Al Bu Falah) has provided the leader for the Bani Yas in Abu Dhabi. The Al Bu Falasah of Dubai seceded from the Abu Dhabi family in 1833 and established its own branch in Dubai under the leadership of Maktum bin Butti.

Abu Dhabi's power originated from the broad coalition of tribes which supported it through the centuries. These populations varied in their size,

---

[7] Sultan Al Qasimi, *The Myth of Arab Piracy in the Gulf* (London: Croom Helm, 1986), 24.
[8] J. E. Petersen, 'Britain and the Gulf', in *The Persian Gulf in History*, ed. Lawrence Potter (London: Palgrave Macmillan, 2009), 278.
[9] Onley, *Arabian Frontier*, 18.

lifestyles and locations within the Abu Dhabi territory. Some, like the Rumaithat and Qubaisat, were largely settled and formed fishing and pearling communities along the coast, and the latter group also settling in some areas of Liwa. The Mazari (Mazrui, s.), however, were a nomadic tribe that migrated across large swathes of territory. The Al Nahyan of the Bani Yas also benefitted from strong alliances with other tribal groups including the populous Manasir (Mansouri, s.) and Dhawhir (Dhahiri, s.), along with the Awamir (Al Amri, s.) who migrated through territories which adjoined Abu Dhabi.[10]

The largest trade and merchant network on this coast consisted of the Qawasim located primarily in Sharjah and Ras Al Khaimah, with additional numbers located across the Gulf at Qishm and other small islands.[11] The Qawasim encompassed a confederation of groups tied to the patronage and political power of the Al Qasimi family which ruled in Sharjah town and the port of Ras Al Khaimah that juts out from the Arabian Peninsula to the north of Oman. Contemporary British sources often cite the Qawasim as the Joasem or Joasemi, reflecting the local pronunciation of the Arabic *qaf* as a *jīm*. The sources also refer to the Qawasim as a single political entity, though in fact the population under Qasimi authority and protection consisted of Arabs, Persians and Indians. They traded in and transported pearls, gold and textiles, which they transported across mercantile networks connected to Persia, India and through the Arabian and Red Seas.[12] The Qasimi fleet consisted of an estimated 18,760 men and over 700 ships in the latter part of the eighteenth century, constituting the largest locally based fleet in the region.[13]

Competition between the Qasimi traders and smaller fleets in the Persian Gulf, including those of Bahrain and Qatar, led to maritime conflicts that disrupted trade. The Qawasim posed a threat to the EIC's ambitions to control trade in and out of eastern India and to minimize interruptions of trade and loss of goods through raids on sea. Sporadic, short-lived conflicts broke out in the eighteenth century between British-protected Omani ships and Qasimi traders. On occasion, the Qawasim allied with Oman against the Saudis when they spread to al-Hasa and Buraimi in 1800. Through most of the latter half

---

[10] Lorimer's *Gazetteer* provides the most extensive detail on tribes and populations from the eighteenth and nineteenth century based on an extensive survey of the Persian Gulf region and tribes along the Arab coast. For a relatively concise discussion of the most significant tribes in Abu Dhabi in the late nineteenth and early twentieth century, see Frauke Heard-Bey, *From Trucial States to United Arab Emirates* (Dubai: Motivate Publishing, 2004), 27–80.
[11] Al-Qasimi, *Myth of Arab Piracy* (1988).
[12] Charles Davies, *Blood-Red Arab Flag: An Investigation Into Qasimi Piracy, 1797–1820* (Exeter: University of Exeter Press, 1997), 57–79.
[13] Al-Qasimi, *Myth of Arab Piracy*, 31.

Table 1.1 Sheikhs Signatory to the General Maritime Treaty of 1820 and Their Territories Recognized by the British Government

Shakhbut bin Diyab al Talahij	Abu Dhabi
Zaid bin Saif [Syf] (on behalf of Mohammed bin Haza bin Zaal)	Dubai [Debay]
Sultan bin Saqr (Sultan bin Suggur)	Sharjah and Ras al-Khaimah
Hassan bin Rahma (Hassun bin Rahmah)	Hatt and Fahleia (near Ras al-Khaimah)
Rajib bin Ahmed [Kazib? Bin Ahmed]	Jazirah al-Hamra [Jourat al Kamra]
Rashid bin Humaid [Rashed bin Hamid]	Ajman [Chief of Ejman]
Hassun bin Ali	Sheikh of Zyah [Rams and Al Dhayah]
Abdullah bin Rashid	Umm al-Qaiwain [Umm-ool-Keiweyn]
Suleiman bin Ahmed Al Khalifa and Abdullah bin Ahmed Al Khalifa	Bahrain

of the eighteenth century, though, the Qawasim and Oman practiced what historian Charles Davies has described as a 'state of low-level undeclared war', with frequent skirmishes along the northern coast.[14]

As a result of the Qawasim defeat, the Arab tribes of the Persian Gulf became inextricably linked to the EIC. The following year the British negotiated the General Maritime Treaty of 1820 with Arab rulers on the eastern Arabian Coast.[15] The General Maritime Treaty established truces with the leading sheikhs of the coast and Bahrain. These truces required the signatories to surrender all 'vessels of piratical powers' and those which were not used for pearling and fishing and cease all activities pertaining to 'piracy'.[16] The final Treaty of 1820 furthermore required 'friendly' ships to fly the white-pierced red flag, not to fight with one another, and to carry a register of the ship, captain, and crew. This early agreement ostensibly limited the EIC's interference in the Gulf to maritime affairs (see Table 1.1).

The Bombay government sent Captain Thomas Thompson of the British Army, along with a detachment, from his posting at Ras Al Khaimah to Qishm island to enforce the treaties. From there, Thompson and his successors oversaw a 'watch

---

[14] Davies, *Blood-Red Arab Flag*, 60.
[15] Also known as the General Treaty for the Cessation of Plunder and Piracy.
[16] 'The Preliminary and General Treaties with the British Government, January 1820' (2.54), *Arabian Treaties, 1600–1960*, vol. 2, 415–20; and 'The Preliminary and General Treaties with the British Government, January 1820', (2.01) 3–14.

and cruise' policy in which three British naval ships would circulate regularly through the Trucial ports to monitor shipping and trade.[17] The expanded British naval presence may have served as a deterrent, but it certainly did not bring an end to the disputes between the sheikhdoms. Conflicts broke out in the decade and a half following the 1820 truce as Oman and Bahrain in particular sought to establish their sovereignty and spheres of influence. Naval leadership used incidents of maritime violence to establish precedents that would discourage future incidents. In one case in 1825, a Qasimi ship attacked a Bahraini vessel. The Senior Marine Officer met with the ruler of Sharjah, Sultan ibn Saqr, to gain his cooperation in punishing the offenders. This event caused Saqr to take a more proactive role in future incidents in an effort to forestall British interference. When, three years later, an incident between a Qasimi ship and another from Oman broke out, Saqr imprisoned and then killed the Qasimi commander.[18] Such actions were in keeping with the stated goals of non-interference of the British government and the EIC as articulated in the 1820 treaty.

Non-interference was not a disinterested laissez faire policy. Naval officers were warned to avoid directly intervening or becoming entangled in local maritime strife as they continued to patrol even in times of conflict between local forces. In 1829, for example, the Political Resident wrote from Bushehr to Captain Wilson on the Sloop of War, Coote, warning him that 'a war at present exists between the Shaikh of [Bahrain] and His Highness the Imam of Muskat aided by Shaikh Thanoon [sic] of Aboodhabie ... but the Government having avowed a determination not to interfere in this quarrel therefore caution you observe the letter during your stay at this Island'.[19] The war escalated through the spring when the Bombay government attempted unsuccessfully to facilitate a peace between the two sides in May.

The truces, combined with naval patrols, reduced the disruptions in trade during the lucrative pearling season. The Trucial sheikhs also signed additional peace treaties under British auspices in 1835, intended to end disruptive warring and protect the integrity of the pearling season. This was renewed annually until 1843, when the truce was renewed again for ten years. The success of these truces inspired the 1853 Perpetual Treaty, which made the agreements a permanent arrangement.[20] Bahrain signed on to the treaty in 1861.

---

[17] J. B. Kelly, *Britain and the Persian Gulf, 1795–1880* (Oxford: Oxford University Press, 1968), 193–208.
[18] Kelly, *Britain and the Persian Gulf*, 205–8.
[19] Capt. David Wilson, Resident of the Persian Gulf (Bushehr) to Captain Wilson of Sloop of War Coote. 27 January 1829. *Naval Reports*, 1.07, 181–2.
[20] 'Treaty of Maritime Peace in Perpetuity', May 4 1853 in *Arabian Treaties: 1600–1960*. Ed. Penelope Tuson and Emma Quick, vol. 2. 469–72.

These treaties not only extended peace among the Trucial States and with the EIC. They also established an increasingly protective relationship between the British Empire and the Trucial sheikhs and limited the rulers to the administration of internal affairs. All negotiations with foreign governments would go through the British Political Residency. The 1853 treaty lay the groundwork for this principle, stating that 'aggression being committed at sea by any of those who are subscribers with us to this engagement … [the rulers] will not proceed immediately to retaliate, but will inform the British Resident or the Commodore at Bassidore, who will forthwith take the necessary steps for obtaining reparation'.[21] Subsequent agreements with rulers on the Trucial Coast further cemented Britain's navy and the British India Office roles as the exclusive agents of foreign affairs. By signing the Protectorate Treaties of 1892 the rulers of Abu Dhabi, Sharjah, Dubai, Ajman, Umm Al Quwain and Ras Al Khaimah agreed not to correspond with foreign powers, not to accept any official agent and not to cede or sell territory to anyone but the British government.[22] This level of British oversight, argues Ali Hasan al-Hamdani, signified the real mark of occupation of British legal and political control, rather than the earlier treaties and bombardment of the Arabian ports.[23]

The Trucial States would never become colonies of the British Empire; nevertheless, by the twentieth century, British administrative structures guided and dominated the politics and development of the Trucial States. This development was driven first by the EIC's purview – the desire to control shipping lanes and prevent interruption of British trade through the Persian Gulf and Indian Ocean. By the end of the nineteenth century, the British government and India Office took the lead, regularizing the administrative structures and shifting the focus from local trade to broader geo-strategic interests.

The Ottomans, the Saudis and the Trucial Coast

Britain's presence in the Gulf not only shaped the regional politics but also drew the attention of the Ottoman and Russian empires. The Ottoman Empire

---

[21] 'The Perpetual Maritime Treaty', May 4 1853 in *Arabian Treaties*, 467–72. This was further cemented by the 'Protectorate Treaties, 1892', in *Arabian Treaties*, 505–6.
[22] 'Exclusive Agreement of the Shaikhs of Trucial Oman with the British Government, March, 1892', in J. G. Lorimer, *Gazetteer of the Persian Gulf: Oman and Central Arabia* (Calcutta: Supt. Government Printing, 1908–1915), v. 1, 786.
[23] Ali Hasan al-Hamdani, *Dawlat al-Amirat al-ʿArabiya: Nishaʾituha wa Tatawuruha* (Kuwait: Maktaba al-Maʿala, 1986), 18–19.

pursued a resurgence in the Gulf in the latter half of the nineteenth century even as Russia seemed to hover in the background of Persia. Taken together, British policymakers in London and Calcutta viewed these encroachments as a threat to their empire in India. Ottoman and Russian potential for expanding their influence in the Gulf lent a sense of urgency to Britain's defence of its role as singular protector over the Trucial States. British intervention in the affairs of the Trucial States increased as the Ottomans focused more attention on al-Hasa, Bahrain and Qatar.

Ottoman power in the Gulf had waxed and waned since its initial occupation of the al-Hasa region in 1550. At times, the Ottoman sultans exercised direct control; at other times, they competed with local notables from Arabia, Iraq and Basra, exercising indirect or even nominal control through local notables well into the nineteenth century. The nineteenth-century Ottoman Empire, however, initiated a series of reforms, collectively known as the *Tanzimat*, or 'reorganization', to centralize the government and re-establish itself as a world power in the face of European encroachment. The reforms, initiated in 1836 continued through 1876, and were especially transformative in Baghdad and greater Iraq.

Midhat Pasha, one of the most influential Ottoman modernizers of the late nineteenth century carried the *Tanzimat* to the Gulf. Having been sent to Baghdad as governor in 1869, he would spend the next three years transforming Baghdad and Basra. Midhat Pasha oversaw the completion of telegraph communications in Iraq, especially between Baghdad and Basra; improved steamer transportation from Baghdad and Basra; and revived the Basra dockyards in order to open Mesopotamia to the Gulf and, consequently, the world. He also continued to oversee reforms of the Ottoman military which had been in progress for decades and extended Ottoman order to the Iraqi frontiers.[24]

Meanwhile, in the central plains of Arabia, the Saudi tribe had begun to revitalize itself. The Al Saud family had fused its military might with a religious fervour inspired by Muhammad ibn Abd al-Wahhab in 1744. This first Saudi emirate expanded through central Arabia and outward to both coasts of the Arabian Peninsula by the early nineteenth century.[25] Egyptian troops, at the behest of the Ottoman Empire, defeated the Saudis in 1818. A subsequent Saudi emirate grew out of the ashes of the previous one, and by 1830 had occupied

---

[24] Ebubekir Ceylan, *The Ottoman Origins of Modern Iraq: Political Reform, Modernization, and Development in the Nineteenth-Century Middle East* (New York: I.B. Tauris, 2011), 65–7, 187–201.
[25] Madawi al-Rasheed, *A History of Saudi Arabia* (Cambridge: Cambridge University Press, 2011).

al-Hasa once again. After the death of the emir Faisal bin Turki Al Saud in 1865, war broke out between his sons Abdullah and Saud over who would replace him as ruler. The conflict spread to the coast and threatened to spill over into the Trucial States.[26]

Midhat Pasha capitalized on the weakness of the Saudi state to advance Ottoman interests. By 1870, the Ottoman Empire had made substantial progress in asserting control over Iraq. Furthermore, the government needed better positions to defend its interests in western and southern Arabia from British encroachment. Al-Hasa could also serve as a valuable site for protecting Iraq, Syria and the Hijaz from the Saudi expansion. Upon learning that Abdullah sought allies to help defeat his brother in Riyadh, Midhat launched a large-scale campaign to recapture al-Hasa for the Ottomans. The following May, over 7,000 Ottoman forces landed at Ras Tanura and succeeded in attacks on the first Saudi locations at Qatif and Dammam. Once captured, the Ottoman governor set about consolidating new administrative practices in al-Hasa.[27] Ottoman rule would continue in al-Hasa from 1871 until 1913, when Abdulaziz ibn Saud and his forces conquered the region. Despite the Ottoman attempt to expand, Britain maintained its hold over the Trucial States and extended it to Bahrain and Qatar. All of this would be managed through its Political Residency system into the twentieth century.

British administration on the Trucial Coast

The Trucial States' relationship with the EIC began as truces, or peace treaties, meant to protect British and British-allied trade interests. Almost immediately after the first treaties were signed, however, the EIC's role in India began shifting from economic to geopolitical aims. Anthony Webster has shown how philosophical shifts in London away from mercantilist policies to a belief in liberalist free trade combined with financial difficulties in the EIC to fundamentally change the role of the EIC in Asia and the subcontinent. The Charter Act of 1833 shifted the EIC from a commercial venture to a governmental body acting on behalf of, but with great autonomy from, the British government.[28] From 1833 to 1858, administration of indirect British rule through the EIC was organized around

---

[26] Al-Rasheed, *History of Saudi Arabia*.
[27] Anscombe, *Ottoman Gulf*.
[28] Anthony Webster, *Twilight of the East India Company: The Evolution of Anglo-Asian Commerce and Politics, 1790–1860* (London: Boydell & Brewer, 2009), 2–3, 101.

a residency system that had originated in factory and trade centres of the EIC's eighteenth-century commercial ventures.

The diplomatic and military arms of the EIC were hardly distinguishable in the eighteenth and early nineteenth centuries in the Persian Gulf. The nineteenth century witnessed the decline of the EIC as a financial powerhouse and its rise instead as a political engine for the British in India. The EIC, to maintain its political and protective role in the Persian Gulf and over the Arab states, reinstituted a system of 'residencies' created as part of its earlier mercantile mission. At Basra, the EIC created the position of 'Resident', or senior merchant, who was subordinate to the Persian Agent posted at Bandar Abbas. The EIC had reinstated this role in 1764, creating residencies to administer the growing political commitments and interests of the EIC in India and expanding control outward to the frontiers of EIC purview.

The first expression of this in the Gulf came in 1820. Captain Thompson's posting at Qishm Island marked the beginning of the political agency there. Two years later, this post moved to Bushehr and combined with the Bushehr Residency (established in 1763) and became the Office of the Resident in the Persian Gulf until 1850, when the title changed to Political Resident in the Persian Gulf. The Resident served as the point of contact between the Trucial Coast and the Bombay Office. The Resident answered directly to the Bombay Political Department under the Governor-General of India appointed by the EIC until 1858. Administration of India at that time transferred from the EIC to the British government following the Indian Uprising of 1857. Administration of Anglo-Trucial affairs consequently shifted to the newly established India Office.[29] A Secretary of State for India in London directed the Viceroy in India on behalf of the British government. From 1858 until 1947, the India Office also appointed a Political Resident for the Persian Gulf, who acted as the mediator between the British government in India and the rulers on the Trucial Coast.

The Political Resident oversaw agents and officers in locations throughout the Gulf. On the Trucial Coast, agents and officers were usually a local Arab, Indian or Persian who acted as the coastal extension of British authority in the Persian Gulf until the end of the nineteenth century. The appointment of George Curzon as Viceroy of India in 1899, however, marked an expanded British presence in the Gulf. Not long after settling in India, Curzon took his famed 1903 tour of

---

[29] Rosemarie Said-Zahlan, *Origins of the United Arab Emirates: A Political and Social History of the Trucial States* (New York: Routledge, 1978), 22–5, describes the ambiguities of administration in the Gulf in greater detail. Essentially, the Political Resident answered to both the Colonial Office and the India Office, which coordinated Gulf policy through interdepartmental committees.

the Gulf, stopping at ports along the western coast. Curzon held an expansive view of British power and importance in the Gulf and on his tour expressed his desire to take an active role in pacifying the Gulf to maintain the security of the Indian Empire. As part of this effort, Curzon oversaw a shift from native agents and officers to British political officers, both to strengthen relationships with the local rulers and to increase British authority while simultaneously fending off European and Ottoman attempts to gain influence.[30]

To accomplish his goals in the Gulf, Curzon appointed Percy Cox to the position of Acting Political Resident, Persian Gulf.[31] Cox had served in the Indian Army in 1884. Following several years in the Scottish Rifles, he was posted to Aden and then the Somali Coast. In 1899, however, Curzon promoted Cox to Political Agent in Muscat. There, he was expected to improve relations with the Sultan of Muscat and Oman, Faisal bin Turki Al Said, as well as monitor developments between the French presence in the Gulf. Cox proved successful on both accounts, and in 1904, Curzon appointed him to the office of Political Resident at Bushehr. Cox became responsible for the enforcement of treaties and for upholding British interests in the Gulf through 1920. As his biographer John Townsend has noted, Cox's appointment held jointly as British Consul General and thus was also under the auspices of the Foreign Office.[32] This would place him in a unique position at the outbreak of the First World War as a high-ranking British official with a proverbial foot in both London and Bombay.

The European launch of the war in June 1914 came to the Ottoman Empire several months later. In November, the Allied Powers declared war on the Ottoman Empire for harbouring German warships in the Black Sea. The first years of Ottoman involvement in the war focused on the Russian border and the Mediterranean, but by November 1914, the British government sought to open up a front in Mesopotamia. The British Indian armies invaded from the Persian Gulf via the Shatt al-Arab and on to Basra in the summer before bogging down south of Baghdad at Ctesiphon. They fell to Turkish forces at Kut the following Spring. More than a year passed before British and Indian forces regrouped and continued on to take Baghdad in March 1917. Before the war ended, the British continued on to capture and occupy Kirkuk and Mosul.[33]

---

[30] Onley, *Arabian Frontier*.
[31] Cox's title would be formalized as Political Resident in 1908; in 1911, he would become Sir Percy Cox.
[32] John Townsend, *Proconsul to the Middle East: Sir Percy Cox and the End of Empire* (London: I. B. Tauris, 2010), 11.
[33] Reeva Spector Simon, 'The View from Baghdad', in *The Creation of Iraq: 1914-1921*, ed. Reeva Spector Simon and Eleanor H. Tejirian (New York: Columbia University Press, 2004), 41-3. Kristian Ulrichson has argued that the initial British failure to advance on Baghdad was the result of the 'fragmented policy-making process' created by the shared decision making of the War Office and

With the British landing at the Shatt al-Arab, Percy Cox received a new assignment as Chief Political Officer to the British Expeditionary Force from the Government of India. He was tasked with traveling to Mesopotamia in 1915 to help coordinate British strategy there during the war. As an official of the British government in India, he would carry the interests and perspectives of the India Office as the basis for his policies and approaches. After the occupation of Baghdad, he relinquished his role as Political Resident but continued on as High Commissioner through 1923. While there he hired native agents to serve in administrative positions, thus extending the influence of the India Office into Mesopotamia until he left. After that time, the Arabists would increase their influence and press for the Foreign Office's Arabian department to take over the administration.[34]

Meanwhile, a second development would further reshape the post-war Middle East and would draw the Trucial Coast further into the Arab core's political sphere. Britain sought to force the Ottoman Empire into opening up yet another front in the war in Palestine. A disgruntled Ottoman official in the Hijaz provided an opening that the Arab Bureau of the Cairo Intelligence Agency was prepared to exploit.[35] Husayn bin Ali al-Hashemi, who was appointed Grand Sherif of the Hijaz in 1908, had become increasingly worried that his deteriorating relationship with the Ottoman government would lead to his removal. He looked instead to break away and establish a state of his own. In 1915, he initiated correspondence with the British High Commissioner in Egypt, Sir Henry McMahon.[36] Their exchange outlined British support for Husayn's establishment of an Arab state in exchange for an Arab insurrection.

The Arab Revolt began in June 1916. Husayn's sons, leading an irregular army of bedouin forces, engaged the Ottomans through subterfuge, skirmishes and battles. The revolt's success, and the outsized celebrity status of T. E. Lawrence and the Arabists who helped to orchestrate it, had significant, if indirect,

---

Government of India. Kristian Coates Ulrichsen, *The First World War in the Middle East* (London: C. Hurst, 2014), 124.

[34] Townsend, *Proconsul to the Middle East*; Spector Simon, 'View from Baghdad', 36–49.
[35] Priya Satia, *Spies in Arabia: The Great War and the Cultural Foundations of Britain's Covert Empire in the Middle East* (New York: Oxford University Press, 2008), 23–58.
[36] Conversations had previously been initiated in February 1914, but the British consulate in Egypt demurred, based on the state of goodwill between the Ottomans and Britain at the time. Later in the year, in anticipation of the Ottomans joining the war, Ronald Storrs suggested that Herbert Kitchener reconsider the offer. Kitchener directed Storrs to follow up, but this time Husayn hesitated. Eugene Rogan, *The Fall of the Ottomans: The Great War in the Middle East* (New York: Basic Books, 2015), 275–309.

implications for the future of the Gulf and Britain's administration of it. As it would turn out, the British government had no serious intentions of supporting Husayn's bid for a greater Arab state. British operative Mark Sykes and French diplomat François Georges-Picot agreed to form a partition plan for the Arab territories among the two European nations, thus effectively cutting Husayn out of his claims for an Arab state. His claims were further eroded by British promises under the Balfour Declaration, which carved out the region of Palestine for British supervision. These agreements made during the war were enacted after the war through a series of treaties and the subsequent establishment of British and French Mandates under the League of Nations.

British lack of support for Husayn's ambitions became apparent after the war. His attempt to occupy Syria failed when the French military pushed his son, Faisal, out of Damascus. He subsequently battled with Saudi ambitions. In late 1924, Saudi forces made forays into the Hijaz, which destabilized Husayn's rule and led him to abdicate in favour of his son Ali. The Saudis attacked the Hijaz again in January 1925. Following a year-long siege, the British government negotiated Ali's retreat, leaving the Hijaz open for the Saudis to extend their authority to the west coast of the peninsula.[37] This set the stage for the 1927 Treaty of Jeddah, in which Britain acknowledged Saudi Arabia's independence and primacy in the interior of the Arabian Peninsula, while the Saudis recognized Britain's control over the Gulf and Arab littoral.

Britain's new position of greater prominence in the Arab world drew Gulf affairs further into the sphere of Foreign Office affairs and consequently the political affairs of the Arab Middle East. Britain had established ties with the new Saudi State following the First World War. The Saudis had gained the upper hand over British-allied Husayn of Mecca. As the Saudis swept through the Arabian Peninsula, British policymakers switched sides and agreed to recognize Saud as the main power in the Arabian Peninsula. The Foreign Office would oversee relations between the Saudis and the British government in most affairs but would coordinate with the India Office, which handled Saudi relations along the Gulf. This combined with the expectations of Iraqi independence and Britain's wish to have a stronger, more effective diplomatic presence in the Gulf. Finally, the rise of anti-British sentiment in Iranian politics in advance of the election of Mossadeq to the Iranian parliament made the relocation of the Political Residency office from Bushehr to elsewhere in the Gulf desirable.

[37] al-Rasheed, *History of Saudi Arabia*, 44–7.

2

The interwar years

In the years between the World Wars, the Trucial Coast experienced significant changes both within the emirates and in their relationships with the Arab world and the British Empire. Technological transformations expanded British power from the seas to the skies – and consequently further inland than the shorelines. The Trucial Coast proved vital to Britain's air route to India and the Far East. The new reliance on air power also underlined the importance of petroleum to the post-war military and industrialization, thus making the prospect of oil deposits in the Arabian Peninsula a significant asset to Britain.

These advances created new opportunities for the sheikhs in the form of much-needed revenue, but also came with political consequences they were loath to accept. Several of the rulers attempted to resist the expansion of British power in the Gulf. By the late 1920s, though, the Trucial Coast was experiencing a significant economic decline due to a global depression and the collapse of its pearling industry. At the same time, the British Political Residents of the Persian Gulf found it relatively easy to dispense with the pretence that they should not interfere with the internal politics of the Trucial Coast. They employed a wide range of tactics to coax and coerce the rulers into agreements that would expand Britain's reach.

The emirates during this time also underwent several significant changes in leadership. These would include a new ruler for Abu Dhabi, shifting leadership and status of Sharjah and Ras Al Khaimah and even British recognition of an entirely new emirate. These rulers would lead the emirates out of the interwar period. This chapter begins with an overview of these changes in the emirates and the economic conditions which increased their vulnerability when Britain would pressure them to acquiesce to terms for airfields and oil concession agreements in the 1930s.

New leaders and an old economy

In the latter half of the nineteenth century, Abu Dhabi had been guided by the steady and long-serving leadership of Zayed bin Khalifah Al Nahyan, or Zayed the Great. He had become the ruling sheikh of Trucial Oman's largest emirate in 1855 and would rule until his death in 1909. During his rule, Zayed bin Khalifah had weathered wars with Sharjah and Qatar, as well as other internal disputes with Dubai and Umm Al Quwain. He had also expanded the reach of Abu Dhabi's influence through a series of marriages and united several new tribes under Abu Dhabi's protection and authority. The result of his long reign was that at his death in 1909, he had increased the annual income of the emirate through control over the largest pearling fleet on the Trucial Coast.

The nineteen years which followed were tumultuous ones. Zayed's oldest son, Khalifa, declined to succeed his father, paving the way for Zayed's second son, Tahnoun, to take over. Tahnoun died in 1912. Abu Dhabi politics descended into a period of disputed succession and fratricide. Hamdan bin Zayed (1912–22) had failed to quell unrest among tribes on Abu Dhabi's frontiers. He was ultimately killed by his brother Sultan bin Zayed whose short reign lasted until 1925. Sultan had angered members of the family when he failed to pay his various relatives an allowance. His brother Saqr (r. 1925–8) then killed Sultan bin Zayed and took the role as leading Sheikh of Abu Dhabi.[1]

Saqr ended up on the wrong side of disputes with his eldest brother Khalifah and Khalifah's powerful allies, the Manasir. Following Sultan's assassination, his sons Shakhbut and Hazza' escaped to Buraimi. British sources indicate that Saqr attempted to have the brothers brought back to Abu Dhabi to eliminate them as a threat to his rule, even sending ships to retrieve Shakhbut and Hazza from an island off the coast. This elicited a response from the British Residency which warned him about violating the maritime peace agreements in his pursuit of is nephews.[2] The following June, Saqr was murdered, apparently at the instigation of Khalifah bin Zayed, who sent for Shakhbut and Hazza.[3] Upon their arrival, the family recognized Shakhbut as the ruler of Abu Dhabi. The following month, the British Agent at Sharjah stopped in to confirm Shakhbut's commitment to

---

[1] Uzi Rabi, 'Oil Politics and Tribal Rulers in Eastern Arabia: The Reign of Shakhbut (1928–1966)', *British Journal of Middle Eastern Studies* 33, no. 1 (2006): 37–50; Jayanti Maitra and Afra al-Hajji, *Qasr Al Hosn: The History of the Rulers of Abu Dhabi, 1793–1966* (Abu Dhabi: Centre for Documentation and Research, 2004); Heard-Bey, *From Trucial States to United Arab Emirates*.
[2] British Resident to Saqr, 23 July 1927. *ROE*, v. 7, 180; Haworth, Political Resident Persian Gulf to Foreign Secretary, Government of India, 13 December 1927. *ROE*, v. 7, 227.
[3] Resident Agent, Sharjah, to Political Resident, Bushehr. *ROE*, v. 7, 189.

Table 2.1 Rulers of Abu Dhabi and Their End of Reign 1855–1928

Zayed I bin Khalifah	1855–1909	Natural death
Tahnoun bin Zayed	1909–12	Natural death
Hamdan bin Zayed	1912–22	Fratricide by Sultan II
Sultan II bin Zayed	1922–6	Fratricide by Saqr
Saqr bin Zayed	1926–8	Assassinated
Shakhbut II bin Sultan	1928–66	Deposed

the treaties with Britain. He provided a positive report, noting that there was 'tranquility and peace' in Abu Dhabi at last: 'When I was there I perceived that all the inhabitants of Abu Dhabi liked Shaikh Shakhboot [sic] and praised him and therefore I obtained a letter from him confirming the treaties.'[4] At twenty-three Shakhbut began his long rule in Abu Dhabi with the approbation of Political Residency (see Table 2.1).

Power in the northern part of the Trucial Coast also shifted significantly in the nineteenth century. The Al Qasimi, who ruled over a confederation of tribes from their port in Ras Al Khaimah until 1820, would spend a portion of the latter half of the nineteenth century attempting to consolidate power between branches of the ruling family. After the British destroyed the port at Ras Al Khaimah, the Al Qasimi capitol moved to Sharjah. In the middle of the century, the Qawasim expanded its influence under the rule of Sultan bin Saqr (r. 1820–66), capturing territory extending to Khor Fakkan, and Kalba and consolidating his control over the coastal areas of Ajman and Umm Al Quwain. Following his death, the region lost its cohesion. Leading sheikhs were sent to different parts of the territory to serve as *walis*, or representatives to the ruler. The latter half of the century saw these *walis* competing to establish themselves as the pre-eminent rulers of the territory. In 1869, Ras Al Khaimah broke away from Sharjah. In the decades that followed the various territories under Ras Al Khaimah and Sharjah frequently engaged in politicking between the two rulers to gain influence for themselves. Ras Al Khaimah remained independent under Humaid bin Abdullah until 1900. Following his death, Ras Al Khaimah returned to the control of the ruler of Sharjah but again operated as a largely independent emirate after 1910 under the control of Salim bin Sultan. Upon his death in 1919, his son Sultan took his place, and in 1921, the British government recognized him as the independent ruler of Ras Al Khaimah. In Sharjah, Saqr

---

[4] Resident Agent, Sharjah to Political Resident Persian Gulf, 1 May 1928. *ROE*, v. 7, 194.

Table 2.2 Rulers and Status of Sharjah and Ras Al Khaimah, 1866–1951

Sharjah		Ras Al Khaimah		
Name	Date	Name	Date	Status
Khalid bin Sultan	1866–8	Ibrahim bin Sultan	1866–7	Independent
		Khalid bin Sultan	1867–68	Under Sharjah
Salim bin Sultan	1868–83		1868–9	Under Sharjah
Saqr bin Khalid	1883–1914	Humaid bin Abdullah	1869–1900	Autonomous wali under Sharjah
			1900–10	Under Saqr bin Khalid
Khalid bin Ahmed	1914–24	Salim bin Sultan	1910–19	Autonomous wali under Sharjah
		Sultan bin Salim	1919–48	Recognized as independent state in 1921
Sultan bin Saqr	1924–51	Saqr bin Mohammad	1948–2010	Independent

bin Khalid died in 1914, and his leadership fell to his cousin Khalid bin Ahmad until 1924 at which time Saqr bin Khalid's son deposed Khalid bin Ahmad. He would remain the ruler of Sharjah until his death in 1951 (see Table 2.2).[5]

The manoeuvrings of these various territories and the extent of their local authority has been documented in the *Gazetteer*. The precise status of sovereignty in each of these emirates is not always clear, as official records of British recognition aligned more frequently with British prerogatives – not necessarily with local perspectives of authority.[6] Formal recognition of the Trucial sheikhs as rulers depended on British recognition of their authority over territories and their willingness to affirm their commitment to the treaties with Britain. This practice would continue through the interwar years until 1952, when the number of recognized Trucial States was fixed at the seven states comprising the United Arab Emirates today.

---

[5] Lorimer, *Gazetteer of the Persian Gulf* v. 1, Historical. Part IA and IB (1915) 759–63; Heard-Bey, *From Trucial States to United Arab Emirates*, 84–5; Said-Zahlan, *Origins of the United Arab Emirates*, 13–15.

[6] Niklas A. Haller, 'Selective Recognition as an Imperial Instrument: Britain and the Trucial States, 1820–1952', *Journal of Arabian Studies* 8, no. 2 (2018): 275–97.

Britain's acknowledgement of a ruler could create significant financial windfalls at a time when the economic forecast of the Trucial Coast looked especially grim. These opportunities would come in two significant forms. One of these would be leases and agreements pertaining to Britain's expanding security needs. The other come through oil exploration agreements. Only those rulers whom the British government recognized through the treaties would find themselves recipients of benefits such as the rents generated from leasing land to the British government, or from concession agreements for mineral and oil rights, as will be seen further on.

Economic decline and new opportunities

The political strength of the rulers depended in part on the overall economic prosperity the rulers enjoyed and the patronage which their relative wealth could provide. The limited economies of the Trucial Coast depended primarily on subsistence-level agriculture and fishing, buttressed by regional trade, date farming and, above all, the pearl trade. The global depression of the interwar years devastated the economy of the Trucial States. International demand for natural Gulf pearls all but disappeared. Amid the collapse of this market, however, the British government was able to provide new sources of revenue through aviation and oil exploration.

At the end of the nineteenth and beginning of the twentieth century the economies of the Trucial Coast were limited in their scope. Agriculture in areas of Sharjah and Ras Al Khaimah, as well as in inland oases such as those at Al Ain and Buraimi on the Abu Dhabi–Oman frontier provided much of the produce that could be consumed on the Trucial Coast. This, combined with fishing and local livestock, provided sustenance to the local populations, though these were supplemented with regional trade, especially in grains such as rice imported from India and Basra. While date production and exportation in much of the Gulf became a significant minority of trade elsewhere on the Arabian coast, Lorimer's *Gazetteer* indicates that the Trucial States did not produce sufficient dates to support both the population and export:

> Except in the Ras-al-Khaimah district and in the Baraimi [sic] Oasis … the production of dates is small … The few dates produced in Trucial Oman are far from satisfying the large demand of the somewhat dense pearl-fishing population; and, during the six years from 1899–1900 to 1904–1905, dates and

date juice were imported to an annual average value of more than £20,000, chiefly from Persian ports and from Turkish 'Iraq.[7]

The primary economic activity of the Trucial Coast into the interwar period, then, was pearl fishing and trade.

The Arabian coast of the Gulf has been the source of natural pearls and mother-of-pearl for millennia.[8] The coast is home to shallow oyster beds stretching from Qatif in the north to Abu Dhabi in the south. At the turn of the twentieth century, pearl diving and sales comprised an extensive market system with elaborate taxation and financing structures that bound the Trucial Coast to Bombay and markets beyond.

The rhythms of daily life, individual employment, population movement and the political structures of the Trucial Coast depended on the success of the annual pearl harvest. Each spring, large numbers of men would migrate from inland territories towards the coastal towns, many of which had been nearly deserted in the off season. Weeks would be spent preparing boats, amassing supplies and assembling crews before the first short diving period. After an initial 'Cold Dive' in April, crews would return for a break and to finish gathering provisions. The 'Great Dive' then was launched around late May and usually continued through September, punctuated with short breaks for crews. In late October, a final short diving period marked the end of the season when the men would return home.

Crew sizes could vary depending on how far out from the coast they were working. According to Lorimer, 'It may be stated generally that the crew of a sea-going boat is from 6 to 42 hands, while that a boat working along the coast only is usually from 4 to 6.'[9] The crews consisted of a captain (*nakhuda*), divers (*ghasah*, s./*ghais*, p.) and haulers (*saib*, s./*siyub*, p.). Some crews would also include hands (*radhafa*) and perhaps a young apprentice (*walaid*). The captain was usually the owner of the boat and hired the crew. Of the crew members, the divers were the most important. Most of them were enslaved or freed Africans, though Lorimer observed that 'many respectable Arabs' had begun to work as divers because the work had become more profitable. Divers would be equipped with weights to help carry them down 8 to 12 fathoms to the seabed where they collected oysters in a bag before haulers pulled them back up

---

[7] *Gazetteer*, v. 1, pt. 2 (1915), 2296.
[8] Robert Carter, 'The Prehistory and History of Pearling in the Persian Gulf', *Journal of the Economic and Social History of the Orient* 48, no. 2 (2005): 140, 143–8.
[9] *Gazetteer*, v. 1 pt. 2 (1915), 2262.

with ropes.[10] The *Gazetteer* estimated approximately 22,045 men worked in some capacity in the early part of the twentieth century, or nearly all the able-bodied men of the Trucial Coast.

Even before the pearls were harvested and brought to land, the crews and their captains were enmeshed in a marketplace of finance and exchange. Auxiliary markets were set up at the outset of the season to supply crews with food and materials necessary to make it through the season. These goods were paid for through loans financed by merchants and taken out by the captains and their crew members. At the end of the season, each crew member was assigned a payout based on a portion of the catch and their jobs minus whatever loans they took out to equip themselves. The captain would usually sell the catch to local or regional pearl merchants. Dubai became the second largest port, after Qatar, in the early part of the century. From there, pearls were exported to wholesalers in Bombay who supplied the global market.[11]

The pearling industry generated additional revenues for the ruler through a variety of taxes. The ruler of each Trucial State could apply tax rates independently of the other states. The most common tax, the *nob*, was assessed per pearling boat, and the amount might depend on the size of each boat. For example, at Rams port in Sharjah, the ruler collected two bags of rice per boat; in Abu Dhabi, the ruler received '1 hauler's share per large or medium boat and 1 diver's share per small boat in autumn; also $100 royalty on every pearl fished worth Rs. 1,000 or more'.[12] Additional taxes could be levied on the number of divers, costs for security or on the size of a crew. These taxes and other earnings from the pearl trade are estimated to have made up most of the rulers' incomes on the Trucial Coast. For Abu Dhabi, two thirds or more of the ruler's income was

---

[10] A fathom is roughly six feet in depth, or 1.8 meters. Of depth, Lorimer says,

> In the choice of a bank, the Nakhuda is limited by the powers of his divers; 8 fathoms is an ordinary depth, and 12 is perhaps the greatest at which work can be carried on without discomfort; boats with good divers, however, will work on banks carrying 14 fathoms. There are men who can negotiate 16 fathoms of water, but the strain at this depth is too great to be endured long, even by the strongest, and fatal accidents sometimes occur in working at such a level. (*Gazetteer*, v. 1, pt. 2 (1915), 2229)

[11] Fahad Bishara, Bernard Haykel, Steffen Hertog, Clive Holes and James Onley 'The Economic Transformation of the Gulf', in *The Emergence of the Gulf States* ed. J. E. Peterson (London: Bloomsbury, 2016), 198–204. There were some variations in processes of finance and sale, depending on the year and the circumstances of the captain's original loan terms. See Victoria Penziner Hightower, 'Pearling and Political Power in the Trucial States, 1850–1930: Debts, Taxes, and Politics', *Journal of Arabian Studies* 3, no. 2 (2013): 215–31.

[12] *Gazetteer*, v. 1, pt. 2 (1915), 2284–9.

derived from the pearl trade, with similar proportions making up the income for the remaining rulers.[13]

So essential to the functioning of the Trucial Coast was the pearling industry that Lorimer observed ominously that without the pearling fisheries the Trucial States would be lost: 'Were the supply of pearls to fail ... the ports of Trucial Oman, which have no other resources, would practically cease to exist'.[14] He was very nearly correct, though it would be the demand for pearls that dried up, not the pearl supply itself.

The decline of the industry has been well documented, as have been its causes. The global depression reduced demand for luxury goods such as pearls from the Gulf. More significantly, however, was the rise of the Japanese cultured pearl. Natural pearls of the Gulf are lustrous but vary in size, shape and colour. In the late nineteenth century, a Japanese entrepreneur, Mikimoto Kokichi, successfully developed a technique for cultivating pearls in controlled pearl farms, allowing him to produce more uniform pearls at scale and for lower prices that those harvested in the Gulf. Combined, the economic crisis and the fashion trends of the interwar period sounded the death knell for the most significant industry in the Trucial States. In 1929, the first year of the global depression, the pearling industry experienced a precipitous decline, with pearl prices dropping as much as 65 per cent in the first year.[15] Though the pearling industry survived on a small scale through the next several decades, it never fully recovered, leaving the Trucial States with little or no indigenous industry to drive its economy. Its location would prove valuable enough. New sources of income arrived in the form of rents collected from the British government and British companies which viewed the Gulf as an ideal bridge to all locations east of Suez.

The air-route to India through the Gulf

The Gulf had become a hub for communication between Britain and its Indian Empire as Britain consolidated its monopoly on the seas and trade routes there in the previous two centuries. As Britain's hold over India became more central

---

[13] Carter, 'The Prehistory and History of Pearling', 181; Lorimer's appendices indicate a period of growth as indicated by the taxation revenues and pearling markets. See *Gazetteer*, v. 1, pt. 2 (1915), 2220–93. Rosemarie Said Zahlan has indicated that the ruler of Abu Dhabi received as much as 86 per cent of his revenue from pearling. Said-Zahlan, *Origins of the United Arab Emirates*, 56–7.
[14] *Gazetteer*, v. 1, pt. 2 (1915), 2220.
[15] V. P. Hightower, 'Pearls and the Southern Persian/Arabian Gulf: A Lesson in Sustainability', *Environmental History* 18, no. 1 (2013): 49.

to Britain's sense of self and of its global identity, so too did the desire to maintain strong lines of communication between London and India. The governor of Bombay, Sir Henry Bargle Frere, requested and received a British mail subsidy for an overland–steamship mail service extension through the Gulf. Service began the following year, and its import only increased after the Suez Canal opened in 1869.[16] The mail service through the Gulf via Basra led to significant expansion in British trade through the port at Basra, and, consequently, infrastructure there and on the Trucial Coast. The India Steam Navigation Company developed regular service to Dubai every two weeks, with the creation of a post office there in 1909.[17] One historian notes that these developments '[provided] the steppingstone for future expansion during the exploitation of the Gulf's oil resources'.[18] But even before the discovery of the region's oil reserves, the Gulf states had become significant to the British Empire and its growing reliance on the new air industry.

Experiments in aviation on a small scale had been taking place in England and elsewhere before the First World War, but it was during the war that Britain came to understand the place air power could play in sustaining its empire. In 1915, planes proved essential in Mesopotamia and more significantly in the Northwest Frontier in India, where they were used to bombard insurgent populations into submission. Throughout the war and after, they were also valuable for surveying land and gathering intelligence against pockets of resistance to British rule.[19] Advocates of air power argued for its potential not only as a weapon of submission but also as an essential instrument for holding the empire together, and for the more Romantic-minded imperialists, for expanding development opportunities to the farthest reaches.[20]

The Arab coast would be an essential component of Britain's strategy to tie the empire together through air power. The First World War had proven the effectiveness of airplanes as a tool of empire, and the Gulf was of fundamental importance to Britain's future strategy: 'The Persian Gulf stands to British air power in almost the exact relation as the Suez Canal to the Royal Navy, namely,

---

[16] Farajollah Ahmadi, 'Communication and the Consolidation of the British Position in the Persian Gulf, 1860s-1914', *Journal of Persianate Studies* 10, no. 1 (2017): 75, 78–9; Stephanie Jones, 'British India Steamers and the Trade of the Persian Gulf, 1862–1914', *The Great Circle* 7, no. 1 (1985): 25–6.
[17] Nicholas Stanley-Price, *Imperial Outpost in the Gulf: The Airfield at Sharjah (UAE) 1932-1952* (Brighton: Book Guild Publishing, 2012), 79.
[18] Jones, 'British India Steamers', 37.
[19] Satia, *Spies in Arabia*, 243–56.
[20] Michael Collins, 'A Technocratic Vision of Empire: Lord Montagu and the Origins of British Air Power', *Journal of Imperial and Commonwealth History* 45, no. 4 (2017): 652–71.

as an essential link in our air communication to the East, particularly for the passage of air forces in time of emergency.'[21]

The first flight from Britain to India left in 1918 from London via Cairo, Basra and the Persian coast in stages. Such flights required frequent refuelling stops (every 200 miles) and emergency landing grounds (every 40 miles). The Persian government exerted little control over its coast, which allowed the British government to operate there without requesting permission. This changed in 1926 when Reza Pahlavi came to power and began centralizing his control over Persia and limiting British interference in Persia's affairs. The British Air Force began looking for alternative landing sites along the Arab coastline.[22]

In 1929, the British Air Force began looking in earnest for anchor points that could support both military and commercial flights. A temporary base had already been established at Basra and was converted into a permanent installation north of Basra. Landing strips at Kuwait and Bahrain were easily established, as was a landing ground near Muscat. But while the Arabian coastline was better suited geographically than the Persian coast owing to its many inlets and sheltered coves, British officials predicted that bringing local rulers in the Trucial Coast on board would be difficult:

> Each state remains strongly independent, and all are hot-beds of intrigue and potential strife. Thus negotiations for the establishment of a refuelling base on this coast were expected to be, and indeed proved to be, of a long and tedious character.[23]

Negotiations took place over three years before arrangements were finally settled. Initial surveys of the coastlines indicated that Ras Al Khaimah would provide the best location for a much-needed air strip. It provided sheltered areas for water landings, and plenty of options for fuel storage, and its proximity to Sharjah added value as additional fuel could be brought in from the British naval base there. Sheikh Sultan bin Salim of Ras Al Khaimah, however, was wary. There would certainly have been benefits to building the air strip in his territory. Rents from the aviation industry would augment the ruler's income, while building and protecting the air strip and other facilities would provide employment for the local populations. Such an agreement, though, would necessarily increase

---

[21] Robert Brooke-Popham (Air Marshal) quoted in G. W. Bentley, 'The Development of the Air Route in the Persian Gulf', *Journal of the Royal Central Asian Society* 20, no. 2 (1933): 173.
[22] Said-Zahlan, *Origins of the United Arab Emirates* is the essential, seminal work on this subject, especially chapter 6: 'Establishment of the Air Route', 92–106.
[23] Bentley, 'Development of the Air Route', 176.

Britain's presence and role in internal affairs, which the ruler knew would face resistance from groups under his jurisdiction.

The *Shihuh* (Al Shehhi, s.) particularly resented British involvement in the region and were wary of any changes that would strengthen the ruler's power over them. British recognition of Sheikh Sultan and Ras Al Khaimah subordinated the Shihuh, who otherwise lived autonomously from the ruler's power. Sometimes described imprecisely as a 'tribe', the Shihuh is a distinct community that has long inhabited the Musandam Peninsula. Ethnically mixed, the Shihuh speak a language mixed with Arabic and Persian and never fully integrated with either Omani or Trucial sociopolitical life. In the second half of the nineteenth century, the Shihuh had exercised extensive power in the town of Dibba (now part of Fujairah) and were frequently at odds with the rulers of Sharjah and Ras Al Khaimah after it became independent in 1921. At the time the British had begun planning for an air strip in Ras Al Khaimah in the 1930s, Sheikh Sultan maintained only a tenuous claim to authority over the Shihuh.

The newly arrived Political Resident to the Gulf, Hugh Biscoe, quickly lost patience with Sheikh Sultan bin Salim's uncertainty. Arguing that the Trucial sheikhs had been given too much latitude, he attempted to move negotiations along through shows of force. He gave permission to air staff to locate a fuel barge in the creek at Ras Al Khaimah in May 1930, without permission from the sheikh. Shihuh fighters and bedouin allies responded to the barge's arrival with resistance, threatening to fire on the boat if it remained in the creek. Sheikh Sultan told the Resident he would not protect the barge. Biscoe responded by sending two British ships to the port in a show of force. The ruler of Sharjah (Sultan bin Saqr) helped convince Sheikh Sultan bin Salim to allow the barge to remain in the creek and to provide a guard detail to protect the fuel supply. He did not, however, concede to landing facilities. By 1931, the need to finalize landing facilities overrode the desirability of Ras Al Khaimah's natural features. Biscoe and the Royal Air Force opened secret negotiations with Sheikh Sultan bin Saqr of Sharjah as an alternative. He, too, balked at their offer initially, but Biscoe gave him an ultimatum: the air strip would be built in Sharjah with or without the ruler's consent. The question was only whether or not Sharjah's ruler would receive payments.[24] On 22 July 1932, Sultan bin Saqr of Sharjah signed an agreement to establish a British air station in his territory. The ruler agreed to provide a landing ground and rest house and guards. In exchange, the British would pay for the guards, in addition to rents for

---

[24] Stanley-Price, *Imperial Outpost in the Gulf*, 20–2, and Said-Zahlan, *Origins of the United Arab Emirates*.

the facilities, a regular payment to the ruler and fees for each commercial flight in addition to military use.[25] One scholar has estimated that this would result in approximately Rs. 30,000, or £2,250, in annual revenues for the ruler.[26] A few years later, the facilities would expand to include a separate meteorological station, a wireless station and a munitions storage building.[27]

Sultan bin Saqr's agreement did not signal the end of difficult negotiations and resistance to the expanded British presence. Sharjah's ruler faced criticism from the rulers of both Ajman and Ras Al Khaimah subsequent to his agreement with Britain, and Hugh Biscoe had again authorized the arrival of naval power off the coasts of those emirates as a warning against their interference. The ruler of Dubai saw the agreement as a potential encroachment on his own position as the main stop for steamer postal service. In 1935–6, the Resident attempted to negotiate with Sharjah for the establishment of a landing strip in Kalba. When he could not be swayed, they instead negotiated with the *wali* of Kalba, Said bin Hamad Al Qasimi, who also initially hesitated to enter into an agreement with Britain, though he finally conceded when Britain agreed to recognize him as independent of Sharjah if he granted permission for emergency landing facilities.

Other Trucial rulers also hesitated to grant Britain rights and used the opportunity to improve their own circumstances and those of their populations. In Abu Dhabi, Shakhbut granted landing rights and allowed for petrol storage. He did so in exchange for rents in addition to extracting a promise that Britain would send geologists to help locate freshwater sources on Abu Dhabi island. When Britain sought to establish a refuelling stop in Dubai in July 1937, Sheikh Said subsequently negotiated better financial terms for himself. Britain increased its rents from Rs. 440 per month to Rs. 940 per month and agreed to pay an additional Rs. 500 per month personal subsidy and additional charges for each plane that landed there.[28] The establishment of the air route to India through the Arab coast of the Gulf further entangled the Trucial Coast in the net of the British Empire.

Oil concessions

Perhaps the most surprising aspect of oil in the Trucial Coast is the extent to which the Trucial States do not figure much in the international competition for

---

[25] 'Sharjah Air Agreement, 22 July 1932', *Arabian Treaties, 1600–1960*, vol. 2, ed. Penelope Tuson (Cambridge: Cambridge Archive Editions, 1992).
[26] Stanley-Price, *Imperial Outpost in the Gulf*, 59.
[27] Stanley-Price, *Imperial Outpost in the Gulf*, 69–71.
[28] Stanley-Price, *Imperial Outpost in the Gulf*, 105–6.

oil monopolies in the interwar Middle East. Britain's search for oil in the Middle East began not in the Arabian Peninsula, but in Mesopotamia and Persia. A 1908 survey of the Trucial Coast suggested that the region was not promising for oil discovery. That same year, the British Anglo-Persian Oil Company (APOC, later the Anglo-Iranian Oil Company, or AIOC) discovered oil in Persia. Little attention was paid to the Arab coast until well into the interwar period, when Britain would worry less about oil and more about how to keep the Gulf and its surrounds under exclusive British influence.[29] Britain's success in this arena would be at the expense of the Trucial rulers who would have little leverage in their negotiations with the oil companies.

The usefulness of oil had certainly not been unknown to Britain before the First World War. American and Russian companies established the earliest oil companies in the mid-nineteenth century in their own countries, and the wealthy Rothschilds of England entered the fray when they began importing and distributing petroleum in 1888.[30] A few years later, they partnered with the British 'Shell' Transport and Trading company which served as the main distribution arm for oil in England.[31] In the decades that followed, capitalists in Europe began pooling resources and looking for ways into the oil world. None of them pursued oil as vigorously J. D. Rockefeller and his associates did from the United States. They managed to extend their control over as many aspects of the fledgling industry under the umbrella of the Standard Oil Company (SOCAL). At the same time, technological innovators sought to find new ways to use oil in the electrifying of homes and the running of railroads. As the potential of oil came to be understood, British and European businessmen began looking for ways to expand from distributors of American and Russian oil to producing oil themselves, and the age of imperialism and colonization provided new opportunities for exploration and exploitation of petroleum reserves. The Royal Dutch Petroleum Company, established in 1890, tapped into the resources of its colonies in Indonesia before merging with the British 'Shell' import–export company and forming the Royal Dutch Shell Group in 1907.

---

[29] Rosemarie Said-Zahlan made this point in her *Origins of the United Arab Emirates*, and subsequent scholars have supported this view as well. Said-Zahlan, *Origins of the United Arab Emirates*, 108–10; Heard-Bey, *From Trucial States to United Arab Emirates* (2002), 295–6; Michael Quentin Morton, *Keepers of the Golden Shore: A History of the United Arab Emirates* (London: Reaktion Books, 2016), 133–4.

[30] Daniel Yergin, *The Prize: The Epic Quest for Oil, Money and Power* (New York: Free Press (a reissue edition), 2008), 19–61.

[31] Toyin Falola and Ann Genova, *The Politics of the Global Oil Industry: An Introduction* (Westport, CT: 2005). The company's legal name included the quotation marks until the early part of the twentieth century.

Britain's real entrée to oil exploration and extraction came through the efforts of William Knox D'Arcy, an Englishman who had become wealthy through gold mining in Australia. In 1901, he expanded his interests to mineral rights and oil exploration in Persia. The Qajar Shah, Mozzafar al-Din, signed what became known as the D'Arcy Concession which granted D'Arcy's company exclusive rights to explore and extract a variety of natural resources including natural gas and petroleum in the majority of Persia's territory in exchange for a cash payment and a percentage of the net profits when oil was extracted. After several years of limited success, the British Admiralty became worried that D'Arcy would sell his exploratory rights to French or Russian rivals. Putting the British government's thumb on the scales to ensure D'Arcy's concession would remain under British ownership by sending in a British agent to purchase a share in D'Arcy's concession, ultimately forming the Concession Syndicate, which would become the Anglo-Persian Oil Company. In 1908, the company struck oil in Persia.[32] The British government's success in monopolizing oil production in Persia made the government complacent in its search for oil elsewhere. In the remainder of the Gulf, there was very little interest or effort on the part of Britain to encourage oil exploration in the region. A 1908 survey of the Trucial Coast indicated there was little likelihood that oil would be discovered there. And with the recent discoveries in Persia, there seemed to be very little sense of urgency for expanded surveys or supporting new concession agreements.

In the wake of the First World War, Britain lost exclusive influence over oil extraction in Mesopotamia. As part of the post-war settlement, Britain and France negotiated a shared interest in any oil discovered in Iraq, which led to protracted negotiations with the United States, Italy and the mandatory government in Iraq. The difficulties in retaining a controlling interest there spurred the British government on to bolster its claims to exclusive rights in the Gulf. The Exclusive Agreement of 1892 had established that the foreign affairs of the Trucial Coast were under the purview of the Political Resident and British government. In 1922, however, the Political Resident was directed to secure further assurances from the Trucial rulers that they would not grant oil concessions, specifically, without permission from the British government. Between February and May, the rulers of Sharjah, Ras Al Khaimah, Dubai, Abu Dhabi, Ajman and Umm Al Quwain each signed a letter to that effect: 'Let it not be hidden from you that we agree, if oil is expected to be found in our territory, not to grant any concession in this connection to anyone except to the person appointed by the High British

---

[32] Yergin, *Prize*, 119–31.

government.'³³ Similar assurances had been granted in Kuwait and Bahrain where Britain also maintained a protective role through the Political Residency.

Britain then brokered the 1928 Red Line agreement with European and American oil companies joined with British oil interests to establish the Turkish Petroleum Company (TPC, which would become the Iraq Petroleum Company, or IPC, the next year). Under this agreement, the APOC, Royal Dutch/Shell Company, French Petroleum Company (CFP/Total) and an American conglomerate each held a 23.75 per cent share of TPC oil production. They further agreed that none of the signatories could operate within a portion of the Middle East without permission from the others.³⁴ When the IPC declined to pursue a concession agreement in Bahrain in 1929, SOCAL made an offer to the ruler and was accepted. Oil was discovered in commercial quantities two years later. The American company's success in Bahrain and subsequently in Saudi Arabia helped create a sense of urgency among British policymakers to ensure they would not lose out on opportunities elsewhere in the Gulf.

The rulers in the Trucial States followed the developments in Bahrain with great interest, especially as the financial benefits of the oil agreements began to manifest. The influx of royalties allowed the Bahraini government to invest in the creation of schools and hospitals, while the oil industry and the auxiliary businesses that supported the industry provided Bahrainis with new job opportunities. Shakhbut in particular seems to have followed the negotiations carefully and watched for opportunities to pursue concessionary agreements that would afford him greater influence over the outcome of negotiations than any deal that might be brokered through the British Residency. Shakhbut requested that APOC survey Abu Dhabi, ostensibly for the purposes of finding freshwater wells, though he also hoped to strike oil.

The survey led geologists to believe Abu Dhabi was likely to have oil in commercial quantities, and in the years that followed, other Trucial rulers requested surveys of their territories as well.³⁵ In 1935, the Petroleum Concessions Ltd. acquired the options to explore for oil. The Petroleum Concessions Ltd., an associated company of the IPC, had the approval of the British Resident over other interested companies with greater American shares

---

³³ Aitchison, *Treaties* XI (1933), 261. The text presented is that signed first by Sheikh Said bin Maktoum of Dubai with the following note: 'Undertakings similar in substance to the above were given by the following Shaikhs on the dates mentioned.' A differently phrased, but substantively similar letter, was signed by the rulers of Sharjah and Ras Al Khaimah.
³⁴ Michael Quentin Morton, 'Narrowing the Gulf: Anglo-American Relations and Arabian Oil, 1928–1974', *Liwa* 3, no. 6 (2011): 39–40.
³⁵ Said-Zahlan, *Origins of the United Arab Emirates*, 107–10.

and influence. Petroleum Concessions Ltd. undertook negotiations with the individual rulers of the Trucial States. Sheikh Said of Dubai signed the first concession agreement of the Trucial Coast on 22 May 1937. The seventy-five-year agreement provided 'The Company' a signing bonus of Rs. 60,000 and Rs. 30,000 per annum for the exclusive rights to explore for, extract and refine oil and natural gas in the emirate. Upon discovery of commercial quantities of oil, Sheikh Said would receive an additional Rs. 200,000 and a share of Rs. 3 per ton of petroleum extracted.[36] The ruler of Sharjah signed a nearly identical agreement a few months later, and Kalba followed suit the next year. These agreements set the standard by which Petroleum Concessions and the British Residency expected the remaining rulers to agree to as well.

Neither Shakhbut of Abu Dhabi nor Sultan of Ras Al Khaimah viewed the proposed agreements as sufficient. Both rulers attempted to negotiate better terms with SOCAL subsidiaries to gain better terms – similar to the more advantageous agreements of Bahrain, Qatar and Kuwait. The 1934 agreement between Kuwait and the Kuwait Oil Company, for example, had promised the ruler of Kuwait an initial payment of Rs. 475,000, and significantly higher annual royalties of at least Rs. 95,000 until oil was discovered in commercial quantities.[37] Sheikh Sultan attempted in 1938 to travel to Kuwait but was prevented from doing so by the British Resident, Trenchard Fowle, because he suspected the ruler's aim was to meet with oil representatives there. Sultan avoided being forced into an agreement with Petroleum Concessions for the time being because of tribal disputes over territory within his emirate. The company consequently withdrew its offer until after the Second World War, when the company offered and agreed to terms with Umm Al Quwain and Ajman.[38]

The ruler of Abu Dhabi, though eager to benefit from the oil agreements, held out until 1939. Frustrated at the lack of progress with Shakhbut an executive from Petroleum Concessions, Stephen Longrigg, offered to come to Abu Dhabi to negotiate directly with Shakhbut, but Fowle believed he could pressure

---

[36] 'File 38/4 Petroleum Concessions Limited Sharjah Concession', British Library: India Office Records and Private Papers, IOR/R/15/2/866, in QDL https://www.qdl.qa/archive/81055/vdc_100000000 241.0x000135 (accessed 28 August 2021).

[37] 'Koweit Concession Agreement', 23 December 1934. Coll 30/91(2) 'Koweit Oil Concession: Agreement between the Shaikh of Kuwait and the Kuwait Oil Co'. British Library: India Office Records and Private Papers, IOR/L/PS/12/3812, in QDL https://www.qdl.qa/archive/81055/vdc_100000000 648.0x00017c (accessed 28 August 2021).

[38] See Said-Zahlan, *Origins of the United Arab Emirates*, 117–20. Negotiations with the ruler of Ras Al Khaimah were signed in 1945. Those with the rulers of Umm Al Quwain and Ajman were completed in 1949 and 1951, respectively. Fujairah would not be recognized by Britain as a sovereign emirate until 1952, and concessionary agreements were settled that same year. Each of the emirates reached the same terms as the agreement between Petroleum Concessions Ltd., and Dubai.

the ruler to agree to the standard terms. Fowle used a limited report of illicit slave trading in the area of Buraimi as an excuse for questioning Shakhbut's commitment to enforce the terms of his treaties with the British government and unilaterally suspended British permissions for him or his subjects to travel outside of the emirates. Fowle also devised a variety of additional ways to force Shakhbut to relent and sign the concession agreements, among them levying heavy fines against the ruler and threatened to confiscate some of his pearling fleet or shell Qasr al-Hosn, the ruler's fort. The India Office disapproved of Fowle's independent escalation of circumstances but was open to the exercise of force to compel Shakhbut's agreement. Before these more severe punishments could be enacted, however, the ruler changed his mind and agreed to finalize terms with Longrigg.[39]

The oil concession agreements provided the rulers with a modest annual income until such time as oil could be discovered, which would not occur for nearly two decades in the Trucial Coast. Nevertheless, the new revenue significantly changed the ways in which the rulers of the Trucial Coast shared economic and political power with the merchant classes. In the years before concession agreements, Gulf merchants held great influence with the rulers. The economic world of the Indian Ocean and the Gulf functioned largely on networks of credit. The rulers frequently required loans in times of economic hardship in order to meet their obligations to their subjects, their creditors and even the British government. These loans typically were financed through influential merchants operating in the Trucial States. The relationships between merchants and their rulers, cemented through financial interdependence, created openings for merchants to hold sway with the rulers in political and social decision making.[40] Royalties from the oil companies severed that relationship by providing the rulers with greater independence and marginalizing merchants' participation in the political life of the Trucial Coast.

The first signs of the destabilization came from further north, in Kuwait and Bahrain in 1938. That year, merchants in Kuwait formed a vocal opposition movement to the Kuwaiti ruler's close ties with the British government and his increasing independence of action relative to the merchant class. By the end of June 1938, the merchants had succeeded in securing an advisory voice in the government through the establishment of a National Legislative Council (*Majlis al-Umma al-Tashri'i*) consisting of fourteen elected members which oversaw

---

[39] Said-Zahlan, *Origins of the United Arab Emirates*, 120–3.
[40] Jill Crystal, *Oil and Politics in the Gulf: Rulers and Merchants in Kuwait and Qatar* (Cambridge: Cambridge University Press, 1990) is the seminal work on this subject.

the budget, education and urban planning, among other subjects.[41] A similar collective movement developed in Bahrain in the same year, with support for the establishment of a popular assembly, or *majlis*, gaining broad support among not only the merchant class but also students and oilfield workers. The Bahraini ruler, with the encouragement and support of the British advisor Charles Belgrave, worked to squash the movement quickly.[42]

Dubai, as the pre-eminent trade centre of the Trucial States, followed in the footsteps of Kuwait and Bahrain. Sheikh Said, who had first come to power in 1912, had already faced opposition from within his family on several occasions, including when he briefly was deposed in 1929 and again in 1934 when he was nearly assassinated by cousins. Support from the British Residency helped the ruler to thwart the attempt, but ongoing disputes over the declining economic conditions in the commercial district of Deira and the weakened financial state of the merchants there continued to undermine Said's efforts to enact any changes without consulting with his family and leaders of the merchant community. A dispute between the ruler's son and another cousin over ownership of taxi services turned into violent confrontations in May 1938 and reignited the fuse of opposition to Said's rule.

Over the next several months, a contingent of family members and local merchants began to occupy the commercial district while issuing demands for reforms, including improved sanitation and access to health care, as well as budgetary oversight and improved security through the establishment of a police force in Dubai. By October of that year, the possibility that Dubai would be subsumed in violence caused the rulers of Sharjah and Ras Al Khaimah concern, and Abu Dhabi's Shakhbut came to Dubai with other leaders from influential tribes to help broker an agreement between the two factions. Said, upon realizing he was about to be deposed again, asked the Political Agent in Bahrain to negotiate terms. On 20 October, Hugh Weightman helped complete negotiations and an agreement was reached. Sheikh Said would establish a *majlis* consisting of fifteen members, who were to oversee the budget, and allocate a limited personal allowance to the ruler. Once enacted, the *majlis* established several reforms for the improvement of Dubai's economic status. The members of the *majlis* regularized customs collections through the appointment of salaried officials. They further established a municipal council

---

[41] Said-Zahlan, *The Making of the Modern Gulf States*, 37.
[42] Said-Zahlan, *Making of the Modern Gulf States*, 64–6; Nelida Fuccaro, *Histories of City and State in the Persian Gulf: Manama since 1800* (Cambridge: Cambridge University Press, 2009).

and a council of merchants to set customs rates, formed a force to patrol the market to ensure order and developed a Director of Education position for the creation of schools. Said resented the *majlis* and the limitations it placed on his authority and on his income. In March the following year, the marriage of Said's son Rashid created an opening for him to invite Said's allies into Deira, where they promptly established control in support of Said. In the days that followed, Said dissolved the *majlis* and replaced it with a weaker advisory council on Weightman's advice.[43]

The movements of 1938 not only indicated a shift in the ways in which rulers exercised authority with respect to their merchant communities but also reflected a rising awareness in the Gulf region of political movements and sentiments in the Arab world more broadly. The leaders of the opposition in Dubai looked to Kuwait and Bahrain as examples for creating stronger representative voices in their government. And those movements had themselves come out of frustrations with not only local politics but also in response to Britain's role in Palestine. News of events in Palestine circulated along the Gulf states through the profusion of newspapers and radio broadcasts, emanating in the 1930s from Cairo, Baghdad and even Italy. The Kuwait movement mobilized in part around the ruler's refusal to send financial support to Palestine during the 1936 General Strike. The strike was a coordinated response among Palestinians in major cities across Mandatory Palestine in opposition to British policies that supported Zionist immigration to Palestine and allowed for ongoing sales of land from Arab Palestinians to Jewish immigrants. Kuwait's Sheikh Ahmad al-Jabir Al Sabah not only refused to send financial support but also forbade public contributions with the understanding that it would violate Kuwait's treaties to conduct foreign relations through the British government. In response, Kuwaitis nevertheless collected and sent out 200 Iraqi dinars in July 1936. In October, a public meeting raised an additional Rs. 9,500 for Palestine. People in the Trucial States similarly took note, if on a smaller scale. In Dubai, public collections were taken in support of Palestine, and Sharjah's own Sheikh Sultan made donations to the Palestinian cause.[44]

At the close of the decade and of his stint in the Gulf, Political Resident Trenchard Fowle reflected the changes wrought by the arrival of oil exploration and extraction in the Arab coast and the ways in which it would transform the

---

[43] Said-Zahlan, *Origins of the United Arab Emirates*, 150–61; Christopher Davidson, *Dubai: The Vulnerability of Success* (London: Hurst, 2008), 32–9.

[44] Said-Zahlan, *Palestine and the Gulf States: The Presence at the Table* (New York: Routledge, 2009), 15–18.

consciousness of the region. Fowle observed of the changing political moods in the Gulf that

> with every year that passes the youths are growing into young men, exercising more and more influence in the States, while behind them are more and more boys following in their footsteps. Of the young Bahraini in a recent letter Weightman wrote:
>
> 'Increased educational facilities in recent years have produced a class of young men with a veneer of education who respond readily to press propaganda, listen to broadcasts and develop political feelings. They believe themselves to be progressive and despise their illiterate parents who, since the youths are earning quite good wages, have lost all influence over them. They are nationalistic, especially since they see foreigners earning more money than they themselves do.'
>
> *Mutatas mutandas* [sic] this is an exact description of a large number of young Indians, Egyptians, Palestinians, and Iraqis ... Some of the local agitations and movements will be directed against the local Rulers, but some will certainly be directed against us, in fact is already being directed against us. Hardly a fortnight passes without an attack being made in the Arab Press of Iraq, Palestine, Syria, or Egypt, against His Majesty's Government and its policy towards the Arab States of the Gulf.[45]

The future of the Gulf states would follow the patterns established in other places where Britain had established control, and that nationalist and anti-British feelings would be fed by the Arab presses. In closing, Fowle added that this fate might be avoided if British policy in the Gulf could maintain the 'goodwill' of the local rulers through the exercise of patience and judicious advice combined with continued protection from neighbouring states.[46]

The interwar period marked many significant transformations in the Trucial Coast and in the Gulf more broadly. Some of the sheikhs who came to power during this time would oversee the region in the decades to come. The agreements rulers signed with Britain for new air facilities and for oil exploration would provide them with greater independence from their subjects but would subject their states to increasing interference from the Political Residents following the Second World War. The air route and promise of oil made the Gulf even more important to Britain's global strategy in the 1950s and 1960s. Increasingly, the Political Residents in the Gulf would view the region in the context of the

---

[45] T. C. Fowle, Political Resident Persian Gulf (Bushire) to Aubrey Metcalf, Secretary to the Government of India. 17 March 1939. *ROE*, v. 8, 58–66.
[46] Ibid.

greater Arab world and the anti-British nationalist movements that arose from the Arab core. The Trucial rulers and their subjects would similarly come to make decisions about their future in the context of Arab politics as they spread to the coast and as British policymakers attempted to persuade them of Arab nationalism's dangers.

3

Building the foundations for a state

The British Empire in India came to an end in 1947, following several years of planning and negotiations for the independence of India and creation of Pakistan. The empire had established a vast bureaucracy which extended well beyond the borders of the subcontinent, including the offices of the Political Resident of the Persian Gulf (PRPG). Following Indian independence, the India Office ceased to exercise its capacity as the caretaker of Britain's affairs concerned with India. It would merge with the Commonwealth Office, and the civil servants who had reported to its office would be redirected through new channels. The interwar period had increased the linkages between the British Empire and the Gulf states. The Foreign Office wished to strengthen these ties and ensure that the emirates' eventual independence would preserve Britain's strategic and economic interests in the region.

The decisions made in Whitehall about where and how to administer the PRPG laid the groundwork for the eventual evolution of the Arab Gulf states into independent territories. The Foreign Office ultimately inherited responsibility for oversight of the Gulf territories. Under the jurisdiction of the Foreign Office, the Trucial States would be expected to become entirely independent of the British government at some future date. Just as significantly, the path towards eventual independence would be forged through policies and decision makers who viewed the region through the lens of the Arabian Department of the Foreign Office. They increasingly viewed Arab nationalism as an inevitable force for decolonization, and they pressed the rulers to establish policies they believed would prevent anti-imperialist, nationalist sentiment from taking hold in the Trucial States.

Between 1947 and 1955, several significant transformations took place in the administrative and political relations of the Trucial States and these would create the framework for their eventual federation as the United Arab Emirates. This chapter considers several of the ways in which the eventual formation of the

United Arab Emirates grew out of state-building practices in the period under consideration. The first key change was the British government's decision to place the Persian Gulf in the Foreign Office's portfolio, rather than that of the Colonial Office. This was more than a simple bureaucratic choice. It established a direction for future independence of the Arab states on the coast. It also shifted the residency away from the Colonial Office, which viewed the world in connection with the Indian Empire. The Foreign Office, the Arabian Department and the Residency would approach the Trucial Coast from the perspective of its place in the Arab world. Thus, this chapter begins with a discussion of both the physical and bureaucratic move of the Political Residency to Bahrain under the Foreign Office's direction.

The formation of a Trucial Council consisting of the rulers of the Trucial States marked a second crucial development. The Political Resident and his officers presented the council as a way to coordinate communication and efforts between the rulers and improve cooperation between them. It would eventually serve as the basis for future resource sharing and unification. Its early activities and the rulers' initial involvement were limited in scope, but these early meetings established structural foundations for the future of the emirates. We conclude with the delineation of boundaries between the sheikhdoms in the mid-1950s. In defining the extent of much of the territories, the British government introduced a foundational component of the modern nation state to the region. This process transformed the nature of territoriality and politics on the Trucial Coast. Taken together, these three components would define the future of the Trucial Coast and pave the way to nation statehood.

The British Residency from the India Office to the Foreign Office

The Indian Empire dissolved in 1947, and consequently so did the India Office, which had overseen British relations to the Trucial States since 1858. The transition led to both the political and physical restructuring of the British presence on the Trucial Coast. Physically, the transfer entailed moving the office of the Political Resident from Bushehr to Bahrain. This was accompanied by the establishment of a permanent British presence on the Trucial Coast in the form of a Political Officer located in the emirates. Politically, it required internal debates within the British government over the future of the Trucial States. Abdullah Taryam argues that the ultimate decision to identify the Trucial States as 'independent states under British protection', managed by the Foreign Office, presented an essential contradiction.[1] In some ways, Indian independence represented an opportunity to extend independence to the nominally sovereign Trucial rulers. It was, however, a contradiction which gave the British government very little pause. Control over the Gulf states had been an extension of British interests in India, and the end of the British Empire in India negated Britain's original purpose. In the interwar years, however, Britain had found new reasons to continue its hegemony in the Gulf. The looming possibility of nationalist, anti-British movements in the region would further inform British policymakers' vision for the Gulf states.

In some ways, India's independence might have created an excellent opportunity for Britain to shed its responsibilities and expenses in the Gulf. The thorny negotiations with the Trucial rulers over landing strips and oil concessions had contributed to souring relationships between them and the British government. But Britain had expanded its own infrastructure in the Gulf during the interwar period. The presence of oil, the air route to India, the expanded military presence in Aden and the Gulf all contributed to the Foreign Office's desire to sustain Britain's primacy in the Gulf.

A British India Office official would oversee the transition of the Political Residency from the India Office to the Foreign Office. Rupert Hay had served as an officer in the Indian Army from 1915 until 1920, when he joined the Indian Political Service. In 1941, he was posted briefly as the PRPG before being stationed in Baluchistan. He returned to the Gulf in 1946, where he finished his career in 1952.[2] The residency's location at Bushehr had been a flashpoint in tense negotiations between the British and Iranian governments for several years. In 1930 and again in 1936, the British government had considered shifting the Residency from Bushehr to Bahrain, but the Second World War had placed those plans on hold. In 1946, the Political Resident was directed to start his post in Bahrain. The Resident and his staff would reside at the naval base at Juffair until a new Residence could be built on Muharraq (see Map 3.1).

In the same year, more changes within the British government would need to be made, including where to house the Political Residency within the larger British government. By 1946, the British government had begun internal plans

[1] Abdullah O. Taryam, *The Establishment of the United Arab Emirates, 1950–1985* (London, UK: Croom and Helm, 1987), 11–12.
[2] Rupert Hay, *The Persian Gulf States* (Washington, DC: Middle East Institute, 1959), ix–x.

Map 3.1 Map of Bahrain.

to withdraw from India and to transfer power to the Indian government. The end of the Government of India necessitated further discussions about the future of the Political Residency and Britain's role in the Gulf. The resulting decisions would have significant implications for development plans and political decision making in the Trucial States.

The first question regarding the Gulf and the British system related to whether the Arab Gulf states would fall under the jurisdiction of the Foreign Office or that of the Colonial Office. While these considerations were underway, the India Office would begin shifting to the Commonwealth Office but would retain the Persian Gulf Residency portfolio until a final determination could be made.

A number of concerns played into the ultimate decision to place the Persian Gulf under the umbrella of the Foreign Office. J. P. Tripp would later author a rather cynical summary of some of these debates as a retrospective in preparation for Britain's withdrawal from the Gulf:

> [The choice was made] out of concern for world opinion about the intrusion of British 'imperialism' in this region and because the major problems which arose for decision in the Gulf were seen as political in character ... It was recognized that the Colonial Office was better qualified than the Foreign Office to assist State Governments in developing medical, educational and welfare activities for which increased revenues from oil were likely to provide opportunities. The Colonial Office was also recognized to be able to provide the administrative staff required by the Sheikhdoms, to have already local associations with Arabia and to have more experience in indirect rule involving ... interference in the internal affairs of protected States. Despite this great experience of the Colonial Office in administering backward areas, it was held to be undesirable in this case, for the reasons mentioned above, and because the foreign relations of the 'petty sheikhdoms' in the area were assuming vastly increasing importance in view of the rapid development of oil production there.[3]

From Tripp's perspective, shifting the Political Residency to the Foreign office represented a 'political' rather than a pragmatic outlook. It reflected an international mood that favoured decolonization, or at least the appearance of it.

In his official history for the British government, Rupert Hay described a tidier deliberation of Britain's future role:

> (a) to continue the policy of not intervening except when compelled, or
>
> (b) to introduce a policy of more direct administration approaching the colonial model, or
>
> (c) without introducing colonial methods to intensify their efforts to promote good administration, social progress, and economic development through the existing Rulers and administrative machinery, largely by means of British advisers and technicians in the service of the Rulers.

They chose the latter.[4]

---

[3] 'The Arab states of the Gulf since 1947: their evolution and development, with particular reference to their neighbours, Arab Nationalism and the British Presence' by Mr. Tripp, December 1966. William Luce Special Collections MS 146 at Exeter University.
[4] 'Historical Summary of Events of the Persian Gulf Shaikhdoms and the Sultanate of Muscat and Oman, 1928–1953'. IOR/R/15/1/731(1). QDL.

Both assessments, as different as they were, would mean that at some future date the states in the Gulf were expected to become independent of Britain. On 1 April 1948, a year after Indian independence, the Political Residency formally transferred to the Foreign Office.[5]

The Foreign Office sent a team to tour the Gulf and prepare a report on the status of the Gulf states and their prospects. Among them were Sir Roger Makins, the Deputy Undersecretary of State, and future Political Resident Bernard Burrows. The Foreign Office men viewed the future of the Trucial States and Gulf more broadly from the perspective of the Arab Middle East and anti-British sentiment building in Iran. At the end of the visit, Makins reported concerns to the Foreign Office that while there was not yet an overt feeling of anti-imperial nationalism or the overt influence of the Arab League, he had 'no doubt that national feeling is not far below the surface' and that it would not be very long before the British government could expect such activity to manifest in the region.[6] To that end, he argued in favour of promoting development and education. This would need to be done carefully to prevent education from leading to an anti-British 'political consciousness'.[7] From the standpoint of the Foreign Office, the arrival of some form of Arab nationalism in the region was inevitable and a careful balance of development and caution was necessary to preserve the status quo.

Hay's view contrasted markedly with that of Makins. Coloured by his years in the India Office, and with the Gulf divorced from British policy in the rest of the Middle East, Hay perceived the Gulf states as safe from nationalism. He argued that the sheikhdoms were not nations, but 'city states under patriarchal rule and with a cosmopolitan population', and that the rulers themselves would rather have British protection than be absorbed into another Arab state.[8] Hay would hold onto his belief that the 'traditional' character of the Trucial States would protect Britain's position in the Gulf from nationalist designs.

---

[5] 'Historical Summary of Events of the Persian Gulf Shaikhdoms and the Sultanate of Muscat and Oman, 1928–1953'. IOR/R/15/1/731(1). QDL. Several authors indicate the transfer date as coincident to the formal transfer of power to India on 1 April 1947. Hay's Historical Summary, however, indicates that the transfer to the Foreign Office would not take place until 1 April of the following year.
[6] H. S. Stephenson (Foreign Office) to Anthony Eden (Foreign Secretary). 20 May 1952. FO 371/98333. TNA.
[7] H. S. Stephenson (Foreign Office) to Anthony Eden (Foreign Secretary). 20 May 1952. FO 371/98333. TNA.
[8] Rupert Hay (Political Resident, Bahrain) to Anthony Eden (Foreign Secretary). 11 June 1952. FO 371/98333. TNA.

The real danger comes from without, not from Middle Eastern neighbours, but from doctrinaire politicians in the West. There are many who think that because democracy suits the West, it is the panacea for all ills in the East, and that any remaining vestiges of imperialism should, as such, be incontinently swept away. Such doctrines could lead to premature abandonment by Great Britain of her position in the Gulf States with disastrous results.[9]

Foreign Secretary Anthony Eden took Hay's views seriously, conceding that some of the Arab Gulf states were more likely to experience waves of nationalism than others. Kuwait and Bahrain appeared more susceptible given that they already had a politically active intelligentsia, and both states had experienced calls for political reforms in the 1930s. Eden nevertheless sided largely with Makins's report.[10] When he appointed Bernard Burrows to the position of Political Resident after Hay, Burrows would carry with him the belief that Arab nationalism would arrive in the Arab states of the Gulf before long.

A Trucial States council

In 1952, the Political Residency formed a cooperative council of the Trucial rulers, which would come to serve as the first regular, cooperative body of the Trucial coast. The Trucial States Council would meet for the first time in March 1952 and would continue meeting approximately twice yearly through 1968. The establishment of the council was meant to serve two goals. The first of these was to streamline communication between the Political Residency and the various rulers, and as Abdullah Taryam has observed, served to 'consolidate British interest' over the Trucial Coast and protect British interests in oil exploration.[11] The second, more long-term goal, was to establish a lasting cooperative relationship between the small sheikhdoms of the Trucial Coast. In his Annual Report for 1952, Hay noted that the Trucial Council was, perhaps, the most important development in the Gulf because it could encourage the rulers there to take an active and cooperative approach to matters that concerned them collectively. This would ultimately help to fulfil the longer-term goal of uniting the states in some form of federation at some future date. While the exact date of that future federation remained unspecified in official minds, Rupert Hay had, upon leaving his post,

---

[9] Hay, *Persian Gulf States*, 153.
[10] Anthony Eden (Foreign Secretary) to H. S. Stephenson (Foreign Office). 2 September 1952. FO 371/98333. TNA.
[11] Taryam, *Establishment of the United Arab Emirates 1950–1985*, 16.

Table 3.1 Political Residents and Political Agents during the Formative Years of the Trucial Council

Political Residents at Bahrain	Political Agents at Sharjah (until 1953) and Dubai (after 1953)	Political Agents at Abu Dhabi
Rupert Hay, 1946–53	Various, 1948–52[13]	
	Michael Weir, 1952–3	
Bernard Burrows, 1953–8	Christopher (C. M.) Pirie-Gordon, 1953–5	
	J. P. (Peter) Tripp, 1955–8	
George Middleton, 1958–61	Donald Hawley, 1958–9	
	E. R. Worsnop (Acting), 1959–61	
William Luce, 1961–6	James Craig, 1961–4	Hugh Boustead, 1961–5
	Glencairn Balfour-Paul, 1964–6	Albert (Archie) Lamb, 1965–8
Stewart Crawford, 1966–70	David Roberts, Dubai 1966–8	
	Julian Bullard, 1968–70	James Treadwell, 1968–71
Geoffrey Arthur, 1970–1	Julian Walker, 1970–1	

considered the federation a possibility in twenty years, while in 1958 Burrows himself thought it would be more likely to occur in the next ten years.[12]

The architects of the Trucial Council were the Political Residents of the Persian Gulf, and more significantly their Political Agents, the latter of whom conducted the council meetings and served as chair of the meetings until 1965. After 1965, the rulers rotated the position among themselves. Until then, the presiding Political Agents called the meetings, set the agendas and directed discussions. The results of the meetings were recorded in minutes and the agents reported back to the Resident their impressions of the meetings' success. These sources provide valuable insights into the process of state building on the Trucial Coast, as well as into the various rulers' feelings about British policies and priorities (see Table 3.1).

---

[12] Bernard Burrows, *Footnotes in the Sand: The Gulf in Transition, 1953–1958* (Norwich, UK: Michael Russel Publishing, 1991), 24.

[13] A political agent was stationed year-round at Sharjah beginning in 1948, but the post changed hands several times per year through 1952. From 1937 to 1948, a British political agent only resided at Sharjah in the winter season. See Said-Zahlan, *Origins of the United Arab Emirates*, 249–50; Heard-Bey, *From Trucial States to United Arab Emirates*, 309.

The early meetings of the council proved inauspicious. The first meeting took place on 13 March 1952 at the British Agency at Sharjah. Michael Weir had urged all seven rulers to come to the first meeting, but neither Shakhbut (Abu Dhabi) nor Said (Dubai) attended, sending representatives in their stead. At the second meeting, held in May, Shakhbut again failed to attend. One aim of the council was to encourage the rulers to take an active role in local affairs, but the tone and agenda of the first meetings did little to convince them to participate actively in the council's proceedings.

Early agenda items included locust control, traffic rules, domestic slavery and nationality and travel documents. Weir hoped the topics would interest all the sheikhs and encourage discussion and cooperation among them. Each of these topics, though, placed the rulers in the position of angering their people or surrendering their closely guarded sovereignty over their local populations to collective decision making. Locusts, for example, had been doing significant damage to farms on the Trucial Coast, including the gardens of the rulers of Umm Al Quwain, Ras Al Khaimah and Ajman. The British government had attempted various methods of locust control in the past, including an arsenic-based insecticide, and then gammaxene-based locust control. A British Locust Control Squad had been traveling through the coast to apply the insecticide but kept coming into conflict with tribesmen in the area who were suspicious of the chemicals and frequently interrupted the squad's work.[14] In the first meeting, Weir encouraged the rulers to 'enjoin the bedouin not to interfere' and to provide guards to accompany the workers.[15] The rulers all assented, but at the next meeting, Weir returned to the subject. The sheikhs 'finally admitted' that the bedouin could not be convinced that the insecticide was safe. Weir pressed the rulers to reason with the bedouin and even handed around a slice of gammaxene and bread for the rulers to eat so as to demonstrate its safety for people and livestock.[16]

Likewise, the question of nationality for the Trucial States proved a difficult subject to navigate. While the Residency would have preferred to establish a single standard for naturalization in all of the Trucial Council, Hay considered the time 'not ripe for a federal administration that could issue passports and

---

[14] Hay, *Persian Gulf States*, 124. According to Hay, the bedouin resented the locust control for two reasons. One was that locust provided a 'change of diet'; the other was that they believed the pesticides produced plants that would kill their camels.
[15] Minutes of the First Trucial States Council Meeting. 23 March 1952. FO 371/98331. TNA.
[16] Minutes of the Second Trucial States Council Meeting. 1 May 1952. FO 371/98331. TNA. Gammaxene is a carcinogen.

grant citizenship for all the sheikhdoms'.[17] And in fact, while the rulers professed a need for standards for citizenship, especially due to the influx of foreign workers in Sharjah and Dubai, they did not have uniform ideas about who should or should not meet requirements for citizenship. Citizenship would continue to be granted over the years based on rulers' declarations until a process for establishing duration of residence and tribal affiliation was established prior to statehood.

One significant matter discussed at the first two meetings was sure to stifle the rulers' contributions to the council then and in future, as it served as a stark reminder that their sovereignty was granted only at the British government's pleasure. The British government had written the sheikhdom of Kalba into existence in 1936, after opening direct negotiations with Said bin Hamad and circumventing the ruler of Sharjah, Sheikh Sultan bin Saqr (1924–51). In 1951, the second ruler of Kalba, Hamad bin Said, was assassinated by the son of the former ruler of Ras Al Khaimah, who then attempted to establish himself as the ruler of Kalba.[18] At the first meeting of the Trucial Council, Weir notified the rulers present that the British government was abrogating its recognition of the emirate of Kalba and would be re-incorporating the territory into Sharjah. Weir 'reminded [the rulers] of Her Majesty's Government's refusal to recognize Saqr bin Sultan bin Salim as ruler of Kalba, or to accept murder as a title to succession in any Shaikhdom' and warned the rulers against providing asylum to Saqr bin Sultan should he seek it.[19]

At the same meeting, Weir also formally announced British recognition of treaty relations with Fujairah at the same time. The newly recognized ruler of Fujairah had, in fact, been actively ruling in his territory since the family had seceded from Sharjah in 1901. Though Muhammad bin Hamad had expressed interest in being recognized officially in the previous decades, the British government had 'considered [it] undesirable to bring into being another petty Trucial State', until 1952, when Hay became concerned that Muhammad would seek out protection from Saudi Arabia.[20] The ruler of Sharjah opposed the decision and refused to recognize the ruler of Fujairah as a 'brother ruler'

---

[17] Rupert Hay (Political Resident, Bahrain) to Anthony Eden (Foreign Secretary). 9 May 1952. FO 371/98331. TNA.

[18] 'Historical Summary of Events of the Persian Gulf Shaikhdoms and the Sultanate of Muscat and Oman, 1928–1953'. IOR/R/15/1/731(1). QDL.

[19] Minutes of the First Trucial States Council Meeting. 23 March 1952. FO 371/98331. TNA. At the second meeting, the agent notified the rulers that all the arrangements for dissolving Kalba had been completed.

[20] 'Historical Summary of Events of the Persian Gulf Shaikhdoms and the Sultanate of Muscat and Oman, 1928–1953'. IOR/R/15/1/731(1). QDL.

following the announcement, and the minutes of the meeting reflect that both Saqr bin Sultan of Sharjah and Saqr bin Muhammad of Ras Al Khaimah greeted the announcement with silence.[21] In short order, the British had erased one emirate and created an entirely new one.

The Trucial States Council continued to meet on average twice per year, but the Political Agents complained time and again about the lack of meaningful participation from the rulers during the early meetings. The rulers either did not come or did not speak much during the earliest meetings. In the third council meeting, Christopher Pirie-Gordon (Political Agent, Dubai) complained that Sheikh Shakhbut only 'spoke once to opine when his opinion was directly asked that H.M.G. knew best' and that the only other significant contribution from the rulers came from Sheikh Saqr of Sharjah, who Pirie-Gordon said criticized 'every item' on the agenda.

Occasionally, Political Agents would express optimism that the meetings might lead to greater cooperation, as was Pirie-Gordon's hope following the fifth Trucial States Council meeting in July 1954. Burrows reported to the Foreign Office that the meeting indicated the development of 'happy relations'.[22] Pirie-Gordon's own summation indicated an informal but talkative gathering of the rulers, who were cooperative and seemingly productive: 'The audience appeared genuinely interested in the items of the Agenda which were eagerly discussed by the rulers in a series of impromptu sub committees round the table.'[23] The group generally was lively and in, 'cheerful and affable spirits'.[24] By the following meeting in December, however, the Political Agent described a more subdued council meeting with several of the rulers remaining quiet and acquiescent throughout.[25]

Pirie-Gordon's successor, J. P. Tripp, expressed even greater frustration in the years that followed. Tripp complained that the council as late as 1956 did not have the capacity for dealing with communal problems. 'These meetings serve the purpose of giving rulers a regular meeting place and a general sense of community interests and problems, but I do not consider the Council is keeping pace with progress in other spheres in the Trucial States.'[26] For Tripp

---

[21] Minutes of the First Trucial States Council Meeting. 23 March 1952. FO 371/98331. TNA.
[22] B. A. Burrows (Political Resident, Bahrain) to Anthony Eden (Foreign Secretary, London). 23 July 1954. FO 371/109814. AGDA.
[23] C. M. Pirie-Gordon (Political Agent, Dubai) to B. A. Burrows (Political Resident, Bahrain). 5 July 1954. FO 371/109814. AGDA.
[24] C. M. Pirie-Gordon (Political Agent, Dubai) to B. A. Burrows (Political Resident, Bahrain). 5 July 1954. FO 371/109814. AGDA.
[25] C. M. Pirie-Gordon (Political Agent, Dubai) to B. A. Burrows (Political Resident, Bahrain). 2 January 1955. FO 371/132900. TNA.
[26] J. P. Tripp (Political Agency, Dubai) to Foreign Office. 28 June 1956. FO 371/120553. TNA.

and other policymakers, the failings of the council meeting were often related to British institutional perceptions of the rulers' personalities themselves. In his impressions of the seventh Trucial State Council meeting, Tripp despaired of the rulers accomplishing much because their view of government was driven by the view that '*l'état c'est moi*', ruling by their 'personal whims'.[27]

Tripp's own views echoed many of those expressed by Hay. In his historical summary of events in the Persian Gulf 1928–53, Hay had labelled the rulers variously as courageous but 'volatile and untrustworthy' (Rashid bin Humaid of Ajman), unsatisfactory as a ruler and 'mentally ill-balanced' (Shakhbut of Abu Dhabi), or of having 'much force of character' despite being 'colourless' (Saqr of Ras Al Khaimah).[28] Even rulers the British Residents and agents described favourably were nevertheless characterized in orientalist terms. Hay describe Rashid bin Said, who acted as regent to his father in 1953, as 'astute but given to intrigue and not at all times trustworthy'.[29] The description would be repeated almost verbatim by subsequent policymakers in the Gulf. Glen Balfour-Paul, the Political Agent at Dubai from 1964 to 1968, would describe Rashid as one of the rulers he 'most enjoyed' as 'enormously energetic' but also as being always busy with checking on the 'proceeds of smuggling and the gold trade'.[30] British policymakers stumbled again and again over their repetitive perception that the sheikhs' personal failings prevented them from modernizing their emirates and employing the same phrases and tropes to explain away the rulers' lack of enthusiasm for, or overt disagreement with, British recommendations.

Cooperation

Despite the pessimism of the Political Agents, the rulers themselves did take action in several areas to improve their states through the Trucial States Council. Though some of the progress seemed slight in the eyes of British policymakers who wished to see the rulers take on modernization projects with enthusiasm

---

[27] J. P. Tripp (Political Agent, Dubai) to Charles Gault, 27 August 1955. *ROE, 1820–1958*, v. 9 (1947–1958), 223–6.
[28] 'Historical Summary of Events of the Persian Gulf Shaikhdoms and the Sultanate of Muscat and Oman, 1928–1953'. IOR/R/15/1/731(1). QDL.
[29] 'Historical Summary of Events of the Persian Gulf Shaikhdoms and the Sultanate of Muscat and Oman, 1928–1953'. IOR/R/15/1/731(1). QDL.
[30] Glencairn Balfour-Paul, *Bagpipes in Babylon: A Lifetime in the Arab World and Beyond* (London: I.B. Tauris, 2006), 196–7.

and rapidity, the rulers did find their way to prioritize development projects that seemed most likely to meet the urgent needs of their subjects.

Some cooperative efforts were limited in their initial scope. The Trucial Coast lacked paved roads well into the 1960s, but the activity from Sharjah's military and air installations combined with Dubai's trade had led to an increase in automobile traffic, nevertheless. Within the first two years of the Trucial Council's history, the rulers of Dubai and Sharjah had begun to cooperate on developing some initial traffic laws. These would later serve as the basis for future traffic regulations across the coast. The rulers likewise shared frustrations over protecting the quality and integrity of the local pearl market. Together they agreed to issue declarations against the sale of off-market pearls in the Trucial States.[31]

The rulers also tackled some more difficult topics, including the matter of domestic slavery on the Trucial Coast. The residents had pressed the rulers to end the practice of domestic slavery often over the years. The maritime slave trade in the Persian Gulf had slowed significantly in the second half of the nineteenth century, as Muscat and Persia had both banned maritime slave trade in 1846 and 1848, respectively.[32] In the northern Gulf and the Trucial Coast, however, enslaved men continued to work as divers on pearling ships, performing other forms of maritime labour at the ports. Significant numbers of enslaved men worked as agricultural labour, especially irrigating and maintaining date farms in oases such as Liwa and Buraimi. Enslavers additionally hired out men in the twentieth century to perform wage labour for oil companies and adjacent industries, providing additional income to the households. Women were also enslaved for domestic labour in individual households in smaller numbers. Estimates of the enslaved population in the Trucial States range widely from 10 per cent to 25 per cent of the population, though Zdanowski has suggested an average along the Arab coast of 14.5 per cent.[33]

British efforts to curtail slavery in the Gulf were half-hearted well into the twentieth century. In theory, British treaties with Oman and the Trucial rulers as early as 1820 forbade maritime transportation of some enslaved people from east Africa through the Gulf and later used naval patrols to discourage slave trade. In reality, however, Britain made little concerted effort to curb transport

---

[31] Minutes of the First Trucial States Council Meeting, 23 March 1952. FO 371/98331. TNA.
[32] Behnaz A. Mirzai, 'The 1848 Abolitionist Farmaan: A Step Towards Ending the Slave Trade in Iran', in *Abolition and Its Aftermath in Indian Ocean Africa and Asia*, ed. Gwyn Campbell (New York: Routledge, 2005), 94–102.
[33] Jerzy Zdanowski, 'The Manumission Movement in the Gulf in the First Half of the Twentieth Century', *Middle Eastern Studies* 47, no. 6 (2011): 864.

of enslaved people or dismantle enslaved labour on the coast or inland, preferring stability over possible conflict.[34] British Agents and Residents granted certificates of manumission to any enslaved person who requested it, but this was a relatively rare phenomenon in the Gulf until the oil industry provided alternative employment in the form of wage labour.[35] Several households on the coast still maintained enslaved servants well into the twentieth century. At the third meeting of the Trucial Council, Weir introduced the subject of slavery and encouraged all the rulers together to issue proclamations ending domestic slavery in their emirates. Domestic slavery was on the decline in the Trucial Coast, but an estimated 2,000 people remained enslaved. Though some of the rulers objected at the meeting in 1953, by 1954 they had all officially banned the practice, though trade in enslaved labour continued from Oman through the Trucial States into Saudi Arabia for another decade.[36]

In two other areas, the Trucial States Council laid the foundations for significant areas of future development. The first of these was the expansion of the Al-Maktoum Hospital in Dubai. Founded in 1949, the hospital boasted of a single British doctor and twelve beds.[37] The oil companies previously had been persuaded to provide services via their own private hospital at Sharjah in the 1930s for subjects of the emirates, but this proved inadequate and had only been offered begrudgingly. Under the Trucial States Council, the Dubai hospital became a joint interest for all the Trucial States, with each ruler agreeing to contribute an annual sum to its upkeep and expansion at the fourth council meeting in 1953.[38] They further coordinated the circulation of dispensers who rotated through clinics on a regular basis until more hospitals could be built in other emirates in the 1960s. The second significant area of development the Trucial States Council addressed was the question of education. Sharjah established its first modern school in 1953, with aid and teachers from Kuwait. In the second year, Sharjah introduced a second programme for girls. Over the next five years, each of the emirates sent students to Sharjah for education. This

---

[34] Benjamin J. Reilly, 'A Well-Intentioned Failure: British Anti-slavery Measures and the Arabian Peninsula, 1820–1940', *Journal of Arabian Studies* 5, no. 2 (2015): 91–115.

[35] Suzanne Meirs, 'Slavery and the Slave Trade in Saudi Arabia and the Arab States of the Persian Gulf, 1921–1963', in *Abolition and Its Aftermath in Indian Ocean Africa and Asia*, ed. Gwyn Campbell (New York: Routledge, 2005), 120–36. Hopper, *Slaves of One Master*.

[36] Third Meeting of the Trucial States Council, 25 April 1953. FO 371/104261. TNA; Trucial States Annual Report for 1954, C. M. Pirie-Gordon. 1955. FO 371/114576. TNA. Meirs, 'Slavery and the Slave Trade', 128–9. This declaration did not end the practice of slavery on the Trucial Coast entirely. See Zdanowski, 'Manumission Movement', 863–83; Hopper, *Slaves of One Master*.

[37] Julian Walker, *Tyro on the Trucial Coast* (Durham, UK: The Memoir Club, 1991).

[38] C. M. Pirie-Gordon (Political Agent, Dubai) to Bernard Burrows (Political Resident, Bahrain). 1 December 1953. FO 371/104261. TNA.

programme, too, would lay the groundwork for the expansion of education for primary and vocational schools later in the decade.[39]

What was accomplished, however, was small in comparison to what Bernard Burrows and his Political Agents wished for. What Tripp and other Political Agents considered to be the failing of the personalities and individual 'jealousies' of the rulers, however, Burrows recognized as a problem connected to the status of the council itself. For all its formality, the council remained for more than a decade as little more than a consultative body, with no meaningful authority.

Drawing borders

Borders remained a particularly difficult subject among rulers, but one which British policymakers were eager to resolve. The frontiers on the Trucial Coast were not fixed for the whole of the nineteenth and early twentieth century. The political structures of the Gulf depended on the amount of territory a tribe or collection of tribes could exercise control over at any given time.[40] The British and Ottoman governments initiated negotiations over frontiers just before the First World War. Those discussions demarcated boundaries which served to delineate where British protection began and ended. Then, when oil companies came to the Gulf to establish concession agreements and mark out areas for early exploration, borderlines became much more critical.[41] More precise boundaries came later through arbitration and mediation as disputes between the rulers necessitated. Some of the borders between the emirates continued undefined until well after the Trucial States became the United Arab Emirates. Those borders with Saudi Arabia, Oman and Qatar remained contentious well into the 1970s, with some of those boundaries still undefined today. The question of boundaries was a point of frustration from the outset of the Trucial Council but would take on greater urgency when Saudi Arabia staked claims to territory in Abu Dhabi and Oman at the site of Buraimi. Tensions over the question of boundaries came about in part because they came to be seen not as respecting

---

[39] Taryam, *Establishment of the United Arab Emirates 1950-85*, 17.
[40] See especially, John Craven Wilkinson, 'Britain's Rôle in Boundary Drawing in Arabia: A Synopsis', in *Territorial Foundations of the Gulf States*, ed. Richard Schofield (New York: St. Martin's Press, 1994), 94–108.
[41] John Craven Wilkinson, *Arabia's Frontiers: The Story of Britain's Boundary Drawing in the Desert* (New York: St. Martin's Press, 1991) is a comprehensive study of the legal debates surrounding the Anglo-Ottoman boundaries and their subsequent adaptation by Britain and Saudi Arabia.

local boundaries, histories or traditions; rather they were imposed borders decided by British policymakers.

Julian Walker, a young British civil servant, arrived on the Trucial Coast in late 1953 to serve as assistant to Pirie-Gordon. Almost immediately, he was tasked with setting internal boundaries for each of the Trucial States. The oil concession companies intended to begin exploration parties in offshore seabeds in 1956, and the future of the coast's development, power sharing and stability would require clearly defined ownership of those seabeds. More importantly, the establishment of internal boundaries served a significant role in transforming the Trucial States into modern states. Borders would allow the nascent state apparatuses to develop regulations, control the movement of populations and make rulers responsible for the actions of those within their territories. Delineating the territories of the Trucial States would transform the nature of rulers' responsibilities over the coming years. Where the earlier Anglo-Gulf treaties had limited the flexibility of the local political and territorial reach of the Trucial rulers, these new boundaries would form an increasingly rigid state structure that adhered to modern international standards of statehood.

Until the mid-twentieth century, boundaries in the southeast Arabian Peninsula were nebulous and permeable. Rulers controlled the territory that the strength of their tribal alliances allowed them to control. Powerful tribes and federations might lay semi-permanent claims to areas where they established fortresses and outposts, oases and migration routes (the *dirah*), but as tribal allegiances shifted, so might rulers' claims to sovereignty over areas.[42] Very few boundaries had been set in the peninsula before the 1950s, and even those were open to interpretation and change. Prior to the First World War, the British and Ottoman governments negotiated what became known as the 'Blue Line' and the 'Violet Line', which delineated the two empires' spheres of influence.[43] The Blue Line had been proposed in 1913 but was never ratified. Nevertheless, the British government treated it as an internationally recognized principle. The line begins on the Arabian Coast just north of where Saudi Arabia meets Qatar and runs south to terminate in the Rub al-Khali, or Empty Quarter. The Violet Line indicated a basis for the boundaries of South Arabia and Oman. It runs westward at an approximately 45-degree angle from the coastline starting near Ibb and terminates at the Blue Line in the Empty Quarter. In the 1930s, Saudi

---

[42] J. E. Peterson, 'Sovereignty and Boundaries in the Gulf States: Settling the Peripheries', in *The International Politics of the Persian Gulf*, ed. Mehran Kamrava (Syracuse, NY: Syracuse University Press, 2011), 21–49, 23.

[43] Wilkinson, *Arabia's Frontiers*.

Arabia expanded its claims farther into the Empty Quarter. Other boundaries were established piecemeal through the 1930s and 1940s, as disputes arose between the rulers.

One such dispute was that between Shakhbut of Abu Dhabi and Said of Dubai. As early as 1936, Shakhbut had approached Said about clarifying the boundary between them in order to prevent a dispute regarding oil concession agreements. Negotiations dragged on, however, until the Second World War placed the subject on hold. In the years that followed, client tribes from both territories clashed with one another until warfare broke out in 1945. The conflict lasted through 1948, when a battle at Ruweihah ended with more than fifty members of Abu Dhabi's Mansouri tribe killed.[44] Shakhbut intervened to end raiding from Abu Dhabi tribes, and in the following year, Said established a peace with the Manasir as well. The following year, the Political Agent at Bahrain set a boundary between the two states, running forty miles inland from the coast. The settlement went against Shakhbut's claims, which he remained resentful about for many more years.

By 1954, boundary disputes threatened to prevent the British Residency's progress on matters of economic and civil development in the Trucial States. Disputes between the rulers themselves prevented the Trucial Council from developing rules and regulations for administering the day-to-day affairs, such as traffic regulations, citizenship and resource-sharing. It also hampered the movements of the rulers, British Political Officers and the oil exploration parties. Sheikh Saqr of Ras Al Khaimah found himself at the centre of conflict with each of his neighbours by 1954. At the time of his accession in 1948, Saqr began investing in development projects, especially in agriculture. The fertile plain produced a number of locally consumed products, including dates, tobacco, onions and tomatoes.[45] More agricultural land in the Hajjar mountain range came under dispute with Sharjah. Boundaries became even more complicated in 1952 after Kalba was dissolved and Fujairah was recognized. Sharjah moved to gain control over the territories of Kalba, and Ras Al Khaimah came into conflict with the ruler of Fujairah. These disputes were more than academic debates. In January 1954, Saqr of Ras Al Khaimah was traveling through Fujairah when he was fired on by tribesmen allied with Muhammad of Fujairah. Despite the

---

[44] 'Historical Summary of Events of the Persian Gulf Shaikhdoms and the Sultanate of Muscat and Oman, 1928–1953'. IOR/R/15/1/731(1). QDL; Heard-Bey, *From Trucial States to United Arab Emirates*, 300–2. Heard-Bey states fifty-two were killed, while Hay's summary indicates fifty-four.

[45] Matthew Maclean, 'Spatial Transformations and the Emergence of "The National": Infrastructures and the Formation of the United Arab Emirates, 1950–1980' (PhD diss., New York University, 2017), 45–7, 107.

Political Agent's attempts to arbitrate the dispute, violence continued, and in one incident, guards working for Sheikh Muhammad shot at the Political Agency's Arab Assistant by mistake.[46]

Burrows and Pirie-Gordon assigned a newly arrived Political Agent to determine the boundaries of the Trucial States in 1954. Julian Walker was twenty-four when he landed in Sharjah and toured the emirates before beginning the task of determining the 'squiggly tribal frontiers' of the emirates.[47] Over the next two years, Walker travelled throughout the region. According to his own accounts, he drew on a combination of sources to determine borders. These included historical accounts and records from Lorimer's *Gazetteer*; the oral accounts of tribal leaders, and the rulers; as well as payments of the *zakat* – the annual donation of charity to the rulers for distribution.[48]

After nearly two years of work, Walker had prepared most of his recommendations. These were not complete. Walker submitted his proposed boundaries, which mapped out hundreds of miles for much of the emirates. There remained some areas around key landmarks, especially at disputed wells, where rulers could not agree and where further negotiation and arbitration would be necessary. In 1956, the boundaries between Ras Al Khaimah and Umm Al Quwain, those between Ras Al Khaimah and Fujairah, and some of those between Ajman and Sharjah, were finalized. Said of Dubai and Saqr of Sharjah remained at odds over Walker's recommendation that the Dubai–Sharjah boundary be set at Abu Hail, five kilometres northeast of Al-Fahidi fort and Dubai Creek. Said maintained his claims, but, 'for several reasons it was decided to override his objections', according to Burrows's report to the Foreign Office.[49] The Resident offered the ruler an opportunity to come to a decision with Sharjah himself by August or the British decision announced in April would stand.

Many of the other boundary decisions would be held back until after disputes with Saudi Arabia over the Buraimi oasis were settled (see Chapter 4). Julian Walker would return to the Trucial States over the years to revisit boundaries. In 1959, he settled what he called '190 erratically wriggling miles' along Oman

---

[46] Trucial States Annual Report for 1954. C. M. Pirie-Gordon (Political Agent, Dubai), 1955. FO 371/114576. TNA.
[47] Walker, *Tyro on the Trucial Coast*,
[48] Two accounts in particular are helpful in tracing Walker's decision making: Walker, *Tyro on the Trucial Coast* and Julian Walker, 'Practical Problems of Boundary Delimitation in Arabia: The Case of the United Arab Emirates', in *Territorial Foundations of the Gulf States*, ed. Richard Schofield (New York: St. Martin's Press, 1994), 109–17.
[49] Bernard Burrows (Political Resident, Bahrain) to Selwyn Lloyd (Foreign Secretary, Foreign Office). 20 April 1956. FO 371/120604. AGDA.

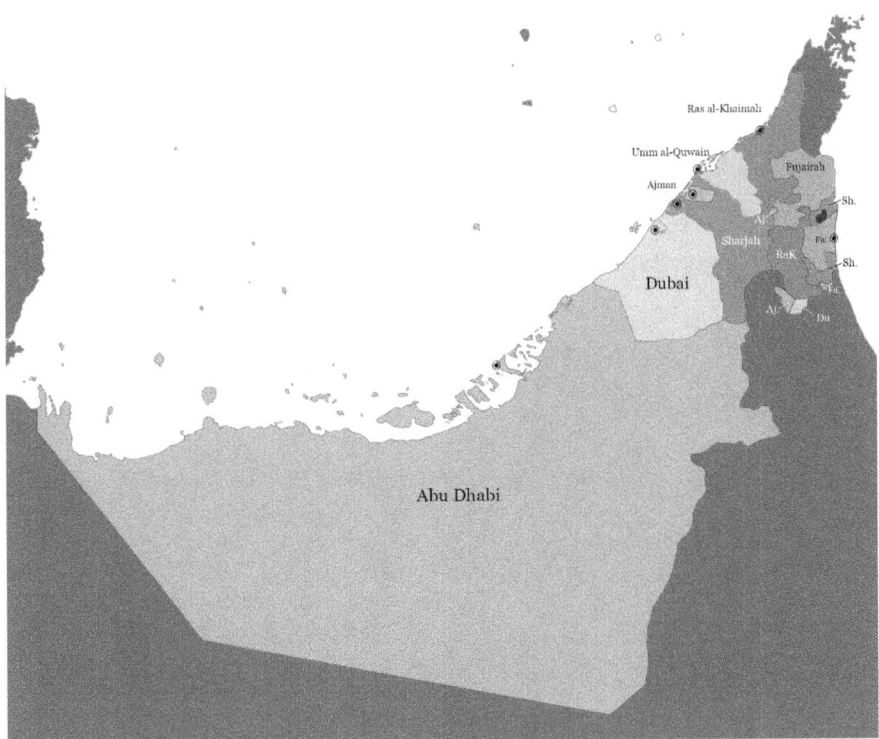

Map 3.2 Map of internal boundaries of the Trucial States.

and the Trucial States.⁵⁰ He returned once again in 1964 to settle further internal boundaries between several emirates. These included the seabed boundaries between Abu Dhabi and Dubai. Those of Dubai and Sharjah were settled in 1965, and the following year so were those of Sharjah and Fujairah (see Map 3.2).

The seeds of statehood in the Gulf germinated in the years immediately following the dissolution of the India Office and the shift of British administration in the Gulf to the Foreign Office. The trappings of modern statehood began to take shape as the rulers participated in a shared council and legislative efforts and coordinated communications. The Political Residency would establish the early structures and shape them within the context of an Arab and Middle Eastern world. This would become increasingly important as the rise of nationalist and anti-imperialist movements in the 1950s and 1960s informed the Residency's policies, and, through them, influenced the rulers.

---

[50] Julian Walker (Political Agency, Dubai) to Bernard Burrows (Political Resident, Bahrain). 24 May 1959. FO 371/140134. AGDA.

Boundaries and territoriality would bring the sheikhdoms greater international recognition as political entities. It would also bring them into conflict with Saudi Arabia. Even as the Residency worked to define the internal boundaries of the Trucial States, Saudi Arabia sought to undermine the external boundaries and political legitimacy of Abu Dhabi at the Buraimi Oasis.

4

The dispute at Buraimi and the consequences of poverty

On the eve of Eid al-Adha in 1952, a party of approximately eighty Saudis with seven vehicles descended in the area of the Buraimi Oasis between Abu Dhabi and Oman. Leading them was the Saudi emir of Ras Tanura, Abdullah al-Otaishan. In celebration of the holiday honouring Abraham's willingness to sacrifice his son Ishmael, al-Otaishan provided a feast for the inhabitants of the village of Hamasa and its surroundings. Over the next several days, sheikhs from surrounding villages and nomadic tribes arrived to meet with the Saudi delegation, whose members settled in for a prolonged stay in the area. Al-Otaishan's arrival amounted to a Saudi invasion and occupation of a porous territory. More than two years of simmering conflict followed. The Trucial Oman Levies (TOL), along with local bedouin forces, ejected the Saudis in 1954.

The Buraimi Dispute is a tense and action-packed episode – one which changed very little in terms of realities on the ground. In the end, the Saudi occupiers were forced to withdraw, but it did not put an end to their ambitions to dominate the frontier. The Saudi government continued to test its influence in the region into the next decades just as it had done in the decades preceding the dispute. Similarly, the frontier boundaries remained just as unsettled after the Saudis left as it had been. No changes to the border came from the dispute, and the borders between Saudi Arabia and Abu Dhabi remained undefined until 1974.

Scholars have nevertheless examined the Buraimi Dispute in an effort to identify it as a significant moment in Britain's imperial twilight. When viewed narrowly, the Buraimi dispute can be seen as a moment when Britain flexed its imperial muscle to protect the rulers on the coast and demonstrate Britain's continued relevance to post-war global defence. Many of the past British Residents, agents and officers provide fodder for this approach, with vivid descriptions of the tense atmosphere and tenuous grasp Abu Dhabi and Oman held on the ground.¹ As America's relationship with the Saudis grew in conjunction with ARAMCO's oil production, Britain sought to assert its relevance as the lynchpin in the Gulf. Some have viewed Saudi encroachment as a sign of Anglo-American rivalry and a first step in the inevitable rise of American primacy in the region.² Other scholars have emphasized the creation of the TOL and its legacy.³ Michael Morton has provided a strong addition to our understanding of the interplay of local politics with British priorities and wider concerns about the oil industry's role in shaping the politics of the Gulf.⁴

This chapter considers the Buraimi Dispute at the intersection of local, regional and imperial circumstances. I draw on Ann Stoler's approach to reading the 'pulse' of the archive to identify the significance of the Buraimi episode in the creation of the Trucial States. Stoler argues that periods of high archival activity can be understood as a bureaucratic quickening of the pulse – points of imperial anxiety reflected in the record which provide insights into institutional priorities.⁵ The British policymakers' reports and telegrams from this period reveal a deep anxiety about Britain's ability to retain its position in the Trucial States. Adopting Stoler's imagining of the archive as a living being, taking the pulse of the archive before, during and after the Buraimi crisis, reveals a steady beat emphasizing the link between development and Britain's ability to maintain its position in the Trucial States.

The conflict illustrates the degree to which the poverty of the Trucial Coast under British 'protection' made the people of the Trucial States and their rulers receptive to outside promises of resources. The Saudi government used food and money to entice sheikhs to change their allegiance and promised healthcare, school and jobs in the future. While Britain and local forces were able to end Saudi occupation with force, the Buraimi Dispute is significant because it showed

---

[1] Glencairn Balfour-Paul, *Bagpipes in Babylon* and *The End of Empire in the Middle East: Britain's Relinquishment of Power in Her Last Three Dependencies* (Cambridge: Cambridge University Press, 1991); Edward Henderson, *This Strange Eventful History: Memoirs of Earlier Days in the UAE and Oman* (London: Quartet Books, 1988) are examples.

[2] Tore Tingvold Petersen, 'Anglo-American Rivalry in the Middle East: The Struggle for the Buraimi Oasis, 1952–1957', *The International History Review* 14, no. 1 (1992): 71–91 and *The Middle East Between Great Powers: Anglo-American Conflict and Cooperation, 1952–7* (London: Palgrave Macmillan, 2000), 36–47. Simon C. Smith, 'The Anglo-American "Special Relationship" and The Middle East, 1945–1973', *Asian Affairs* 45, no. 3 (2014): 425–48.

[3] Tancred Bradshaw, 'The Hand of Glubb: The Origins of the Trucial Oman Scouts', *Middle Eastern Studies* 53, no. 4 (2017): 656–72; Muna M. Al-Hammadi, *Britain and the Administration of the Trucial States, 1947–1965* (Abu Dhabi: Emirates Center for Strategic Studies and Research, 2013), 51–76.

[4] Michael Quentin Morton, *Buraimi: The Struggle for Power, Influence, and Oil in Arabia* (New York: I.B. Tauris, 2013).

[5] Stoler, *Along the Archival Grain*.

British policymakers that the real threat to their position on the Trucial Coast was its failure to raise the standard of living for the people of the Trucial States.

Against this backdrop, the Saudi government attempted to assert its political power and claim the territories which Abu Dhabi and Oman (with the support of Britain) viewed as their own. The chapter continues with al-Otaishan's arrival and occupation of Hamasa and his bid to sway local sheikhs towards Saudi patronage. Britain tried to counteract the Saudis but struggled to parley the complexities of tribal relations and politics into the frameworks of international diplomacy and negotiations. Where Shakhbut, Zayed and their tribesmen wanted swift action to preserve their legitimacy, British diplomats attempted to present incomplete records of customary and religious taxes as well as spotty local reports into arguments suitable for an international tribunal. The chapter ends with the armed confrontation and the arbitration that followed. The dispute over Buraimi solved few problems but drew the Trucial States into the international spotlight and forced both Britain and the Trucial rulers to consider their continuing relationships with one another, and with the broader Arab world, in a new light.

The villages at Buraimi

The Buraimi Oasis is situated approximately 150 kilometres east of Abu Dhabi at the base of the Jabal Hafit of the Al Hajar mountain range. Archaeological evidence suggests prehistoric settlement in the area, and more significant settlements in the early Islamic period, made possible through innovations in irrigation using *aflaj* (*falaj*, s.) directing water into the area for cultivation. Sometime in the seventeenth or eighteenth centuries the Omani Yarubids, who had gained control over the region, instituted works to expand and develop intensive date palm cultivation. Evidence from recent archaeological digs in Al Ain indicate the digging out of sunken gardens and the expansion and elaboration of the *aflaj* system for collecting and carrying run-off from the nearby mountain, as well as direction of water from wells into the gardens.[6]

Agriculture constituted the primary economic activity in the oasis well into the early part of the twentieth century. At the turn of the twentieth century,

---

[6] Timothy Power and Peter Sheehan, 'The Origin and Development of the Oasis Landscape of al-'Ain (UAE)', *Proceedings of the Seminar for Arabian Studies* 42 (2012): 301–2; Timothy Power, Nasser al-Jahwari, Peter Sheehan and Kristian Strutt, 'First preliminary report on the Buraimi Oasis Landscape Archaeology Project', *Proceedings of the Seminar for Arabian Studies* 45 (2015): 233–53.

the villages of the Buraimi Oasis flourished. Percy Cox, a British officer and Political Agent at Muscat (1899–1903), published a description of his travels into the oasis, painting a vivid picture of a lush landscape amid the desert.[7] Cox departed from Muscat to Abu Dhabi in the company of the Omani Sultan via ship to Abu Dhabi, where they met with 'the grand old man of the pirate coast', Zayed bin Khalifah.[8] From there, Cox continued on into the interior of the emirate by camel accompanied by various men 'responsible to the Shaikh of Abu Dhabi' for his safe passage for much of his travels.[9] He described the oasis as follows:

> At the time of my visits the population of the oasis was estimated at about 5000. The habitations, which are for the most part dotted about in clusters among the gardens, are built of mud and date screens combined. The water supply is from numerous fuluj [sic] or underground aqueducts coming in from the hills to the east, and one or two also from Jabal Hafit. Light though it is the soil is evidently most prolific, and it was calculated that the oasis supported not less than 60,000 date palms besides all the fruits and vegetables to be found in that region, e.g., grapes, melons, limes, figs, pomegranates, a few mangoes, and in the way of crops, wheat, barley, and jowari and quantities of lucerne.[10]

Farming provided one significant area of economic activity, but the oasis also provided for two other areas of the economy: pearling and the slave trade.

As discussed in the previous chapter, enslaved people performed a significant portion of agricultural labour and served on pearling vessels throughout the Gulf. Enslaved labourers worked seasonally in both agriculture and on pearling ships and in maritime trade, sometimes migrating from inland to the coast and back as needed. Demand for enslaved labour declined within the Trucial Coast in part because of the decline of the pearl trade. During the Second World War demand for enslaved labour rebounded, particularly in Oman and Saudi Arabia. Hamasa village housed the inland slave market where men, women and children were brought from the Makran and Batinah coasts and housed in barracks before being sold and transported further into Arabia. While many enslaved people

---

[7] Cox's account was published in 1925 but should be dated to some period between 1899 and 1904. Rosemarie Said-Zahlan dates his trip to 1905, but John Townsend suggests it occurred in 1902. Townsend is more likely to be correct, as Cox had left his post in Muscat by 1904 and would not have departed from there for his travels. Townsend, *Proconsul to the Middle East*, 10; Said-Zahlan, *Origins of the United Arab Emirates*, 139.

[8] Percy Cox, 'Some Excursions in Oman', *The Geographical Journal* 66, no. 3 (1925): 197.

[9] Cox, 'Some Excursions in Oman', 201–2. At different stages of the journey, Cox was accompanied by Saqr bin Zaid as well as a sheikh from the Dhawahir tribe. At other times, he would be accompanied by those under the direction of the sultan.

[10] Cox, 'Some Excursions in Oman', 207.

in the nineteenth century were of Persian or African origin, by the twentieth century most came from Baluchistan. Many sold themselves into slavery, but a more significant number were kidnapped from the Makran Coast. In Buraimi, enslavers could purchase fraudulent papers indicating that the enslaved people had been born into slavery, thus making their travel into Saudi Arabia legal. Once in Saudi Arabia, they would be placed in domestic labour.[11]

The region underwent a series of wars in the eighteenth and nineteenth centuries, but no permanent power established sustained control over the largely independent tribes. In the nineteenth century, Buraimi comprised nine separate villages settled in a six-mile radius. The villages of Buraimi and Hamasa were under the nominal control of the Sultan of Oman and Muscat for much of this period, though in fact they were more directly under the control of the Naimi and Bani Qitab among other tribes who functioned autonomously, if not independently, from the sultanate. The remaining villages comprised a mixture of tribes which would coalesce around the Bani Yas.

Sandwiched between the Saudi emirates and the Omani sultanate, Buraimi and its surroundings experienced the tugs of war between the two. The first Saudi emirate attempted to expand its control into the area in 1800, and that year Saudi forces captured Buraimi. Over the next several years, it established fortresses at al-Subarah and al-Khandaq. Buraimi became the base for Saudi attacks against Oman until the first Saudi emirate fell to Egyptian–Ottoman forces in 1818. The Saudi state revived itself in 1824 and in the 1850s began to make incursions into the oasis again. British records show several short-lived efforts on the part of the Saudis to establish a presence in and around Buraimi in the second half of the nineteenth century. In 1853, for example, a Saudi representative came to Buraimi to collect tribute from the sultan. Over the next decade, Saudi forces and their allies made additional visits to Buraimi to attack Omani positions along the coast. Saudi incursions into Oman in 1865 extended deep into Omani territory and the Batinah coast. These events led to the murders of two British Indian subjects and the capture of others. Following the death of Saudi emir Faisal bin Turki (r. 1834–8, 1843–65), his son, Abdullah, sent a communication to the Political Agent at Bushehr in an attempt to reaffirm Saudi friendship with Britain and to indicate the release and return of British Indian subjects from Saudi control. A subsequent envoy delivered further affirmations of friendship with Britain, a desire for peace and reiterated that the Saudi emirate would

---

[11] Miers, 'Slavery and the Slave Trade', 126–8.

respect British subjects and not pursue aggression against the Trucial sheikhs and the Sultan of Oman.[12]

Saudi advances on Buraimi and the outlying areas did not go unanswered throughout this period. The Naimi sheikh requested British aid to rebuff Saudi encroachments, but Pelly refused aid indicating that he could not become involved in the internal affairs of the sheikhs.[13] Saudi attacks on Bahrain and the Omani coasts, however, did give Britain opportunities to use naval force to attack Saudi forces. The combination of British shows of naval force, internal disarray in the Saudi emirate and the advancing threat of the Ottomans against the Saudis created an important opportunity for Abu Dhabi's ruler, Zayed bin Khalifah (Zayed the Great or Zayed the first) to consolidate his rule over a significant amount of territory. Zayed had already begun building a powerful base. In 1870, he allied himself with the Naimi and Oman to defeat and eject the Saudis and their allies from the oasis.

Zayed the Great's victory established a strong Al Nahayan presence in the Buraimi Oasis. Abu Dhabi controlled numerous fortresses in the oasis' villages in his purview. He would go on to build several watchtowers in the area as well as a series of additional fortresses in Ain al-Dhawahir, or al Ain, to defend against future Saudi expansionism. Abu Dhabi's and Oman's control over the territory of the Buraimi Oasis remained largely unchallenged through the end of the nineteenth century and well into the twentieth century.

The villages of Buraimi continued to thrive for a time. While Zayed lived, his influence in Buraimi continued to expand. In the years after his death, the rulers of Abu Dhabi who followed him remained predominant in most of the oasis. However, their influence over the tribes waxed and waned with the strength of their rule and, accordingly, their ability to ensure the economic well-being of the tribes and enforce security measures when tribal disputes broke out. For the most part, they were successful in maintaining relative peace in Buraimi through 1926. Zayed's sons Tahnoun (r. 1909–12) and Hamdan (r. 1912–22) both built alliances with local tribal leaders and forged agreements with the ruler of Dubai and the sultan to maintain peace on the occasions when internal disputes threatened stability. When, in 1912, a dispute between the Al Nahayan and Al Bu Shamis broke out, Tahnoun succeeded in gathering sufficient forces

---

[12] This exchange of communications is sometimes referred to as the 1866 Anglo-Arabian Treaty or Anglo-Saudi Agreement. According to Lorimer's historical summary in the *Gazetteer*, there was no treaty or agreement but a unilateral declaration on behalf of the emir. Lorimer, *Gazetteer* 1, pt. 2, 1124. See also Gary Troeller, *The Birth of Saudi Arabia: Britain and the Rise of the House of Sa'ud* (London: Routledge, 2013) (a reprint edition of a 1976 version), 17–18.

[13] Lorimer, *Gazetteer* 1, pt. 2, 1118.

and the help of the local Bani Qitab sheikhs to mediate the dispute. In sporadic disputes between 1913 and 1919, Hamdan sustained Abu Dhabi's importance in Buraimi by cultivating good relationships with the Manasir and marshalling sufficient forces to quell the disturbance.[14] This was not enough, however, to keep animosity from bubbling up again and again. Combined with the onset of the pearl trade's collapse and the economic hardships created by the global depression, Hamdan found himself at odds with members of his own family over the distribution of allowances to maintain their loyalty.

In addition to managing the internal affairs of Buraimi, Hamdan once again faced the rise of the Saudis. The Saudi emirate's ambition to be the paramount power on the Arabian Peninsula brought conflict to the frontiers of Abu Dhabi. Prior to the outbreak of the First World War, the revived Saudi state succeeded in wresting control of al-Hasa from the Ottomans. Hamdan, suspicious of Saudi expansionism, joined the ruler of Dubai in preparing to confront the Saudis in the eastern frontier. He was put off from the idea by British assurances – and warnings – that the Anglo-Turkish agreement on boundaries was sufficient protection. By 1917, Hamdan had determined that the best path forward with the Al Saud would be through an exchange of letters, which put the enmity between the two parties on pause.[15]

Hamdan's assassination at the hands of his brother Sultan (r. 1922–6) in 1922 marked the beginning of a period of instability in Abu Dhabi that continued until Shakhbut's accession in 1928. Sultan found himself unable to balance the tribal politics and family intrigue any better than Hamdan. Continued tribal disputes led some of the western tribes to invite help from the Saudis through their representative at al-Hasa. Their requests for support gave the Saudi governor of the eastern province, Abdullah bin Julawi, the opening he needed to send officials to collect *zakat* from those tribes on the Abu Dhabi frontier. He also made attempts to collect from tribes in the Liwa and Buraimi oases. These ventures met with limited success, as the tribes farther away from al-Hasa were more successful in ignoring or rejecting Saudi claims to taxes or tribute. Sultan's rule lasted until his brother Saqr (r. 1926–8) assassinated him. Unable to garner sufficient support within the family for his rule, Saqr sought to court Saudi support in the hopes they would support him against any attempts within his family to overthrow him. This proved insufficient insurance. He was

---

[14] Maitra and Al-Hajji, *Qasr al-Hosn*, 204–22.
[15] Ibid., 223. In addition to the exchange of letters and assurances from Cox that the Anglo-Ottoman borders were sufficient deterrent, the British government also sent a ship to Abu Dhabi as a warning against the ruler's preparations for attack.

assassinated two years later and Shakhbut ascended to the role of ruling sheikh of Abu Dhabi.

Shakhbut ushered in a period of stability in Abu Dhabi's frontier. He appointed his brother Hazza as the *wali* of the western region (Liwa), and successive loyal *walis* projected the Al Nahyan's power in the eastern region. From the perspective of the Political Residents, Shakhbut's leadership and importance in Buraimi remained steadfast through the 1930s and 1940s. As will be seen further on, there were occasional instances where the question of Saudi influence arose, but British Agents and the Residents remained confident that Shakhbut's influence in the oasis was strong. Trenchard Fowle observed as late as 1939 that in Buraimi Abu Dhabi is 'the big power at the threshold' and commanded the 'considerable respect' of the most important tribes in the area, making him 'the strongest influence in Buraimi and much of Dhahira'.[16] When, in 1948, British explorer Wilfred Thesiger followed in Percy Cox's earlier footsteps, he described Abu Dhabi as still the paramount power in Buraimi under the representation of Shakhbut's 'universally popular' brother, Zayed, who had become the *wali* of the eastern region in 1946.[17]

Precursors to the dispute

Attempts to determine claims to areas of the frontiers led to more questions as oil concessions were being sorted. When oil concessions were signed in 1933, it raised questions about the boundary lines, particularly those boundaries between the Trucial States collectively and the Saudi frontiers. As discussed in the previous chapter, these boundaries had remained as general agreements between the British and the Ottomans prior to the First World War. The Foreign Office informed the United States of these boundaries subsequent to the Iraq Petroleum Company (IPC) concession agreement. The Saudi foreign minister, however, rejected the Anglo-Ottoman boundaries as irrelevant as the Saudis had not signed onto the agreement and the Ottoman government no longer existed (see Map 4.1).

---

[16] Political Agency (Bahrain) to Trenchard Fowle (Bushehr), 1939. IOR R/15/1/706.
[17] Wilfred Thesiger, 'Desert Borderlands of Oman', *The Geographical Journal* 116, nos. 4–6 (1950): 139. In his own writings, he spells his destination as 'Muwaiqih', but this seems to be an incorrect transliteration of al-Muwaijih, an area in Al Ain, and a fortress. In the Gulf dialect, the *qaf* becomes a *jīm* and the *jīm* sometimes becomes a *yah*. The spelling of al-Muwaijih in Arabic, however, is ٱلْمُوَيْجِعِي.

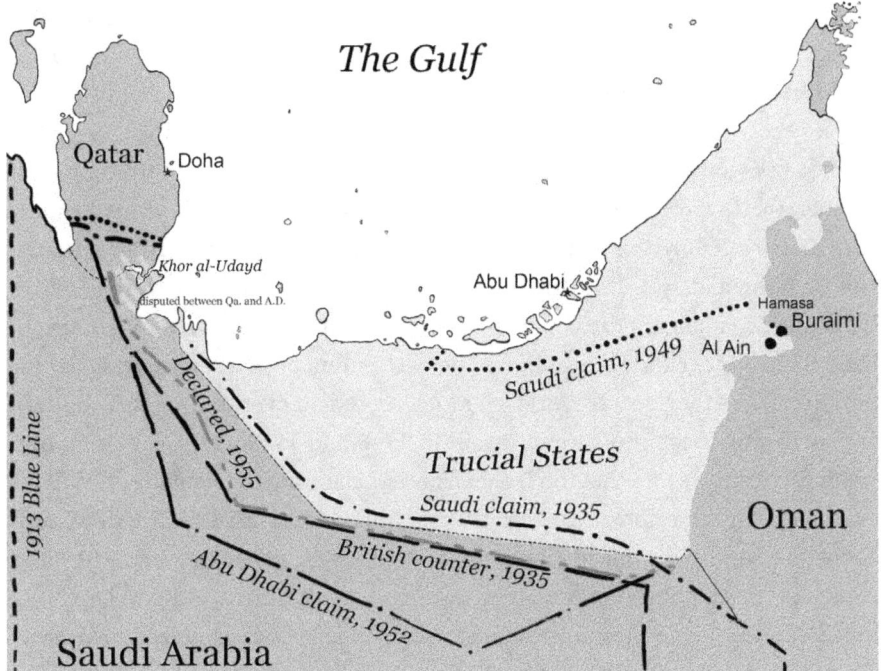

Map 4.1 Map of boundary claims between Qatar, Abu Dhabi and Saudi Arabia.

The Saudis put forward their own claim in 1935. The 'Hamza Line' or 'Red Line' claimed all of the Rub al-Khali far south into Oman's claimed territory and far east into territory claimed by Qatar, Abu Dhabi and Oman. The basis for the claim, according to the Saudi government, was the historical influence and tax collection from the Al Murrah tribe and the wells which they claimed to control. They also claimed the territory of Khor al-Udayd, located on the Qatar peninsula. Internal discussion among the British seems to indicate that while the British found these claims to be unreasonable, they would be willing to make some small concessions in exchange for a quick settlement that would protect Qatar and Abu Dhabi from the future spread of Saudi interest into their territories. They hoped that a concession in the Rub al-Khali would be a 'generous concession to Saudi aspirations' and would help facilitate agreement on the Qatari border with the Saudis while also preserving the eastern coast south of Qatar for Abu Dhabi.[18] While the British believed they would be close to an agreement on Qatar in October 1935, the question of the southeast frontier

[18] Mr. J. C. Walton to the Secretary of State for Foreign Affairs, 12 January 1935, *Buraimi Dispute*, v. 1.

remained deadlocked. In November, Britain proposed the Riyadh Line: this would set a boundary between Qatar and Saudi near the base of the Qatar peninsula; Khor al-Udayd would remain in Abu Dhabi territory, and the thin strip of coast south of the peninsula would remain with Abu Dhabi, though the boundary lay far east of the original Blue Line to Saudi Arabia. In the southeast frontier, the Riyadh Line came relatively close to meeting much of the Hamza/Red Line by ceding the Rub al-Khali, but Saudi Arabia rejected the proposal almost immediately.[19] The British offered a small modification to the Riyadh Line in 1937, adjusting the Qatar-Saudi border, but the Saudis remained firm in their claims under the Hamza Line. The parties remained at an impasse for the next decade, as the Second World War took precedent over settling the frontiers.

The frontier began to simmer again in 1948 and 1949. On a few occasions, Saudi parties came into the Abu Dhabi frontiers claiming the right to collect taxes or *zakat* from their nomadic client tribes. Hazza complained to British officials about the Saudis' arrival in the eastern province in the spring of 1948.[20] But while the frontier question remained unsettled, the Resident and Foreign Office urged caution while they investigated the claims. Hay considered the activity 'no new matter' and suggested that it may be tribes moving on the frontier to avoid paying taxes to the Saudi government. The British ambassador at Jeddah was urged to ask about it in order 'show that we are taking an interest', on behalf of Abu Dhabi.[21] The following February and March, Hazza and Shakhbut again reported Saudi forces entering Abu Dhabi, the latter traveling as far inland as thirty-five miles outside of Abu Dhabi town.[22] At least one other Saudi party accompanying ARAMCO surveyors once again travelled out into Abu Dhabi territory. Following the latest incident, the Political Office, Patrick Stobart, went out with Hazza to look at the situation.

Stobart discovered two ARAMCO camps and a makeshift air strip accompanied by Saudi guards on April 21. In an exchange with an ARAMCO employee, Stobart learned that the company men knew they were operating within Abu Dhabi's territory. The following day, Stobart returned and informed the party that the British government viewed their presence as an act of aggression and ordered the party to withdraw. Saudi guards held Stobart at gunpoint along with two of Shakhbut's men before releasing him while detaining the Abu Dhabi guards for a longer period. The Saudi government lodged a protest to the British

---

[19] Telegram: Jedda to Secretary of State for Foreign Affairs, 8 December 1935, *Buraimi Dispute*, v. 1.
[20] British Agency (Sharjah) to Political Agent (Pelly), Bahrain, 27 April 1948. IOR R/14/4/3.
[21] WR Hay (Bahrain) to Ernest Bevin (FO), 8 May 1948. IOR R/15/4/3.
[22] Political Agent (Sharjah) to Pelly (Bahrain), 9 March 1949. IOR R/15/4/3.

ambassador at Jeddah, claiming they had been in Saudi territory. The British government responded on Abu Dhabi's behalf; they rejected the Saudi claim and reproached the Saudis for having violated Abu Dhabi's sovereignty. With this, the dispute over the territory once again threatened to disturb the *status quo* on the peninsula – with the Saudis yet again asserting an expanded claim to the territory on Abu Dhabi's and Oman's frontiers. This time, they insisted that the strip of coast from the Qatar peninsula was historically Saudi territory, as well as most of Abu Dhabi's eastern province and further west to include the Buraimi Oasis – they claimed that neither Oman nor Abu Dhabi could rightfully claim to exercise authority over the tribes there.[23]

The diplomatic side of the dispute continued over the next several months. British policymakers were operating carefully in order to avoid complicating their relationship with the United States. In July, both the Saudi and British governments agreed to establish a commission for a fact-finding mission to be followed by negotiations or arbitration upon completion. A subsequent agreement in September called for maintaining the status quo in the contested area. The commission was scheduled to begin work the following fall but never actually took place. British policymakers would spend the next several years weighing whether or not they would be able to win a case submitted for arbitration at an international tribunal.

Meanwhile, on the ground in Abu Dhabi, the situation remained unstable. In February, a party of Saudis travelled into Abu Dhabi territory as far east as Bainunah, and a group of seven travelled south into Liwa. There, they attacked one of Shakhbut's subjects and stole his camel and robbed others.[24] This apparently coincided with another party of Saudi guards further to the north in Qatar, which led to an exchange of fire and two of the Saudi guards being killed. The Political Agent at Doha also reported there was an uptick in Saudi influence among the sheikhs in the Qatar-Saudi frontier area, with the Saudis paying an 'allowance' to some of the sheikhs there.[25] By the middle of 1952, tensions had escalated to such a degree that Shakhbut and his brothers were fighting among themselves over how best to maintain control in Abu Dhabi. Reports in the Agency's Trucial States Diary indicated that the 'rift' between Shakhbut on the one hand and Zayed and Hazza on the other continued for several months

---

[23] For details of the foregoing, see Morton, *Buraimi*, 75–85 and Kelly, *Eastern Arabian Frontiers*, New York (1964), 142–9.
[24] Translation of letter dated 22 February from Sheikh Hazza bin Sultan of Abu Dhabi to PD Stobart. 15 March 1950. FO 371/82015. TNA.
[25] Wilton (Doha) to Pelly (Bahrain), 10 April 1950. FO 371/82015. TNA; C. J. Pelly to G. W. Furlonge, 24 June 1950. *Buraimi Dispute* v. 2.

because the latter believed Shakhbut was not doing enough to counter Saudi activities.[26] A month later, rumours circulated that Shakhbut had increased his guards around the Maqta watchtower to prevent his brothers' allies from coming into Abu Dhabi town and that there may have been an armed clash between the guards and several Manasir tribesmen. The situation seemed to improve by late July, however, when Shakhbut invited Zayed to Abu Dhabi to reconcile their differences.[27] Their good relations mended just in time, as a month later they would have to present a united front in the struggle to eliminate the Saudi presence from Buraimi.

Arrival and blockade

The tribes that populated the unsettled frontier territories between Abu Dhabi, Oman and Saudi Arabia exercised dynamic, liminal power that was outside the reaches of any single ruler. 'Barbaric by design', the tribes which roamed these territories maintained shifting allegiances between the centres of power in an effort to maintain their autonomy.[28] The mobile and seemingly ungovernable nature of the polities of nomadic tribes made it difficult to substantiate the claims of any one aspiring ruler by any single measure. British archival sources reveal the varied angles by which the British sought to substantiate Abu Dhabi and Oman's claims while countering those of the Saudis, using both the local measures of degrees of sovereignty in combination with the modern international framework of nationhood. All sides of the disagreement used a number of different bases to make their arguments for sovereignty over the territories.

Saudi claims to the territory in dispute hinged on two primary components. The first of these were 'ancestral' claims based on the extent of past Saudi emirates' boundaries. In the first Saudi state, Abdulaziz bin Muhammad had expanded the Saudi territorial claims across the Trucial Coast and briefly south along the lower Omani coast (1800–24). The second Saudi state again expanded across the Trucial Coast before being defeated by Zayed I in 1870 as discussed earlier on. From that time forward, the Saudis never held any sustained uncontested control over the territory or settled populations in those

---

[26] Trucial States Diary No. 6, 25 May-30 June 1952. FO 1016/169. TNA.
[27] Trucial States Diary No. 7, 1952. FO 1016/169. TNA.
[28] Scott, *Art of Not Being Governed*.

territories. Nevertheless, two of the larger nomadic tribes that circulated on the contested frontier acknowledged allegiance to the Al Saud. The Al Murrah was recognized by the British and Abu Dhabi as primarily loyal to the Saudis.[29] The Manasir, however, comprised nomadic sections, which had sometimes aligned with the Saudis, but the remainder settled primarily in villages claimed by Abu Dhabi. The Saudis used this ambiguity as their basis for sending tax collectors into al-Hasa, Dhafrah and the Buraimi Oasis.[30]

The nature of tax collection provided significant fodder for debate over the degree of power exercised in the area of Buraimi in particular. Records of sustained tax collection could serve as the basis for legitimizing both rulers' claims to territories inhabited by tribes, but the precise nature of what constituted 'taxes', *zakat* payments and exchanges of goods as acts of hospitality and diplomacy proved just as ambiguous as the territorial boundaries. *Zakat*, or charitable giving, is a religious obligation for Muslims. In non-Muslim countries, Muslims and their families manage their *zakat* contributions individually. Historically, however, Islamicate empires and states could and did collect *zakat* as a government tax for redistribution to the poor. The ability of an empire to collect and administer *zakat* could be understood to signal recognition of the legitimacy of a state's claim to govern a people, while refusal to pay *zakat* to a state power could be a sign of non-recognition or resistance to a state's legitimacy.[31]

Several times in the 1930s and 1940s, Political Residents requested information from the frontiers regarding the nature and extent of tax collection in the frontiers. In one such case in 1934, the Residency requested an agent to find an 'intelligent man' who could be sent to Buraimi, Dhafrah and other areas to 'secretly' discover:

> i. What tribes and subsections of the tribes with the names of their Shaikhs have paid *zakat* to King Bin Saud or to the Amir of Hasa, 'Abdullah ibn Jiluwi.
>
> ii. In what years they have paid zakat and when did the payments first begin.
>
> iii. On how many camels and sheep each tribe and sub-section paid zakat and at what rate for each camel and sheep.
>
> iv. At what place and to whom were the payments made.[32]

---

[29] Extracts from a Summary of the History of the Dispute, *Buraimi Dispute*, v. 1.
[30] Foreign Office Minute, 30 September 1950, *Buraimi Dispute*, v. 2.
[31] Samantha May, 'Political Piety: The Politicization of *Zakat*', *Middle East Critique* 22, no. 2 (2013): 149–64.
[32] Political Agent (Bahrain) to Residency Agent (Sharjah) 3 July 1934. IOR R/15/4/3.

Reports over the year on who paid *zakat* to whom reflect inconsistencies. In 1924 and 1925, for example, the Emir of al-Hasa reportedly collected *zakat* on behalf of the Saudis from the Al Bu Shamis and later in Buraimi.[33] The following year, 'someone' tried again to collect taxes from the Nuaimi in Buraimi and Hamasa but was apparently unsuccessful. In the years 1922 and 1926, Sultan bin Zayed of Abu Dhabi had collected *zakat* in the area of Buraimi instead.[34] In another incident in 1934, Saudi collectors attempted to collect taxes in Liwa and other frontier areas and were rebuffed by force, leading to a formal apology to Hazza bin Sultan from the Saudi official who had sent them.[35] Almost two decades later, the information on *zakat* payments proved just as spotty, with Saudi *zakat* collectors attempting to collect taxes in the frontier region around fourteen times between 1934 and 1948 – but usually only with some tribes and sections.[36]

The social and political nature of tax collection and exchange signified the deep complexity behind the question of whether or not Abu Dhabi, Oman or Saudi Arabia exercised authority in a given territory. The collection of taxes and the exchange of gifts as hospitality could be conflated with one another. When British officials asked Sultan bin Zayed about the nature of his payments to Abdulalziz ibn Saud in the 1920s, Sultan indicated that the exchange of gifts was a matter of demonstrating friendly relations with neighbouring rulers.[37] Similarly, when a *zakat* collector travelled into the frontier to collect from subject tribes, they would stay at the home of a local sheikh. The hospitality and gift giving of the host sheikh did not necessarily constitute payment of *zakat*, but was instead the social obligations of a host and their guest.

Finally, the collection of *zakat* did not necessarily connote any sustained sense of legitimacy corresponding with territoriality. Nomadic peoples' allegiance to a polity did not align with continuous or majority presence in any given location. The Al Murrah could travel through Abu Dhabi frontiers for some part of the year and pay taxes to Saudi collectors while located in Abu Dhabi territory; however, they did not circulate permanently within just Abu Dhabi territory. Neither did they constitute a majority of the population in any of the settled

---

[33] Extract from Muscat News No. 12 for the Period 16 to 30 June 1925 in Political Residency (Bushehr) 'Ibn Saud's Relations with Trucial Chiefs'. 18 March 1923–5 October 1939. IOR R/15/1/706. BL.
[34] Translation of a letter, 19 September 1934 from Residency Agent, Sharjah to Col. Loch with enclosures: information about Buraimi and its surroundings: information obtained secretly from the people who are reliable and have knowledge about Dhah'frah. *Buraimi Dispute*, v. 1.
[35] Telegram, British Agent Sharjah to Political Agent Bahrain, 12 September 1949. IOR R/15/4/3. BL.
[36] Telegram, British Agent Sharjah to Political Agent Bahrain, 29 July 1949. IOR R/15/4/3. BL.
[37] Extract from Muscat News No. 12 for the period 16 to 30 June 1925 in Political Residency (Bushehr) 'Ibn Saud's Relations with Trucial Chiefs', 18 March 1923–5 October 1939. IOR R/15/1/706. BL.

areas they frequented. In the case of some nomadic Manasir, they may have sometimes allied themselves with the Saudis, but the majority of settled Manasir in Liwa and Dhafrah recognized Abu Dhabi's rule. Even this distinction between 'wandering' Manasir and 'settled' Manasir could be questioned; for example, Thesiger had observed that the Manasir in the 1940s were firmly allied with Abu Dhabi and to his knowledge had never been claimed by any ruler other than that of Abu Dhabi.[38]

The strongest foundations for Abu Dhabi's claims in the frontier versus those of the Saudis lay, on the one hand, in their treaties and boundary agreements of the nineteenth and early twentieth century and, on the other hand, the facts on the ground about tribal sheikhs' professions of loyalty. The Saudis might reject the Blue and Violet lines as invalid based on the extinction of the Ottoman Empire, but they could not as easily dismiss the 1915 and 1927 treaties which had recognized British primacy on the Trucial Coast and Oman. The Hamza Line and Ryan Line of the 1930s created a frontier that had brought the two claims more closely in line with one another. It was this frontier which the 1949 Status Quo agreement assumed as the basis for creating a rough frontier zone in which no oil exploration was to occur.

The parties to the dispute laid out their arguments at a conference in Dammam in the early part of 1952. Between 28 January and 14 March a delegation from Saudi Arabia and one representing British and Abu Dhabi's position met for extensive and heated discussions over the boundary claims of the two parties. Emir Faisal, along with his deputy foreign minister, the governor of al-Hasa and the Saudi ambassador to London represented the Saudi position. Rupert Hay led the British-Abu Dhabi contingent accompanied by the rulers of Abu Dhabi and Qatar.[39] The conference came to an abrupt close when Hay indicated that Britain would only continue discussions on the frontier line based on the Hamza/Red Line of 1935. The Saudis rejected this position. With no changes agreed to, the London Agreement remained in place.

Later that summer, the Saudis initiated a new strategy in an attempt to change facts on the ground in the western frontier and Buraimi to strengthen Saudi claims. In late August and early September, a flurry of telegrams traveling between Bahrain, Sharjah and Muscat reported that a Saudi party was traveling through Abu Dhabi's western frontier and were expected to arrive at Hamasa village in the

---

[38] Sir W. R. Hay to G. W. Furlonge, 3 June 1950, *Buraimi Dispute* v. 2.
[39] J. B. Kelly, *Eastern Arabian Frontiers* (London: Basic Books, 1964), 151–9. Kelly provides a clear and detailed summary of the sessions of the Dammam conference and its conclusion.

Buraimi Oasis. Zayed cabled from Buraimi to the sultan confirming that 'about 80 Saudis in seven cars have arrived' to a mixed welcome.[40] Some forty of them were armed and others may have been varied tribesmen or Saudis in 'ordinary civilian dress'.[41] Turki bin Abdullah al-Otaishan led the Saudi contingent in the company of the Al Bu Shamis sheikh, Rashid ibn Hamad of Hamasa. The leading sheikh of the Nuaimi, however, was reportedly not pleased with their arrival.[42] Within a matter of days, al-Otaishan established himself in a house just west of Hamasa. Some of his party travelled on to Dubai to obtain a variety of supplies, including tables, radio equipment and other materials that made it clear that al-Otaishan planned to stay.

Inquiries sent through the British ambassador at Riyadh returned a response to the Gulf that the Saudis were sending al-Otaishan to deal with an internal security matter.[43] Moreover, the Saudis argued that that they had not violated the status quo and were within their rights to be in Buraimi because the villages in the Buraimi Oasis was not explicitly in the London Agreement.[44] The Foreign Office and Political Residency expressed some internal confidence that they could easily demonstrate that Saudi Arabia had never actually claimed Buraimi for itself prior to al-Otaishan's occupation in their previous explanations of boundaries.

Al-Otaishan's presence in Buraimi was intended not to defend past claims so much as to change popular allegiances on the ground before any final international arbitration or settlement would be undertaken. Upon his arrival, al-Otaishan began a campaign to win the loyalty of local tribesmen and persuade the local population to declare their allegiance to Saudi Arabia. He issued invitations to all surrounding sheikhs to visit him. Within the first two weeks, tribal leaders appeared to be shifting their alliances away from Zayed and Abu Dhabi. Sheikhs from Dhak and Ibri reportedly visited al-Otaishan, where he asked them to fly the Saudi flag to show their allegiance. Furthermore, some members of the Bani Yas appeared to be defecting from Abu Dhabi to the Saudis.[45] In exchange, al-Otaishan was reportedly providing money and recruiting tribesmen to serve as guards.

---

[40] Sultan Said bin Taimur to Major F. C. L. Chauncy, 4 September 1952, *Buraimi Dispute* v. 2.
[41] M. S. Weir to W. S. Laver, 7 September 1952, *Buraimi Dispute* v. 2.
[42] Kelly, *Eastern Arabian Frontiers*, 159; Sultan Said bin Taimar to Major F. C. L. Chauncy, 4 September 1952, *Buraimi Dispute* v. 2.
[43] Telegram, Riches (Jeddah) to Foreign Office, 8 September 1952. FO 371/98371. TNA.
[44] Telegram, Richards (Jeddah) to Foreign Office, 18 September 1952. FO 371/98372. TNA.
[45] Telegram, Hay (Bahrain via Sharjah) to Foreign Office, 12 September 1952. FO 371/98371. TNA.

Alarmed at the shifting environment in greater Buraimi, Zayed travelled to Bahrain to request help from the Resident. Upon his return to Buraimi, he sent regular messages reporting on the need for a show of support and force from Britain and reinforcements to demonstrate Abu Dhabi's power and assure his allies that they would be protected.[46] In response, the Political Resident requested a small force to travel to Buraimi. The TOL were a newly established force meant to help support internal security in the Trucial Coast and serve as security for the Political Resident and agents.[47] The TOL's commander gathered a force of about forty men to travel to Muwaiji as a show of support, but the slow response contributed to despair on Zayed's part.[48] By 11 September, Zayed was sending regular reports indicating defections of not only other local tribes to al-Otaishan but also some of the Bani Yas. The Political Resident requested additional support from the Royal Air Force to perform flyovers, but the Foreign Office resisted a quick escalation. Instead, they suggested planes fly over the coast as a 'morale boost' but would not allow planes over Buraimi.[49]

Zayed and Saqr bin Sultan al-Nuaimi both reported further defections while the Foreign Office waited for a response from the Saudis to respond to their demand that al-Otaishan withdraw. By mid-September, al-Otaishan could boast that twelve sheikhs had joined him, including the lead sheikh of the Bani Kaab whose defection from Oman might be attributed to the lack of action by the sultan and the British government.[50] The Saudis' reply was not forthcoming, and the Foreign Office finally approved moving forward with RAF flights. Jets began to fly over Buraimi from Sharjah and continued daily for several weeks. The flights had the effect of shaking up the Saudi party and the local population. The Saudis protested the flights, but Hay ignored the Saudis' request and argued for them to continue.[51]

Tensions continued to escalate into October as Oman sent men to defend his claim to Buraimi and Hamasa, with some sixty men traveling as reinforcements for Saqr al-Nuaimi. He held another 8,000 men ready on the coast. Meanwhile, Zayed and Shakhbut worked to gather bedouin forces from across Abu Dhabi to send to Al Ain, and additional TOL moved into the area to bring their number

---

[46] For example, Telegram, Hay (Bahrain) to Foreign Office, 15 September 1952. FO 371/98371. TNA.
[47] Athol Yates, *The Evolution of the Armed Forces of the United Arab Emirates* (Warwick: Helion, 2020), 177. The Trucial Oman Levies would be renamed the Trucial Oman Scouts in 1956.
[48] Telegram, Hay (Bahrain via Sharjah) to Foreign Office 13 September 1952. FO 371/98371. TNA.
[49] R. F. G. Sarrell (Foreign Office) to Rupert Hay (Bahrain) 12 September 1952. FO 371/98371. TNA.
[50] Telegram, Hay (Bahrain) to the Foreign Office, 18 September 1952. FO 371/98372. TNA.
[51] Telegram, Hay (Bahrain) to the Foreign Office, 22 September 1952. FO 371/98372. TNA.

up to 100.⁵² More Saudis arrived in October to augment al-Otaishan's numbers. It appeared violence could break out at any moment, especially as the Omani forces were preparing to set out for Buraimi. On 26 October, British and Saudi representatives in Jeddah agreed to sign a standstill agreement. The agreement would allow the parties to maintain their positions but not augment them; they could provide supplies and would allow people to move freely. The parties also agreed not to provoke or interfere with one another. Finally, they would issue no propaganda or take action to impact circumstances in such a way that might influence a final settlement of the frontier. In truth, the latter issue would be difficult, if not impossible, to enforce.

The tense situation around Buraimi remained relatively quiet through the end of the 1952. Britain had convinced the sultan to stand down, and he remained cautious about doing anything that could be perceived as violating the Standstill Agreement. The Saudis, however, took advantage of this relative quiet to continue supplying goods and to continue courting the local populations' loyalties. In March, however, activity on the frontier seemed to be picking up. First, an armed confrontation between TOL forces and Abdullah Salim of the Bani Kaab led to a short exchange between the Foreign Office and the Saudi government. Salim and fifty men approached a TOL post in Sharjah and demanded the force surrender. Salim, though not a Saudi subject, had been known to visit with al-Otaishan and had received supplies and money. The Saudis disavowed any knowledge of Salim's connection with al-Otaishan.⁵³

Only a few days later, the Residency and Foreign Office received new reports of Saudi parties traveling far into Abu Dhabi territory. This time, a Saudi official named Muhammad Ibn Mansour travelled with a sizeable armed escort into Abu Dhabi territory to collect *zakat* from tribes in the area. The TOL stopped their progress on 12 March, and Ibn Mansour's party diverted to Buraimi. Buraimi became his base of operations as he attempted to expand Saudi claims for the right to collect taxes in the surrounding area, even offering to pay greater *ikramiyah* (a gratuity payment) than the *zakat* he was there to collect.⁵⁴ Once again, the Foreign Office made noise over the Saudis' violation of the Standstill Agreement, but the Saudi government responded by not only denying that Ibn

---

[52] Trucial States Diary No. 10 of 1952 for the period of 29 September to 28 October. FO 1016/169. TNA; Kelly, *Eastern Arabian Frontiers*, 161.
[53] The Secretary of State for Foreign Affairs to G. C. Pelham (Jeddah), 12 March 1953. *Buraimi Dispute*, v. 3.
[54] In modern parlance, *ikramiyah* connotes bribery payments. According to J. B. Kelly, ibn Mansour was offering Rs. 200 in *ikramiyah* in exchange for the tribes' payment of Rs. 100 for *zakat*. See Kelly, *Eastern Arabian Frontiers*, 168.

Mansour's actions were a violation of the agreement, but they also asserted that his collection of *zakat* was part of the maintenance of the agreement.

The incident marked a new phase in the conflict over the eastern frontier. Shakhbut and Zayed, as well as the British Residency, had already been frustrated that the Standstill Agreement allowed al-Otaishan to continue courting public opinion in the disputed frontier areas. There had been little, if anything, Britain could do to counter his activities without appearing to violate the Standstill Agreement or agitate local opinion against their presence. Ibn Mansour's appearance, however, created an opening to cancel the Standstill Agreement. Britain responded swiftly and imposed a blockade meant to stop the movement of supplies to the Saudis in Hamasa. The Levies imposed sanctions meant to limit the resources that could travel into Hamasa but allowed free movement of local residents. Saqr al-Nuaimi would coordinate the blockade from Buraimi.

Poverty and promises in the oasis

The blockade created new problems for Abu Dhabi and the Buraimi Oasis, as its existence served to both undermine and underline the Saudi strategy for winning over the people of Buraimi and the frontier to its side. Al-Otaishan's primary responsibility in the Buraimi Oasis was to distribute wealth and convince people of the area that their futures would be more prosperous if they aligned themselves with Saudi Arabia rather than with Abu Dhabi and Oman. Immediately following his arrival and for the duration of his stay, al-Otaishan had set about disbursing wealth and making promises of development to the tribes in the area. In turn, the Saudi government and press used the depressed and isolated economy of Buraimi as a flashpoint. They depicted the people of the Trucial States as being under the thumb of the British and their allied sheikhs and painted the Saudis as their anti-imperialist saviours. This strategy would continue to shape British policy and fears in the years that followed, feeding Arab anti-imperialist and nationalist rhetoric in the Gulf through the remainder of the Trucial States' dependence.

Even before the blockade, the Buraimi Oasis, like other parts of the Trucial States, had seen a decline in economic status following the collapse of the pearling industry. Without the revenues from pearling and related industries, the tribal sheikhs had little in the way of resources to support and maintain the patronage and loyalty of those under their leadership. In Buraimi, this economic stagnation was compounded by its distance from other centres of power, such as Abu Dhabi, Dubai and Muscat. Furthermore, locals reported a long period of poor rainfall lasting fifteen to twenty years which contributed to a significant decline in potable water and irrigation. The result was smaller yields from farming, the fall in the water table and the drying up of many of the wells and *aflaj*.[55]

Al-Otaishan began a campaign meant to draw the attention and loyalty of local tribes in the area upon his arrival at Hamasa. The following day, he began distributing food and resources as part of the Eid celebrations. These holiday fasts for the community turned into a regular soup kitchen open to people in the surrounding community. He also immediately offered hospitality to all the leading sheikhs in the area, and even those beyond the oasis, such as tribes with ties to Sharjah and Ajman. Al-Otaishan frequently invited sheikhs to visit for coffee and meals where he asked them to profess their allegiance to the Saudi government with loyalty oaths.[56] Al-Otaishan reportedly granted some Rs. 15,000 to one of the sheikhs of the Bani Qitab, contributing to further competition within their ranks before the month was even up.[57] Some others were invited to travel to Saudi Arabia, and upon their return they were gifted Rs. 7,000 each.[58] Zayed and Saqr bin Sultan al-Nuaimi complained to the Residency about al-Otaishan's early successes in persuading some of the sheikhs to align themselves quickly with ibn Saud.

Al-Otaishan locally and the Saudi government in the Arab press contrasted the poverty in the Trucial States with Saudi generosity. Though Shakhbut had often expressed a need to provide a hospital or clinic in Buraimi, he had not been able to persuade the British to help him establish one. Al-Otaishan brought two Syrian doctors with him to provide medical services to the oasis. Ibn Saud also promised additional benefits of a modern, developed state in the form of education and agricultural development – promises which transformed Turki al-Otaishan's encampment into a 'magnet'.[59] Local inhabitants who wished to go to Saudi Arabia to find work for wages were also invited to do so.

The Political Resident and Foreign Office recognized the situation as politically sensitive from the outset. The poverty that Burrows had found in the Trucial States during his tour in 1948 and Roger Makin's subsequent report had indicated the need for development to stave off future threats to the British

---

[55] 'Report on Water Supplies of Part of the Trucial Coast', 12 December 1953. FO 371/104332. TNA.
[56] Pirie-Gordon to LeQuesne, 2 November 1953. FO 1016/246. TNA.
[57] Trucial States Diary No. 9, 26 August-28 September 1952, FO 1016/169. TNA.
[58] Trucial States Diary No. 10 of 1952 to 29 October. FO 1016/169. TNA.
[59] ADM Lane (Foreign Office) to Drake (Treasury), 27 January 1953. FO 371/104332 TNA.

primacy in the region (see Chapter 3). The Saudi publicity pointed to the poverty of its neighbours and connected that poverty to Britain's stranglehold over the Trucial States. Burrows and his allies in the Foreign Office quickly began drawing up grant proposals and funding requests for support from the Treasury so that they could credibly counter Saudi claims.

Burrows initiated several requests for funds which he believed would significantly improve Britain's reputation in the Trucial States at a relatively modest cost. A first request in 1952 asked for funding to start several important projects. Burrows requested funding for the hospital at Dubai and additional support to fund the creation of a mobile clinic. Within the Foreign Office, policymakers conceded that al-Otaishan's arrival in Buraimi placed Britain in a 'most embarrassing position'; they clearly understood that Saudi promises of aid had been so successful because British protection had brought the Trucial States 'so little'.[60] These projects aimed at establishing evidence of development and growth through British support to counter al-Otaishan's generosity on Saudi Arabia's behalf. But the continuous stream of supplies to Buraimi from Saudi Arabia meant that al-Otaishan could demonstrate with immediate effect the potential for wealth, whereas British development schemes were long-term projects with tenuous funding and bureaucratic obstacles.

Allies in the Foreign Office endorsed Burrows' request and reiterated the political necessity of the expenditure. The Foreign Office requested a modest £10,000 for development in 1953–4 from the Treasury, which subsequently authorized this as a one-time grant. The funds would provide £2,000 in support for the Dubai hospital and to extend the contract of the doctor. Five thousand pounds would go towards establishing schools in Sharjah. The Foreign Office hoped this investment in education would encourage the oil companies to contribute as well, since it would provide training to develop a larger local work force. Another £1,500 would be set aside for water surveying and expanding cultivation, while £1,000 would go towards work improving the Dubai creek, which had silted up. While acknowledging that substantial and sustained funding for the Trucial States was undesirable, the British justified the expenditure as a defensive measure: 'We do feel however that expenditure on this relatively modest scale is an inevitable corollary to our decision to stand up for the Rulers in the face of Saudi encroachment.'[61] Britain disbursed the funds in the hope they

---

[60] Minute, A. D. M. Greenhill, 3 November 1953. FO 371/104332. TNA.
[61] A. D. M. Lane (Foreign Office) to A. E. Drake (Treasury). 27 January 1953. FO 371/104332. TNA.

could persuade the Trucial rulers that there were benefits to staying steadfastly aligned with Britain.

The blockade, introduced in April 1953, created a new set of dilemmas for Abu Dhabi's claims. On the one hand, a total freeze of movement would strangle al-Otaishan's generosity and potentially weaken his appeal. On the other hand, doing so could create hostility among the bedouin who were used to moving across the frontiers – and could tip their support towards al-Otaishan's camp. Rather than halt all movements between Saudi and Abu Dhabi territories, the early blockade allowed free movement for the local populations.

The porous blockade proved ineffective. The first sign of trouble came in May. The TOL and bedouin forces supporting the desert patrol began hearing of trouble from travellers in the territory between Sharjah and Buraimi. Obaid bin Juma al-Kaabi, the leading sheikh of the Bani Kaab, had openly supported the Saudis shortly after al-Otaishan arrived in Hamasa. Between May and June, he and his tribesmen began confiscating goods from several individuals and even fired on a British government vehicle. While Zayed had wanted to make a show of force, Britain had discouraged him from retaliating.[62]

The following month, al-Kaabi and his men clashed with British Levies. The Saudi government protested that British armed forces and an aircraft attacked the Bani Kaab at their post, firing on homes with machine guns and dropping bombs on 'innocent inhabitants including women and children'.[63] According to the Political Resident's accounts, the clash was not one sided. Rather, British forces combined with Zayed's forces to push through roadblocks Bani Kaab forces were using to stop vehicles and confiscate goods. Pirie-Gordon reported to the Resident that British forces only fired when they were fired upon. Forces were able to surround and enter Obaid al-Kaabi's house after al-Kaabi had fled the post.[64] At the end of the operation, at least four tribesmen were killed while some others were wounded. Zayed and his men had also managed to find supplies and Rs. 54,000, in Obaid al-Kaabi's house.[65] Clearly, goods were getting past the blockade.

Efforts to tighten up the blockade continued through the summer and into the fall, with the aim of reducing supplies to al-Otaishan. The TOL built up its numbers to nearly 500 men and established new checkpoints along coastal

---

[62] Translation of Letter Dated 10th Shawal 1372 (22 June 1953) from Zayed bin Sultan to the Political Agent (Sharjah). FO 1016/243. TNA.
[63] Telegram, Jedda to Foreign Office, 1 July 1953. FO 1016/243. TNA.
[64] Pirie-Gordon (Sharjah) to Hay (Bahrain), 1 July 1953, FO 1016/243. TNA.
[65] Telegram Bahrain to FO, 1 July 1953, FO 1016/243. TNA; Telegram, Bahrain to Foreign Office, 2 July 1953, FO 1016/243. TNA.

and overland routes. This included camel patrols supplemented with 'friendly tribesman'. Zayed recruited approximately 100 men who supplemented posts at Masaid and Liwa. An additional 40 men came from Muscat to boost forces at Buraimi village.[66] By October, it seemed these adjustments had succeeded in making things harder for al-Otaishan's camp. Reports from Zayed suggested that al-Otaishan's generosity was diminishing to 'a war time austerity level' and that his own morale was reaching a low point. Zayed further indicated that though al-Otaishan continued to pursue an alliance with Saqr al-Nuaimi, he appeared to be 'holding up' under the pressure.[67] While British reports from Zayed and others in the area estimated that al-Otaishan's resources had diminished by late 1953, nevertheless, he still retained a stockpile of 100 bags of rice.[68] As time wore on and his resources decreased, support for al-Otaishan was waning. Some of the goals of the blockade were being met at least.

These measures created new points of friction and left other problems unresolved. The rapid build-up of troops from 100 to nearly 500 allowed for wider ranging and more effective patrols, but the quality of the troops recruited in such a short time left much to be desired. Recruits were diverted from the Aden Protectorate Levies. Many of them had not served for long while others had been rejected in Aden as unsuitable or un-recruitable. The Levies suffered under organizational and disciplinary issues. Reports from the British commander, Major Otto Thwaites, described low morale and poor discipline within the ranks. He described infractions ranging from bribery to illegally selling arms and ammunition.[69] Tensions within the force escalated as Thwaites attempted to introduce order and end corruption. Ultimately, at least three of the Levies murdered Thwaites and two other officers along with injuring several others.[70]

The blockade also undercut the goodwill efforts Burrows hoped his development plans would improve Abu Dhabi's and Oman's territorial claims. The multitude of new checkpoints created new tensions with tribesmen who were stopped and searched for contraband. Several times between June and

---

[66] Chief Staff Officer to Minister of Defence, 7 September 1953, DEFE 7/1477. TNA; Report on Operations Trucial Oman for the week ending 8 October 1953, FO 1016/246. TNA.
[67] Pirie-Gordon, Sharjah to Le Quesne (Bahrain), 12 October 1953, FO 1016/246. TNA.
[68] Pirie-Gordon to LeQuesne, 2 November 1953, FO 1016/246. TNA.
[69] Bradshaw, 'The Hand of Glubb', 656–72. Bradshaw provides details of the creation of the Levies and goes into some detail about the makeup of and problems in the Levies in 1953. See also Pirie-Gordon, Sharjah to Le Quesne (Bahrain), 12 October 1953, FO 1016/246. TNA; Pirie-Gordon (Sharjah) to LeQuesne (Bahrain), 17 October 1953, FO 1016/246. TNA.
[70] Burrows (Bahrain) to Eden (London), 23 November 1953, WO 32/15497, TNA. The murder occurred on 7 November, when Thwaites and others went to investigate a murder and theft in Sharjah that was committed by Levies. Burrows' culminating report cited here details of the results of the investigation into Thwaites' murder.

November 1953 toll posts and other checkpoints became locations of conflict, sometimes small and other times of greater consequence. By October, the Political Agent at Sharjah requested that they loosen up these checkpoint stops, as it was 'causing undue worry and enquiry' and doing more harm than good. Zayed posted some of his tribesmen at key points to visually confirm locals' travels rather than perform the more invasive searches.[71] Additionally, the blockade was fuelling local criticism against British policies. When the TOL commander visited Hamasa, he was 'subjected to a harangue' from al-Otaishan for the 'inequity and inhumanity of the British efforts to starve the innocent men and women and children of Hamasa'. Newspapers in Jedda reported that women and children in Hamasa were starving because Britain refused to allow the Saudis to send food.[72] These kinds of incidents played out in other instances when British and international visitors travelled to the area: a Red Cross representative witnessed a large crowd of women and children protesting ill treatment by the British during his visit in the summer of 1954.[73] The regional spotlight on the Gulf could only serve to highlight the poor conditions on the Trucial Coast and expose Britain to criticism for its neglect.

Britain developed a ration system to ensure the local population had food and that they received it from Britain rather than from al-Otaishan. The British agent's office oversaw distribution of staples to Hamasa at fixed intervals. This plan created new tensions between the British and local sheikhs. For the ration programme to work, British forces relied on local tribesmen to provide population numbers and to distribute the food. Local smuggling in the area provided a black market for goods, which the British were loath to shut down as they feared it would foster resentment in the population. The black market deprived Saqr of his share of sales on goods in the legitimate Hamasa market even as his work securing the blockade placed him in a tenuous position with the local populace.

Burrows judged that the development projects that had begun in 1953 had met with 'considerable satisfaction' in the Trucial States. This prompted him to follow up with another detailed request for an additional £20,000 for the following year.[74] As he prepared for Trucial Council meetings in late 1953, he urged the Foreign Office to forward approval for future expenditures so that

---

[71] Report on Operations Trucial Oman for the week ending 8 October 1953, FO 1016/246. TNA.
[72] Pirie-Gordon to LeQuesne, 2 November 1953, FO 1016/246. TNA; Telegram, Pelham (Jedda) to Foreign Office, 26 May 1954, FO 371/109833. TNA.
[73] Reports of Walker (undated) and Bustani, 10 July 1954, FO 371/109837, as referenced in Morton, *Buraimi*, 128–32.
[74] Minute, A. D. M. Greenhill, 3 November 1953. FO 371/104332. TNA.

he could announce the programme at the council meeting in mid-November.[75] Reports from the Trucial Coast indicated that new irrigation works being dug by Zayed in Al Ain were proving successful and labourers from Oman were undertaking more improvements.

Further funds would be needed to begin drilling for wells based on a recently completed water survey. The Treasury granted the additional £20,000 but also stressed to the Foreign Secretary that this funding could not become an annual expenditure. Water projects provoked the most interest among the Trucial rulers, and most especially that of Shakhbut, and funding such projects could go a long way to engendering cooperation and even gratitude from those living on the Trucial Coast. By March of 1954, it was clear that several of the projects were underway. Schools in Sharjah were contracted to be built in 1954. Plans for digging new wells in the following year were being developed, while new equipment had been ordered for the Dubai hospital. None of these projects, however, had yet led to tangible improvements on the ground. Equipment deliveries were slow to arrive, the wells had not yet been dug and completion of the schools had been delayed due to rains. The project at Dubai Creek depended on getting staffing from England, or perhaps Kuwait, to complete a survey before any work could be done.[76]

Much more was needed, but British funds for the projects were limited. The Treasury official who had approved the funds explained to the Foreign Secretary that 'I agree that in the interests of maintaining their boundaries and of our general influence over [the Trucial rulers], we are justified in giving some tangible assistance' but insisted that the recent grant would be a 'self-contained scheme', without additional funding in coming years.[77] The future funding for development would need to come from oil money – but this would only come to pass if Britain could sustain Abu Dhabi's claim to the frontier territory where they expected oil would most likely be found.

Burrows persevered in his efforts to develop the Trucial Coast as the best insurance for continuing a long-term presence in the Gulf. While the projects were underway and were met with apparent approval from the rulers, they did not nullify the success of Saudi propaganda. The Saudis publicized their efforts to bring benefits to the people in the Buraimi Oasis and vilified the British blockade as harming the people of Oman and Abu Dhabi.

---

[75] Telegram, Burrows (Bahrain) to Foreign Office, 2 November 1953. FO 371/104332. TNA.
[76] W. S. Bill Laver (Bahrain) to A. C. I. Samuel (Foreign Office), 11 March 1954. FO 371/109859. TNA.
[77] Butler (Treasury) to Anthony Eden, 12 November 1953. FO 371//104332. TNA.

Confrontation, arbitration and denouement

Little changed over the next several months as the blockade continued to remain in place. Abdulaziz ibn Saud died in November and his son, Saud, succeeded him. The new Saudi king made no significant shifts in his father's policy towards Buraimi, until May 1954 when he would employ an ARAMCO exploration party to break the stalemate. This decision would draw the international community, as well as the US government, into the conflict. But while the American oil company would figure into the dispute, the American government remained hands-off in pressing towards a resolution.

Burrows learned through back channels that the Saudis planned to test British resolve in the Abu Dhabi frontier in late May. An ARAMCO party, accompanied by armed Saudi guards, planned to travel into Abu Dhabi territory; Saud had instructed the party to go as far into the frontier as they could before the British turned them back.[78] On 31 May, news arrived that five or six Americans, accompanied by seventy armed tribesmen, had stopped at Salwa, on the Saudi side of the frontier to wait out unfavourable weather. The party was much larger than the usual exploration parties that travelled with six to ten vehicles on surveys.[79] They clearly intended to do more than sample soil or test drill.

Given the potential for open conflict, the Foreign Office operated quietly behind the scenes. Information about the party's size and mission filtered from ARAMCO staff to the British embassy office in Washington to the Foreign Office and Residency. The Foreign Office directed the Resident to act carefully and provided strict instructions for engaging – or more precisely, not engaging – with the ARAMCO party. The Foreign Office informed the American government that forces would stop the party if it crossed into Abu Dhabi, but it also provided strict instructions to Burrows about how to proceed. Burrows instructed the Levies to prepare to increase their numbers to be able to outnumber any Saudi force in the hopes of deterring any actions on the part of the Saudis. He also relayed strict instructions from the Prime Minister and Foreign Office that the British forces should not be the first to open fire on the Saudi guards under any circumstances. The Americans were thought to be unarmed and all efforts should be made to avoid firing or harming them.

---

[78] Telegram, Makins (Washington) to Foreign Office, 30 May 1954, FO 371/109833. TNA.
[79] Telegram, Burrows to Foreign Office, 31 May 1954, FO 371/109833; Telegram, Makins (Washington) to Foreign Office, 30 May 1954, FO 371/109833. TNA.

The party travelled onward to the Riyadh Line before crossing it in early June. By that time, Burrows had received instructions that the forces should maintain their distance, avoid confrontation and track the party's movement. Air reconnaissance followed the movements of the party as they crossed the line and trekked across lands inhabited by Shakhbut's allies, the Qubaisat.[80] On 5 June, an RAF plane air dropped a notice to the party informing them that they had entered Abu Dhabi territory. The party withdrew four days later without any confrontation, but the anxiety this party provoked on the Trucial Coast and in the Foreign Office makes clear that the stakes of the standoff in the Abu Dhabi frontier had become far too high to sustain.

The Buraimi impasse contained within it several layers of complication. On the face of it, the conflict involved the Saudi government, the Abu Dhabi government and the Omani government (with the latter states' positions represented by the British government). For the local players, the conflict revolved around the national ambitions of the Saudi government to increase its influence on the Arabian Peninsula versus Shakhbut's hope to maintain his position as a powerful tribal leader within his own territory. From Britain's perspective, defending Abu Dhabi and Oman's territorial claims served to justify Britain's continued presence in the Trucial Coast. The final element, the American connection, tempered Britain's ability to act more decisively to defend Abu Dhabi and Oman's claims. The ARAMCO oil company's relationship with the Saudi government also sustained ties between the oil company and the US government.[81] Again and again, the Foreign Office hesitated to take aggressive action to stop Saudi encroachment in part because they wanted to avoid confrontations that might strain the Anglo-American relationship.[82] The high volume of telegram exchanges, sometimes several times a day, which flew between the Foreign Office and the Residency and relayed incremental adjustments in anticipation of the Saudi-ARAMCO party's transgression suggest deep anxiety over something greater than the usual run-ins on the frontier. The close communication with the Washington embassy and with ARAMCO staff members further illustrate the fine line the Foreign Office walked to keep the United States from intervening directly in support of the Saudis and ARAMCO.

---

[80] Telegram, Burrows (Bahrain) to Dubai, 1 June 1954, FO 371/109833; Telegram, Burrows to Foreign Office, 1 June 1954, FO 371/109833. TNA.
[81] Robert Vitalis, *America's Kingdom: Mythmaking on the Saudi Oil Frontier* (Stanford: Stanford University Press, 2007) details the American-ARAMCO relationship and ARAMCO's role in forging the 'special relationship' between the United States and Saudi Arabia.
[82] Petersen, 'Anglo-American Rivalry in the Middle East', 71–91.

Not long after the confrontation-that-wasn't, Prime Minister Eden met with the American vice president Richard Nixon and assured both him and the State Department that they were earnestly pursuing an agreement with the Saudis. As the summer ended, Britain and Saudi reached an agreement on the blockade, a frontier zone and the establishment of a tribunal to arbitrate the dispute. The Arbitration Agreement included the following components: the blockade would end, al-Otaishan and his forces would leave Hamasa and the Levies would leave the other villages, a joint force would patrol to prevent violence and arbitration would commence in Geneva the following September.

In the year between the agreement and the arbitration meetings, conditions on the ground continued to deteriorate. The Saudi force used the new shared police patrol to sustain and expand Saudi payments to tribal leaders in the area. Flights that dropped supplies to the Saudi police forces provided opportunities for smuggling in money and ammunition that was distributed to the headmen of various tribes. By the spring of 1955, even Saqr ibn Sultan had begun accepting monthly payments. The looser frontier patrols also created opportunities for renewing slave trade routes into Buraimi and out to Saudi Arabia, where demand for enslaved labour had expanded as Saudi living standards increased with oil production.[83] The instability also created opportunities to satisfy old grudges, and one disgruntled son of a sheikh assassinated in the 1920s looked to the Saudis to provide the funds he would use to foster an uprising against Shakhbut. Shakhbut's son discovered the plan and Britain responded with weapons to help Shakhbut mount a defence, giving his and Zayed's men a brief morale boost.[84]

Preparation for the arbitration tribunal went on behind the scenes until the first session on 11 September but was doomed from the outset. The tribunal panel comprised five members. Britain volunteered Sir Reader Bullard, a former British diplomat and scholar with decades of experience in the Middle East and Arabia, as their tribunal member. The Saudis put forward Yusuf Yasin, a long-time advisor to ibn Saud and his son. A lawyer from Pakistan and a legal scholar from Cuba served as two of the neutral members. Charles de Visscher of Belgium, who had previously served on the International Course of Justice, acted as chair of the tribunal.[85] The British delegation, along with Zayed and Shakhbut, had

---

[83] Miers, 'Slavery and the Slave Trade', 120–36, esp. 126–7.
[84] The foregoing period is described in excellent detail in Morton, *Buraimi*, 148–6, and Kelly, *Eastern Arabian Frontiers*, 180–4, 187, 190–6. Kelly uses Saudi documents recovered after the Buraimi invasion to fill in a number of gaps in British knowledge of Saudi activities before October 1955.
[85] P. Couvreur, 'Charles de Visscher and International Justice', *European Journal of International Law* 11, no. 4 (2000): 937.

recorded numerous instances of Saudi violations of the Arbitration Agreement in the past year. They submitted their complaint to the tribunal before it had even convened.

Rather than reviewing the arguments on the historical claims to the territory, the six sessions of the tribunal became mired in disputes over Saudi witness tampering and bribery, rather than reviewing the arguments on the historical claims to the territory. Zayed and his brother Hazza both attested that a Saudi agent had offered him a bribe to change his testimony. Within the first few sessions of the tribunal, the British delegation also discovered that a Saudi witness had been seen meeting with Yusuf Yasin upon his arrival at the airport in Geneva. By the middle of September, Reader Bullard resigned from the tribunal in protest of Yasin's conduct. De Visscher suspended deliberations to allow the British delegation to consider their options for continuing the tribunal.

Frustrated with continued Saudi violations of the arbitration agreement but unable to back out of the tribunal without losing international credibility, the Foreign Office provided the tribunal with evidence of Saudi misconduct. An unnamed man posing as an oil representative recorded a conversation with Dr. Abdul Rahman Azzam, the Saudi delegation's lawyer. Azzam confessed in that conversation that he had accepted money from the Saudi government in the previous year. In the wake of this information, de Visscher and another of the judges resigned and the tribunal collapsed entirely. This provided the opening Britain had long been waiting for.

The years of low-grade warfare over the frontier came to a swift end on 26 October. Early that morning, a Levy force exceeding two-squadrons' strength left Kahil in Omani territory northwest of Buraimi. Heading south, the force split in two with one group heading to the closer Saudi police camp, where the Saudi forces were quickly disarmed. The Levies there cut communication lines to Hamasa. The other Levy force continued on to Hamasa where they occupied several houses within the village. Firefights broke out between the levy forces and 200 tribesmen. Additional Levy forces followed in the afternoon, and fighting continued in bursts until late into the evening. The three sheikhs leading the opposition – Saqr, Rashid and Obaid – agreed to a ceasefire and were escorted via Land Rover to Al Ain, where they would be sent into exile in Saudi Arabia. Burrows reported back to the Foreign Office that Operation Bonaparte, as it had been named, had succeeded, with only two Levies killed and three wounded.[86] Omani forces came to occupy

---

[86] Telegram, Burrows to Foreign Office, 26 October 1955. FO 371/114623, TNA; Telegram, Burrows to Foreign Office, 27 October 1955. FO 371/114623, TNA.

Buraimi and Hamasa, where they swept through and forced out any of Saqr's holdouts.[87]

The weeks that followed held numerous revelations about the scale of Saudi operations in Buraimi. The Levies recovered stores of rice, dates and ammunition in addition to approximately Rs. 160,000.[88] More importantly, however, the Saudis had left behind a treasure trove of documents. These included the certificates of loyalty al-Otaishan had issued to tribal sheikhs and detailed allowances paid out to various sheikhs in exchange for their loyalty. The British later presented some of the most salient details from these documents to the American government. The Saudi government attempted to create an international dustup in the coming weeks, declaring to the British government that the British had 'imposed their will … in order to achieve their own gains' and accusing the British rather than the Saudi delegations of sabotaging the arbitration by 'disgraceful manoeuvering'.[89] For several months, the Saudis would threaten to take the matter to the United Nations, but this never materialized.

In the wake of the Buraimi Dispute, the facts on the ground did not change. A crisis between the US and Britain never manifested. As we will see in Chapter seven, their special relationship endured the following decades before Britain's withdrawal. The question of the frontiers, which had been the root of the conflict, remained unsettled for the duration of Britain's protectorate over the Trucial Coast. Though the Saudis came to a direct agreement with Qatar over Khor al-Udayd in 1964, Abu Dhabi was not included in that agreement. Shakhbut, and Zayed after him, continued asserting Abu Dhabi's claims to the territory. The matter remained unresolved until 1974, when Sheikh Zayed and King Faisal reached an agreement that ceded Abu Dhabi's claims to Khor al-Udayd in exchange for settled borders between the emirate and the kingdom as well as Saudi Arabia's recognition of the newly formed United Arab Emirates.

The three years of ongoing warfare had, however, drawn international attention to the Trucial Coast, especially from other Arab states. Saudi propaganda in the Arab newspapers brought the realities of poverty and slavery on the Trucial Coast to Arab newspapers and radio broadcasts at a time when new revolutionary leaders were asserting their independence from European

---

[87] See Morton's detailed and lively description of the operation in *Buraimi*, 180–7.
[88] Ibid.
[89] Telegram, Phillips (Jedda) to Foreign Office, 27 October 1955, FO 371/114623. TNA.

imperialist influence. The Buraimi episode represented a potential flashpoint for anti-British, anti-imperialist rhetoric that reverberated in Cairo, Damascus and even Amman. In the next chapter, we will see how the rise of revolutionary anti-imperialist movements in the Middle East came to reshape the dynamics of Anglo-Trucial interactions.

5

The Trucial States at the height of Arab nationalism, 1956–1967

The period between 1956 and 1967 is often referred to as the height of Arab nationalism in the core Arab states. Set against the broader international trends, this was a period of decolonization and anti-imperialism across the globe. More than thirty African countries gained their independence during this era. Several Asian nations separated from British and French control or found themselves reeling from conflicts over the future of their newly independent states. Similarly, a number of nominally independent nations in Latin America experienced anti-imperialist revolutions aimed at wresting their sovereignty from the influence of American and European countries. In the Middle East, states which had been under British and French mandatory control in the interwar period also began to chafe under the outsized influence and pressure from Britain in particular, and foreign powers generally, which sought to keep Egypt, Syria, Iraq, Jordan and Lebanon firmly oriented towards Western capitalism.

The sleepy Trucial States had remained largely outside the realm of conflict of these larger political and nationalism movements, with a few exceptions noted in the previous chapters. But British policymakers in the Gulf anticipated the eventual arrival of Arab nationalism and anti-British sentiment to come in some forms. Though Arab nationalism(s) could be expressed in a variety of forms, the Political Residents in the Persian Gulf viewed the phenomenon as an extension of Egyptian Nasserist anti-imperialism.

In the Gulf states and especially the Trucial States, Arab nationalism forms an undercurrent of the social and political environment. No major revolutions or sustained resistance movements ever manifested on the Trucial Coast during this period. Nevertheless, the possibility that it might arrive in the Gulf remained a constant concern of the Political Residents and their staff. Their interactions with Trucial rulers would be informed by their persistent fears that the Trucial States might fall under the influence of Nasser or other anti-British leaders.

The rulers of the Trucial States themselves were also aware of the rhetoric coming from other Arab states. Throughout the decade, rulers of each of the emirates actively sought to use British fears to their own advantage. Both the rulers and their subjects displayed a burgeoning awareness of Nasserism, and this coincided with the discovery and extraction of oil in neighboring Gulf states and eventually in the Trucial States themselves. Britain would push the Trucial rulers to shift their states to adopt policies with the goal of sharing resources to fend off anti-British sentiment, and the Trucial rulers would look beyond their borders for help to prioritize the kinds of projects they thought were best for their own states.

The second nationalist bookend is the Aden/Yemen civil war and British withdrawal – the continuation of the British/Egyptian war for influence which, by 1967, brought the realities of the Arab political world closer to home.

The Suez crisis and the Gulf

Several scholars have suggested that the Suez crisis marked the beginning of the end of Britain's position East of Suez.[1] Newer scholarship has begun to re-examine this view. The nationalization of the Suez Canal certainly dislodged the British from their preferred location of power at the canal in Egypt. It did not, however, divest British policymakers of their ambitions to maintain a significant presence in the Middle East and east of Suez. As Simon Smith and Spencer Mawby have argued, Britain attempted to continue their influence from Aden, and then from the Trucial Coast and the Gulf.[2] A full discussion of debates about the precise nature of Suez as a moment in the history of the British Empire falls outside the scope of this work. It is important to acknowledge, however, the far-reaching impact of Nasser's decision to nationalize the Suez Canal throughout the Middle East. Nasser's victorious nationalization represented not only an economic victory for Egypt but also a victory for Arabs over western imperialist powers. Arab leaders across the Middle East sought to harness the energy Nasser

---

[1] Keith Kyle, *Suez: Britain's End of Empire in the Middle East*, reprint edition (New York: I.B. Tauris, 2011); William Roger Louis, *The Ends of British Imperialism: The Scramble for Empire, Suez and Decolonization* (New York: I.B. Tauris, 2005); Glencairn Balfour-Paul, *The End of Empire in the Middle East: Britain's Relinquishment of Power in Her Last Three Arab Dependencies* (Cambridge: Cambridge University Press, 1991).

[2] Simon C. Smith, *Ending Empire in the Middle East: Britain, the United States and Post-war Decolonization, 1945–1973* (New York: Routledge, 2012); Spencer Mawby, *The Transformation and Decline of the British Empire: Decolonisation after the First World War* (New York: Palgrave, 2015); Spencer Mawby, *British Policy in Aden and the Protectorates, 1955–67* (New York: Routledge, 2005).

generated in an effort to project their own visions of anti-imperialist, pan-Arab nationalisms. Syrian, Jordanian and Iraqi rulers especially found themselves trying to outdo Nasser to prove their own anti-imperialist credentials. Nasser's charisma, however, would garner support among Nasserists across the region who sought to realize his brand of pan-Arab nationalism in their own countries. Though the Baathist platform for a pan-Arab future had originated in Syria earlier in the century, Nasser became the icon who made the goal appear attainable.[3] To what extent, though, did enthusiasm for Nasserism extend to the Trucial Coast? Were there instances of support within the Gulf that threatened the status quo of the Trucial States and threatened to force out the British Residency? As we will see, the Suez crisis did lead to celebrations of Egypt's victory and anti-British protests. These were relatively isolated incidents and did not necessarily indicate a brewing anti-imperialist movement which would threaten the rulers or the British presence. Nevertheless, the effects of Nasser's movement and the spectre of Nasserism and anti-imperialism would shape the way Britain advised the Trucial rulers in the years that followed.

The Suez Canal, built at Egyptian expense and with Egyptian labour, opened in 1869 under the control of the Suez Canal Company. It remained under the financial, and sometimes military, control of foreign powers from the time of its opening. The company operated the canal under a lease agreement for ninety-nine years. In the early years, the majority of stakeholders in the company were French, but the canal became an important conduit for British trade with the Indian Empire and points farther east, and in 1875, the British government purchased a 44 per cent share in the company. The British and French finance controllers who took over Egypt's budget enacted austerity measures that contributed to a significant Egyptian uprising in Alexandria in June 1882. In the weeks that followed, the French navy abandoned Alexandria, and the British Royal Navy sailed in, bombarded the port of Alexandria and occupied Egypt. While successive British prime ministers expressed a desire to withdraw from Egypt in the decades that followed, Britain remained as a shadow government in Egypt until the First World War, when it dropped the pretence of political and military advisor and declared Egypt a British protectorate.[4]

---

[3] Gordon, *Nasser's Blessed Movement*; Malcolm Kerr, *The Arab Cold War: Gamal 'Abd al-Nasir and His Rivals, 1958–1970*, 3rd edn (Oxford: Oxford University Press, 1971); Adeed Dawisha, *Arab Nationalism in the Twentieth Century: From Triumph to Despair*, 2nd edn (Princeton, NJ: Princeton University Press, 2016), 160–85.

[4] Kyle, *Suez*, 12–19; Juan Cole, *Colonialism and Revolution in the Middle East: Social and Cultural Origins of Egypt's 'Urabi Movement* (Princeton, NJ: Princeton University Press, 1993).

Egyptians agitated for their independence from Britain after the war. In 1922, Britain declared Egypt independent and handed over official rule to a constitutional monarchy. Britain retained control over a number of areas of British interests in Egypt, thus ensuring a continued military presence and effective control over the Suez Canal in conjunction with the Suez Canal Company. Even after the establishment of the Egyptian Republic in 1953, the Suez Canal remained under the company's control and it remained a significant site of British presence and influence.

Upon ascending to the presidency in 1954, Gamal Abdul Nasser set out to reduce British influence in Egypt and strengthen the country through large-scale economic development. He renegotiated security agreements with the British government, requiring the reduction and removal of British troops from Egypt by 1956. The arrangement would allow for joint British and Egyptian oversight of the military bases. The contract that leased the canal to the company was set to expire in 1968. Meanwhile, Nasser planned to build the Aswan High Dam as the cornerstone of his plans for Egypt's future growth. The project would allow him to dam the Nile River, controlling the flood waters and increasing the amount of arable land in Egypt. It would also generate hydroelectricity, which would help drive industrialization. The United States initially agreed to finance Nasser's dam project, but his plan was thwarted when the State Department withdrew the money because Nasser had turned to the Soviet Union for an arms deal.

With no other major resource at his disposal, Nasser abrogated the company's lease and placed the Suez Canal under the Egyptian government's newly created Suez Canal Authority. Britain called for diplomatic and military intervention to reverse Nasser's actions. Nasser had provided financial remuneration and agreed to the international laws pertaining to the movement of ships through the canal; but for Britain, the Suez was the central locus for British access to India and its positions east of the Suez. In response, Britain conspired with the French and Israeli governments to invade the Suez. On October 29, Israeli forces parachuted into the Sinai Desert. British and French bombers provided support with a bombing campaign. Fighting between the tripartite forces on one side and Egyptian forces on the other continued until American and broader international pressure for a ceasefire brought fighting to an end on 6 November. Despite the military successes of the invading powers, international pressure forced them to withdraw their troops. Nasser's victory solidified his position as an effective leader in Egypt and gained him popularity not only at home but throughout the region. His victory seemed to confirm the power of Arab nationalism in the face of imperial forces and inspired Arab nationalists throughout the region for more than a decade after the Suez crisis.[5]

Following Nasser's nationalization of the canal, there were some initial signs of admiration for him in the Gulf. Propaganda appeared in the Trucial States in the wake of the Suez crisis, and examples of nationalist and Nasserist activities began surfacing in the Gulf over the course of the next decade. Bernard Burrows, British Resident at Bahrain in 1956, reported the discovery of several 'subversive pamphlets' that year. They called on the people of the Gulf to

> rise up and rebel against the enemy as other Arabs have done … [The British imperialists] stay as long as they can and will ignore the desires of the people. They take away the riches of the Gulf to their own countries. The battle is for life and death. The way to complete independence is by general strikes, co-operating together against the colonisers and their spies, demanding independence, joining with our brothers in Egypt and Saudi Arabia, in Syria, Jordan and Yemen in a strong pact to enable us to fight together.[6]

Such examples of print media combined with the rising power of radio to draw inhabitants of the Trucial States more deeply into the orbit of pan-Arab and Nasserist politics. Battery-operated radios became increasingly common in the Arab Gulf in the 1950s and 1960s. A number of local figures recall listening to Radio Cairo and the 'Voice of the Arabs', and British archives include numerous summaries of Radio Cairo broadcasts that reached the Trucial States.[7] Nasser's popularity was particularly apparent in Dubai, where 'most' coffee shops openly displayed his picture. Several coffee shops also played Cairo's 'Voice of the Arabs' on the radio for customers to listen to throughout the day.[8]

In November, the Gulf Residency braced for another wave of activity in the wake of the October 31 invasion of Egypt. Where possible, the political agents along the Gulf coast informed the rulers of the coming invasion the night before in order to get security arrangements in place when the news broke. Some of the largest demonstrations took place in Bahrain, where fifty people were arrested in November. British troops were used to suppress the demonstrations, and

---

[5] Kyle, *Suez*; Robert McNamara, *Britain, Nasser and the Balance of Power in the Middle East, 1952–1967: From the Egyptian Revolution to the Six-Day War* (London: Frank Cass, 2003), 49–59.
[6] 'An Awakening Call to the Arabs of the Gulf': Annex D in Letter from Bernard Burrows (Political Resident, Bahrain) to Selwyn Lloyd (Foreign Minister, London). 9 October 1956. FO 371/120553. TNA.
[7] Mohammed al-Fahim, *Rags to Riches: A Story of Abu Dhabi* (London: London Centre of Arab Studies, 1995), 114–15.
[8] 'Monthly Diary, November': Bernard Burrows (Political Resident, Bahrain) to D. M. H. Riches (Eastern Department, Foreign Office). 10 January 1957. FO 371/126871. TNA. AGDA.

Manama remained under curfew for several weeks. During that time, there were further incidents of political activity, most of which were attributed to younger men and schoolboys who were part of a local club.⁹ In Qatar, the ruler expressed 'extreme disapproval of British actions' but agreed to support the Political Agent in maintaining order in Doha. On the afternoon following the invasion of Egypt, the bazaar closed and 'Levantine artisans' closed their shops to come out on strike. Strikes and demonstrations continued for the next two days, as did incidents of arson and the cutting of an oil pipeline. In an even bigger show of popular support for Egypt, 200 people appeared at the ruler's home on November 9 to volunteer for service in Egypt.¹⁰

In the Trucial States, the response to the invasion of Egypt was much more mixed. In advance of the invasion, the Political Agents informed the sheikhs to gain their cooperation for security measures. The Political Resident at the time, Burrows, later described the situation in Dubai and Sharjah as 'tense', though both Sheikh Rashid and Sheikh Saqr agreed to support British security efforts. In Sharjah, there were multiple incidents of anti-British activity. These included arson attempts, one of which targeted the car of the British commanding officer of the Trucial Oman Scouts on 26 November.¹¹ At least one of the young dissidents included the ruler of Sharjah's own son. A sixteen-year-old Sultan Al Qasimi had watched British guards and planes in Sharjah during the Suez crisis when he would visit the air base to play soccer on the British Labour Ministry team. Frustrated, he exhorted his friends to take action against the British along with him in the late fall of 1956. He recalls in his memoir that: 'We cheer daily for Egypt's victory and the disgrace and humiliation of the aggressors and we do nothing. Now we must do something!'¹² That evening, he and two friends sneaked out to the main communications station between the base and the city and set fire to it. Over the next several days, they also cut pipes that supplied water to the air base and set fire to a British general's car.¹³

The ruler in Dubai immediately offered support to prevent any demonstrations. In the earliest days following the invasion, rumours of possible strikes and demonstrations spread. These never materialized in any sustained,

---

[9] Charles Gault (Political Agent, Bahrain) to Bernard Burrows (Political Resident, Bahrain) 17 January 1957. FO 371/126894. TNA. AGDA.
[10] 'Monthly Diary, November': Bernard Burrows (Political Resident, Bahrain) to D. M. H. Riches (Eastern Department, Foreign Office). 10 January 1957. FO 371/126871. TNA. AGDA.
[11] 'Monthly Diary, November': Bernard Burrows (Political Resident, Bahrain) to D. M. H. Riches (Eastern Department, Foreign Office). 10 January 1957. FO 371/126871. TNA. AGDA.
[12] Sultan ibn Muhammad al-Qasimi, *Sard al-That* (Sharjah, UAE: Al Qasimi Publications, 2009), 187.
[13] Ibid., 187–200.

large-scale sense, quite probably because Sheikh Rashid met with leaders of important families to make it clear that such actions would be unacceptable.[14] There were, however, several small signs of anti-British activity, and the Political Agent at Dubai reported that they had needed to increase security to ensure order.

Reactions in Abu Dhabi and Ras Al Khaimah were much more tepid. In Ras Al Khaimah, students were suspected of defacing property, including painting the ruler's car.[15] Sheikh Shakhbut and his brother Zayed expressed support for the invasion of Egypt and no anti-British demonstrations manifested.

The relative quiet of the emirates in the wake of the Suez crisis and invasion did not mean either the rulers or the British agents could rest assured that anti-British nationalists would never arrive in on the Trucial Coast. If anything, the possibility of interference by the Arab League, Nasserists and anti-British movements seemed to be ever more likely. In the years that followed, British policymakers would try to guide rulers towards projects they believed would blunt the criticisms Nasserists and anti-imperialists might direct at the Gulf states.

Reactive development

Donald Hawley arrived on the Trucial Coast in 1958 to serve as the new Political Agent in Dubai. Upon returning from a tour of the states he observed to the Political Resident that 'there is comparatively little to show on the ground for our long association with the Trucial States and what we have been able to do, of course, pales before what has been done in the oil rich states'.[16] Kuwait and Bahrain had been transformed by the early discovery of oil. In Bahrain, where oil had been discovered in the interwar period, secondary level education was already available to both boys and girls by 1958. In that year alone, nearly 14,000 children were enrolled in school in Bahrain.[17] Kuwait had also begun to establish state education programmes immediately after striking oil. By 1945, Kuwait

---

[14] 'Monthly Diary, November': Bernard Burrows (Political Resident, Bahrain) to D. M. H. Riches (Eastern Department, Foreign Office). 10 January 1957. FO 371/126871. TNA. AGDA.
[15] 'Reactions to the Anglo-French Intervention'. Tripp (Political Agent, Dubai). November 1956. FO 371/120553. TNA.
[16] 'Preliminary Impressions of the Trucial States': Dispatch No. 21, Donald Hawley (Political Agent, Dubai) to Sir G. H. Middleton (Resident, Bahrain). 30 December 1958. FO 371/140087. TNA.
[17] Emile Nakhleh, *Bahrain: Political Development in a Modernizing Society*, 2nd edn (New York: Lexington Books, 2011), 23.

developed schools for kindergarten through secondary education for both boys and girls. By independence in 1961, 45,000 Kuwaiti students were educated through the national school system.[18]

Similarly, Bahrain, Qatar and the Trucial States had all begun building and expanding infrastructure to support their growing economies and to establish greater state power through municipal governance. Farah Nakib masterfully demonstrates the ways in which Abdullah al-Salem rapidly transformed Kuwait's municipal structures under a massive modernization programme in 1950. Under his supervision, the oil revenues that had begun trickling and then streaming in in the late 1940s and early 1950s paid for schools, hospitals and roads, as well as a complete restructuring of the urban landscape of Kuwait.[19] In Bahrain, Britain had been deeply involved in guiding the development of municipal plans and offices through the Bushehr Residency under the India Office and worked closely with the Bahraini government and Manama in the interwar years. Bahrain's municipal government, formed under the British advisor Charles Belgrave in 1926, was prepared to implement modernization plans rapidly when oil revenues became available there. The discovery of oil in 1932 was quickly followed by the creation of a refinery which allowed for some early exports of oil from Bahrain before the Second World War paused production. By 1939, Bahrain could already boast a hospital, movie theatre, commissary and expanding access to paved roads and electricity.

These developments in other parts of the Gulf did not go unnoticed by people in the Trucial States. Those who were able to access training outside of the emirates, or whose family members had taken work in Bahrain, Qatar and Kuwait's oil fields and returned to the Trucial Coast brought back with them knowledge of what other states provided. They were also becoming increasingly informed of developments and living standards beyond the Gulf through radio broadcasts from Cairo.

Mohammad al-Fahim of Abu Dhabi relates the very real hardship and tragedy that the lack of services and infrastructure could have on the lives of people in the Trucial Coast when he describes the circumstances of his sister's injury in an accidental fire at home. The closest hospital was almost eighty-five miles away, in Al Ain.

---

[18] Michael S. Casey, *The History of Kuwait* (Westport, CT: Greenwood Press, 2007), 64; Jill Crystal, *Kuwait: The Transformation of an Oil State* (Boulder, CO: Westview Press, 1992), 68–9.

[19] Farah Nakib, *Kuwait Transformed: A History of Oil and Urban Life* (Stanford, CA: Stanford University Press, 2016).

My father and mother, myself and my other siblings all got into the Land Rover with my injured sister and headed across the desert from Al Ain [in Abu Dhabi] to Sharjah. Of course there was no road other than a sandy track that followed the route of the camel caravans so we got stuck many times along the way and the adults had to get out and push the vehicle. It took us two days to cover a distance that can now be travelled in a couple of hours at most. By the time we arrived in Sharjah it was too late; my little sister had already died from the burns.

It was an unfortunate accident. But equally unfortunate and completely unforgiveable, was the fact that as late as 1957 there was not a single doctor in the Sheikhdom of Abu Dhabi. Most of the rest of the world had easy access to doctors, medicine, and the latest in medical technology to treat the injured and the ill. We, on the other hand, had nothing, not even the simplest and most basic medical services ... it was only in 1961 that the first missionary clinic was established in Al Ain and not until 1967 that a hospital was built in Abu Dhabi.[20]

Accounts such as this, and the growing awareness that the rest of the world had more, had the potential to create resentment and hostility towards the British and Trucial Rulers who cooperated with them, especially as people encountered nationalist ideologies from the rest of the Middle East.

Al-Fahim's narrative demonstrates that the Trucial States not only lacked services but was gaining a growing awareness of the region's standing in comparison to the rest of the world. The increasing sense of frustration stemmed from the awareness that people elsewhere in the Gulf, the wider Arab world and beyond lived better. Older generations of Emirati women today have noted this as well. Before oil and before modernization 'we had no idea what was happening in other places; we did not know that other people took hospitals for granted, we didn't know the whole world wasn't poor like us'.[21] Awareness of the disparity between the Trucial Coast and the surrounding states grew through the 1950s and 1960s as nationalist movements in the Arab world sought to expose inequities created by Western powers. The vast gap between the Trucial Coast and other Arab countries provided fertile ground for the growth of dissatisfaction and disaffection with Britain.

The rulers of the emirates had each made efforts in the past decades to improve the condition of their peoples. The ruler of Ajman, for example, provided Rs. 2,000 as a contribution to shared public health and education projects.[22]

---

[20] al-Fahim, *From Rags to Riches*, 63–4.
[21] Quoted in Jane Bristol-Rhys, *Emirati Women: Generations of Change* (London: Hurst, 2010), 44.
[22] 'Thirteenth Meeting of the Trucial Council: December 1': Hawley (Political Agent, Dubai) to Sir G. Middleton (Bahrain). 8 December 1958. FO 371/132535. TNA.

Sheikh Shakhbut had also funded a number of public works projects in Abu Dhabi. These included building a bridge connecting Abu Dhabi to the mainland, building new desalination plants, a power station and a pipeline connecting the Buraimi Oasis and Abu Dhabi town.[23] The ruler of Dubai and his son, Rashid, had been quite active in economic and administrative development, so that by the end of the 1950s, Dubai enjoyed the claim of being home to not only the only hospital in the Trucial States but also a British-style post office and a branch of The British Bank of the Middle East, as well as a functioning municipal council.[24] Rulers in all seven emirates had also funded dispensaries to serve some of the basic needs of their populations. There were seven dispensaries, located in Abu Dhabi town, Buraimi, Ajman, Umm Al Quwain, Ras Al Khaimah, Kalba and Fujairah, two of which had only opened in 1958. These dispensaries only operated in any area on a quarterly basis, as there were insufficient dispensers to run them year-round. Al Maktoum Hospital, the only one on the Trucial Coast until 1960, was often understaffed and undersupplied.

Education had also been a significant priority for several of the rulers, but by 1958, there was very little to show for their efforts. An agricultural school had been developed in Ras Al Khaimah, and a new British-built trade school opened in Sharjah in 1958 and taught eighteen young male students in its first year. Elsewhere, there were few or no sustained efforts at primary education for students across the coast.

Burrows had pressed for a comprehensive development plan with increased funding from the British government to help pay for it. The government, however, would not invest more than the 'niggardly sum' of £31,000 per year they already contributed.[25] The only ways to enhance the funding for development projects, then, was to pressure the rulers to contribute more to a common fund, or to request resources from other Gulf states. Kuwait and Qatar frequently provided gifts to the Trucial States at the request of the Political Resident. Such funds were used for providing new teachers and improving the harbour in Sharjah.[26] These were insufficient to improve the infrastructure of the emirates in a meaningful way. By the end of the decade, Dubai, though the largest and most prosperous of

---

[23] Christopher Davidson, *Abu Dhabi: Oil and Beyond* (New York: Columbia University Press, 2009), 31–2; Maitra andal-Hajji, *Qasr al Hosn*.

[24] Aqil Kazim, *United Arab Emirates: A Socio-Discursive Transformation in the Arab Gulf* (Dubai: Motivate, 2000), 233–6.

[25] Letter from Malcolm Gale (Commercial Secretariat, British Residency, Bahrain) to M. H. Morgan (Eastern Department, Foreign Office). 1 October 1956. FO 371/120611. TNA.

[26] 'Trucial States Development (Education)'" F. B. Richards (British Residency, Bahrain) to Walmsley (Eastern Department, Foreign Office). 11 December 1956. FO 371/120612. TNA.

the towns, lacked electricity with the exception of a few private generators. None of the emirates boasted paved roads, or permanent roads of any kind, apart from a few neighbourhood paths.

Foreign influence and the spectre of nationalism

The discovery of oil in Abu Dhabi in 1962 dramatically changed the political and demographic landscape of the Trucial Coast. An offshore exploratory expedition in the mid-1950s had made the discovery of an oil field northwest of the Abu Dhabi coast in 1958, but another four years followed before the oil could be extracted and exported in commercial quantities. In the first year, nearly 6 million barrels came out of Abu Dhabi's first oil field. That number increased steadily over the next several years. Annual production in 1965 exceeded 100 million barrels. Suddenly, funds became available for Abu Dhabi. The following year, in 1966, Dubai would also begin exporting oil, though in much smaller quantities. The remaining Trucial States did not find or export oil for another decade.[27]

With the new funds from oil, the Trucial Coast also faced massive population growth, driven largely by an influx of foreign workers. The lack of educational and vocational training in the Trucial Coast resulted in demand for foreign workers in virtually every new field of social and economic development. Expatriates from the Middle East arrived to serve in these capacities throughout the Trucial Coast. Jordanians, Egyptians and Palestinians filled positions as teachers. Iraqis, Yemenis and Adenis poured into Abu Dhabi to take up jobs working in the oil industry, bringing with them their experiences working in the oil industries back home (see Table 5.1).[28]

Little demographic information exists before 1968, when the Residency administered a census of the Trucial Coast for the first time. We have no clear picture of population growth before then. Some estimates from 1939 put the populations in Abu Dhabi, Dubai and Sharjah at 35,000 combined. By 1962, the population in Sharjah had exploded from just 5,000 in 1939 to approximately

---

[27] Taryam, *Establishment of the United Arab Emirates*, 265; Michael Quentin Morton, 'Calypso in the Arabian Gulf: Jacques Cousteau's Undersea Survey of 1954', *Liwa* 7, no. 13 (2015): 20–1. For details about the discovery and production of oil in Dubai, Ras Al Khaimah and Sharjah, see Gerald Butt, 'Oil and Gas in the UAE', in *United Arab Emirates: A New Perspective*, ed. Ibrahim Abed and Peter Hellyer (London: Trident Press, 2001), 231–48. Oil production in Dubai began in 1966 while the remaining emirates began production in much smaller quantities after the formation of the United Arab Emirates.

[28] Fred Halliday, 'Labour Migration in the Middle East', *MERIP Reports*, no. 59 (1977): 3–17.

Table 5.1 Population Growth in the Trucial Coast in the Mid-Twentieth Century

	1939	1962	1968	1970
Abu Dhabi	10,000	28,000	46,500	60,000
Dubai	20,000	50,000	59,000	75,000
Sharjah	5,000	33,000	31,500	40,000
Ras Al Khaimah	–	10,000	24,500	30,000
Fujairah	–	6,000	9,700	10,000
Umm Al Quwain	–	5,000	3,700	4,500
Ajman	–	4,500	4,200	5,500
Total		136,500	179,100	225,000

33,000 largely due to its position as a military post. Dubai had more than doubled to 50,000 in the same amount of time. In the years following the 1962 oil discovery, Abu Dhabi experienced even greater growth. The population in 1962 was estimated at 28,000; it doubled by 1968 and reached an estimated 60,000 by 1970. The total population of the Trucial States in 1968 neared 180,000. Approximately 74,250 of them were foreign workers.[29]

British policymakers watched the growth of foreign workers with some anxiety. Arabs from 'radical' governments were known to bring their anti-imperialist sentiments with them. Local police forces and the Trucial Oman Scouts monitored foreign nationals for signs of political activity. Youth groups arose, often starting as soccer clubs, and in Ras Al Khaimah, the Scouts monitored seventy-one foreign nationals from several Arab states who they believed were tied to such organizations. Among the groups were *Nady al-Itihaad* (the Union Club), *Nady al-Bahri* (the Marine Club) and *Nady al-Ahaly al-Watany* (Club for the National Peoples). The reports identified Iraqis, Syrians, Yemenis, Omanis, Jordanians, Palestinians and Lebanese expatriates as members.[30] Even the local police forces, which were peopled largely by non-Gulf Arabs, came under suspicion from the Trucial Oman Scouts for holding 'subversive meetings'.[31]

To combat external influence from nefarious nationalists, British Residents, agents and officers had sought in the wake of the Suez crisis to discourage rulers from hiring workers from 'radical' states whenever possible. When hiring an

---

[29] Halliday, 'Labour Migration in the Middle East', 3–17.
[30] 'Desert Intelligence Office's Reports', 15 March 1966. WO 337/14. TNA; 'Desert Intelligence Office's Reports' August 1966. WO 337/14. TNA.
[31] 'Desert Intelligence Office's Reports', 3 October 1966. WO 337/14. TNA.

At the Height of Arab Nationalism 115

overseer and surveyor for an agricultural school in Ras Al Khaimah, internal minutes detail a lengthy discussion about who would be most appropriate to fill the positions. One official noted that 'any nationality other than Egyptian' would be preferable as they wanted to 'prevent Egyptian teachers and doctors being employed in the Trucial States'.[32] J. P. Tripp had cautioned against Egyptian and Syrian employees as especially likely to spread 'revolutionary ideas'. He further advised the rulers in a Trucial Council meeting not to

> uncritically accept the flashy and superficially 'advanced' expatriates of other Middle East countries who came to their states purporting to instruct them and to teach their children ... [the Rulers] must be vigilant to see that their States were not undermined by the new and often revolutionary ideas which were being pumped into the Gulf by the emissaries of Egypt and Syria.[33]

In Dubai and Sharjah, Palestinian teachers were particularly dangerous in British eyes.[34] By 1958, the list of countries to avoid had expanded to include Jordan, which had flirted too closely with anti-British nationalism. Iraqis remained acceptable for teaching and other positions, at least until 1958, when a coup there eliminated the British-allied Hashemite monarchy. Instead, they advised the rulers to recruit teachers and experts from other British dependencies. Bahrain frequently provided teachers and teacher training for primary schools when they were built. For technical expertise, such as Trades Schools and the Agricultural programme in Ras Al Khaimah, they could recruit from Sudan. When possible, Kuwaiti money and expertise was both welcome and encouraged, and doctors were hired from India for hospitals and dispensaries.[35]

The rulers often found these limitations frustrating. With such a short list of Arab states from which the rulers could draw, Sheikh Saqr complained to Tripp that they could not find sufficient Arabic-speaking teachers for their vocational programmes in Ras Al Khaimah.[36] Despite the warnings, Arab teachers from non-Gulf countries came to the Trucial Coast to take up posts. The British Resident recorded several instances of protests and teacher-led demonstrations at schools at times when significant international and regional events stirred up political feeling.

---

[32] Minute by John B. Denson (Eastern Department). 17 July 1956. FO 371/120610. TNA.
[33] 'Minutes of the Tenth Meeting of the Trucial Council Held in the Political Agency on 13th May 1957'. 13 May 1957. FO 371/126900. TNA.
[34] Enclosure in Dispatch to Foreign Office no. 43, Tripp to Burrows. 2 April 1957. FO 371/126900. TNA.
[35] Maitra and al-Hajji, *Qasr al Hosn*, 244.
[36] 'Minutes of the Tenth Meeting of the Trucial Council Held in the Political Agency on 13th May 1957'. 13 May 1957. FO 371/126900. TNA.

Development also created increasing tensions within the Trucial States. Abu Dhabi's new position as the wealthiest state on the Trucial Coast exacerbated rivalries among the rulers of the Trucial States. Shakhbut had agreed in 1954 to contribute an additional 4 per cent of his revenues to the shared development funds when Abu Dhabi began receiving oil revenues. But rulers of the smaller states found themselves looking for alternative sources of funds in order to exercise greater control over their own development plans. Two of those rulers found a potential ally in the form of the Arab League.

In 1964, the Arab League requested visas for delegates to travel to the Gulf in October to discuss establishing formal relations with the Gulf states and to talk about matters relating to immigration.[37] William Luce, having arrived from Aden in 1961 to take up the Political Residency in the Gulf, sanctioned the visit despite his concerns that it would open the gates to Egyptian and Iraqi nationalism. Not to do so would open the Trucial rulers to criticism from the Arab world that they were under the thumb of British imperialism. Luce viewed the visit, however, as part of an 'overt form of penetration' on the part of Egypt and Nasserism, aimed at weakening the British position in the Persian Gulf. For him, the Arab League was simply an organ for Nasserist expansion.[38] He warned the rulers to neither make nor accept any formal overtures from the League.[39] Like Burrows before him, he also argued in favour of a proactive strategy on the part of the Foreign Office to create a substantial alternative source of aid: 'In order to weaken the impact of any Arab League aid which may be forthcoming we should do everything practicable to increase aid for the northern Trucial States from other sources.'[40]

The Arab League visit in October 1964 seemed to go smoothly from the British perspective. There were no security breaches and the rulers did not make any formal agreements with the Arab League. There were, however, indications that the Arab League's tour would create important political complications. The rulers reported that the League offered to provide funds for development and the rulers of Sharjah and Ras Al Khaimah, two of the poorest states, seemed inclined to accept the League's offer of funds. When members of the Arab

---

[37] Letter, William Luce (Political Resident, Bahrain) to T. Frank Brenchley (Foreign Office). 23 June 1964. FO 371/174492. TNA. Luce served as political Resident in Bahrain (1961–6) following his time as resident at Aden.

[38] Letter, William Luce (Political Resident, Bahrain) to Stewart Crawford (Assistant Under-Secretary, Foreign Office). 25 January 1965. FO 371/179754. TNA.

[39] 'Relations between the Southern Gulf States and the Arab League': Minute by Brenchley (Foreign Office). 14 October 1964. FO 371/174993. TNA.

[40] Letter, Luce (Political Resident, Bahrain) to Stewart Crawford (Assistant Under-Secretary, Foreign Office). 25 January 1965. FO 371/179754. TNA.

League asked Sheikh Saqr bin Muhammad Al Qasimi of Ras Al Khaimah about support he was interested in receiving, Saqr suggested experts in a variety of technical fields as well as £2 million for building a bridge to connect Ras Al Khaimah and Dubai.[41] The Arab League also continued to make overtures to Sheikh Saqr bin Sultan of Sharjah, who had welcomed the League's visit to the region enthusiastically.[42]

This visit indicated to Luce the need for the Residency to establish a greater appearance of independent action by the Trucial rulers. Until this time funds for development funnelled through the British government, and Luce believed that this made the Trucial States vulnerable to attacks from Nasser and other anti-imperialist, nationalist voices. He made changes to the appearance of leadership within key institutions of the Trucial States to help fortify the rulers against the Arab League's offers. A Trucial States Development Office manned by locals would serve as a better channel for funnelling resources back into the Trucial States, both giving the rulers a sense of control over managing resources and development projects as well as to create an appearance of independence from the British government.[43] To produce a greater appearance of involvement in decision making on the part of the rulers, Luce removed the Political Agent at Dubai from the role of chair of the Trucial Council. The position then would be filled by one of the rulers. The council established a deliberative committee that formed the Development Office, which would oversee the administration of funds for development. The new president of the Trucial States Council presided over the Development Office. In this way, there would be a semblance of local Arab control over the internal affairs of the Trucial States.

The reality of the Trucial Council and the Development Office was that it remained largely in British hands, with British officials and advisors retaining active roles administering and steering development projects. The administration of the Development Fund fell to Development Secretary Bryan Kendall at first, though within a month Luce began pressing for Arabizing the leadership of the Development Office. He appointed a prominent banker from Dubai, Easa Salah al-Gurgh, to the position. Kendall stayed on with the Development Office under

---

[41] Letter, F. D. W. Brown (Political Residency, Bahrain) to J. A. Snellgrave (Arabian Department, Foreign Office). 4 November 1964. FO 371/174493. TNA; Letter, M. A. Marshall (Political Agent, Dubai) to William Luce (Political Resident, Bahrain). 4 November 1964. FO 371/174493. TNA.
[42] Letter, William Luce (Political Resident, Bahrain) to Brenchley (Foreign Office). 11 January 1965. FO 371/179754. TNA.
[43] Letter, Luce (Political Resident, Bahrain) to Stewart Crawford (Assistant Under-Secretary, Foreign Office). 25 January 1965. FO 371/179754. TNA.

a different title.⁴⁴ Higher positions in the Development Office and its subsidiary offices were staffed almost exclusively by British employees and remained that way through 1971.⁴⁵

These superficial changes were not sufficient to deter some of the rulers from continuing to work with the Arab League. Following the visit in 1964, the Arab League proposed setting up an office in Sharjah for funnelling and distributing development funds to the Trucial States. Luce recommended at a meeting of the Trucial States Council that any money from the Arab League should be directed through the Development Office, rather than directly to any of the individual rulers.⁴⁶ Two of the rulers, Sheikhs Shakhbut of Abu Dhabi and Rashid of Dubai, agreed with Luce's position and Shakhbut offered to provide additional funds to the Development Fund to offset the League's offer. King Faisal of Saudi Arabia also offered funds, contingent upon the Trucial rulers' agreement to reject the Arab League. The rulers of the five smaller Trucial States refused those terms. The Political Agent at Dubai attempted to persuade the rulers of Ajman, Umm Al Quwain and Fujairah, but reported to Luce that they had rebuffed him, saying, 'Nobody has helped in the development of their States hitherto and now they have an offer from the Arab League of extensive, cut-and-dried development projects with funds to carry them out.'⁴⁷ Sheikh Muhammad bin Hamad Al Sharqi, the ruler of Fujairah, was eventually persuaded to accept Saudi Arabia's terms for aid to the Development Fund, but Sheikh Saqr bin Sultan of Sharjah remained adamant in his support for the Arab League's offer.

Saqr's willingness to accept the Arab League's presence in the Trucial States would undermine the British position in the Gulf, in the minds of the Political Resident and officials in the Foreign Office. The Foreign Secretary authorized Luce to deny the Arab League members visas for future visits 'and to let the rulers know that Her Majesty's Government are ready to forbid the establishment of an Arab League Office in the Trucial States and to take the necessary action if any ruler should refuse to accept Her Majesty's Government's advice on this point'.⁴⁸

---

44 Telegram, 'Arab Aid to the Trucial States': William Luce (Political Resident, Bahrain) to Stewart Crawford (Assistant Under-Secretary, Foreign Office). 17 February 1965. FO 371/179916. TNA; Easa Saleh al-Gurgh, *Wells of Memory: An Autobiography* (London: John Murray, 1998) talks about his joining the Development Office as well as the degree to which Kendall still held power within the agency.
45 Taryam, *Establishment of the United Arab Emirates*, 52–3.
46 Letter, Brenchley (Foreign Office, London) to R. L. Sharp (Treasury, London). 23 February 1965. FO 371/179916. TNA.
47 Telegram, William Luce (Political Resident, Bahrain) to the Foreign Office. 21 May 1965. FO 371/179917. TNA.
48 Telegram, Stewart Crawford (Foreign Office, London) to Luce (Political Resident, Bahrain). 24 May 1965. FO 371/179917. TNA.

The Foreign Office was absolutely determined that development, as a primary tool of British influence in the Trucial States, should remain the purview of the British officials in the Gulf.

Saqr bin Sultan continued to pursue the Arab League's invitation. Sharjah's economic circumstances were limited. It was not a large trade entrepot, like Dubai. With relatively small territorial scope, it was unlikely oil reserves would be its saving grace. There was great need for external funding if Saqr was going to improve Sharjah's situation. When the Arab League proposed a subsequent visit in 1965 for the purpose of establishing an office, Saqr accepted. This time, however, Luce planned to block the visit.

A burst of telegrams and letters between Luce and the Foreign Office elaborated on the methods at the Resident's disposal to prevent League officials from entering the Trucial States should they try. Owing to British control of air space and immigration, Luce believed he would be able to thwart any attempts by the Arab League to land in the Trucial States. Luce debated the legality and the practicality of using military force to expel the Arab League officials should they succeed in arriving in the Trucial Coast.[49] In June 1965, Luce received consent from the Foreign Office to close the airports at Abu Dhabi, Dubai and Sharjah; he also was allowed to use his discretion in withdrawing British protection to Sharjah, if necessary.[50] The crisis gave rise to instability throughout the Trucial Coast as the rulers and the Political Resident waited to see whether a confrontation would emerge. Saqr's refusal to deny the Arab League an office in Sharjah appeared to imbue the rulers of Fujairah, Ajman, Umm Al Quwain and Ras Al Khaimah with confidence. British officials began to speculate that the rulers in those states might opt to withdraw their relations with Britain.[51]

On 24 June 1965, Luce proved triumphant in his efforts to keep the Arab League officials out of the Trucial States. Technicians from the Arab League attempted to fly into Dubai via Doha, Qatar. The airport at Dubai remained closed. A subsequent attempt to gain entry through Bahrain failed when Arab League officials were denied entry there without visas.[52] He then was informed by the Political Agent-Dubai, Glen Balfour-Paul, that he was being deposed.

---

[49] Letter, William Luce (Political Resident, Bahrain) to P. D. Nairne (Ministry of Defence, London). 2 June 1965. FO 371/179917. TNA.
[50] Telegram, William Luce (Political Resident, Bahrain) to Glen Balfour-Paul (Political Agent, Dubai). 17 June 1965. FO 371/179918. TNA.
[51] Telegram, Glen Balfour-Paul (Political Agent, Dubai) to William Luce (Political Resident, Bahrain). 14 June 1965. FO 371/179918. TNA.
[52] Telegram, William Luce (Political Resident, Bahrain) to the Foreign Office. 28 June 1965. FO 371/179919. TNA.

Balfour-Paul's account remained somewhat circumspect even decades later. He wrote in *End of Empire in the Middle East* that Saqr's family 'with British encouragement, deposed him'.[53] Easa Salah al-Gurg described the circumstances in more detail:

> The official version was that the deposition was the decision of a family council, the result of a loss of confidence in the Ruler's fitness to continue in office. The truth, as I understood it, was rather different.
>
> The Shaikh was invited to a meeting with the Political Agent. He set out, attended by various of his retainers and two armoured cars. On his arrival at the Agency a paper was waved in front of him which was alleged to be the record of the family council's decision. The Shaikh asked to see the paper; this was refused. In fact, it bore only one signature, that of the Shaikh who was to succeed him as Ruler – and who was later to be murdered by the exiled Shaikh. He was led out of the back door of the Agency, avoiding his armed retainers at the front, driven to the airport and put on a flight to Bahrain. He was said to have wept as he saw his sheikhdom disappearing below him.[54]

Plans for cooperation with the Arab League was shelved.

The threat of Arab nationalism could not be contained simply through excluding the Arab League from the Trucial States. The Foreign Office and the Residency viewed the Gulf as an increasingly likely target of anti-imperialist ideology. The Aden Protectorates in southern Arabia were falling; anti-imperialists from Yemen were making their way through southeastern Arabia and Oman and threatening to extend their influence into the Trucial States.

The British government required a more proactive approach if it were going to maintain influence in the Gulf. But British policymakers found themselves facing what they considered to be a significant internal obstacle to meaningful development. Sheikh Shakhbut had ruled Abu Dhabi since 1928 and had held the emirate together through a global depression, Saudi expansionism and through the first years after the discovery of oil in Abu Dhabi. Despite this, historians have largely adopted a negative view of Shakhbut and his rule in Abu Dhabi, based on British response to Shakhbut's deliberative, and sometimes resistant, approach to development in Abu Dhabi.

To Shakhbut, British demands of his funds often contradicted his own priorities for Abu Dhabi. The ruler had built a school in 1956 near Qasr al-Hosn where he lived, but having been warned against foreign teachers

---

[53] Balfour-Paul, *End of Empire in the Middle East*, 121.
[54] Al-Gurg, *Wells of Memory*, 119–20.

from Egypt, Syria and Jordan, he insisted that teachers should come from Abu Dhabi.[55] When he learned that Bahraini teacher-training courses were proving successful for some of the other states, he agreed to look for potential trainees to send from Abu Dhabi and to accept teachers from Bahrain in the meantime.[56] He often indicated, though, that the rulers of each state should retain greatest control over their own territories, likely with an eye to protecting his own sovereignty.

Having ruled for decades with very little income, Shakhbut was understandably cautious in his approach to spending money, and often required more time than British agents and Residents thought appropriate to come to a decision about development projects. In reaction to his reticence, George Middleton pressed for help finding high-quality advisors who could help Shakhbut develop a modern administration and learn to 'spend his income'.[57] In other instances, however, when the ruler became enthusiastic about hiring teachers, customs officers and a secretary to aid in developing his government, the Political Agent sought to reign in his requests. He nevertheless pressed forward in a variety of areas. In 1960, he requested help to recruit teachers from Sudan for the school in Abu Dhabi.[58] By the time oil was discovered in Abu Dhabi, and Shakhbut had the means to develop his state, he had gained a reputation among British officials as 'mean' and 'miserly'.[59]

British policymakers began increasingly to describe Shakhbut as too conservative and, potentially, 'not fit' to rule. The Political Agent in Abu Dhabi in 1960 reported to the Political Resident in late 1960 that he 'ruled in a traditional manner', and though 'honourable and straightforward in his dealings, he will on matters affecting his "rights" sometimes go back on his promises'.[60] In some cases, Shakhbut's conservatism worked to British advantage. He feared foreign influence and rapid modernization would undermine the traditions and social fabric of Abu Dhabi, so when the Arab League offered aid and advisors to the rulers of the smaller states during their 1964 visit, Shakhbut joined Rashid of Dubai in an offer to increase their contributions to the Development Fund to

---

[55] Trucial States Diary No. 10 for the Period October 1–31, 1956. FO 371/120553. TNA.
[56] Minutes of the third meeting of the Education Committee of the Trucial Council, held at the Political Agency on the 13 of May 1958. FO 371/132760. TNA.
[57] G. H. Middleton (Political Resident, Bahrain) to Donald Hawley (Political Agent, Dubai), 5 July 1960. FO 371/148916. TNA.
[58] E. F. Henderson (Political Agent, Abu Dhabi) to Donald Hawley (Political Agent, Dubai), 3 September 1960. FO 371/148916. TNA.
[59] 'Henderson's Valedictory Despatch from Abu Dhabi': Henderson to Middleton, 6 December 1960. FO 371/148918. TNA.
[60] Report by R. McGregor on Abu Dhabi, September 1960. FO 371/148917. TNA.

offset the League's offer.⁶¹ More often than not, however, the British Residents and agents in the Gulf failed to see eye-to-eye on priorities of development. For years, Shakhbut had pressed Britain to search for oil on Abu Dhabi island, where there was only one fresh water well, which no longer supported the growing population. Several times he and British officials argued over whether resources should be diverted to search for water and build more desalination plants instead of searching for oil.⁶²

Twice, the British Residency attempted to orchestrate Shakhbut's removal. The first attempt was in 1963, and the second attempt at 1965. Despite tensions within the Al Nahayan family regarding Shakhbut's leadership, the family refused to support the Resident's proposal.⁶³ By June of 1966, William Luce and the Political Agent at Abu Dhabi had come to view Shakhbut as too great a threat to modernization, and relations between themselves and the ruler had deteriorated significantly. In a lengthy review of events in Abu Dhabi in 1966, Lamb detailed Shakhbut's cancelation of several contracts pertaining to construction and electrification projects. Shakhbut became frustrated with proposals for the Gulf median line with Iran, as well as the terms of a previous agreement with Dubai regarding seabed boundaries, and had developed a dispute with Abu Dhabi Marine Areas, Ltd. (ADMA). His mood apparently improved by April, when a 'row' with his family led him to appoint his brother Zayed to lead the Finance Department and draw up a fixed budget for family members.⁶⁴ Lamb drew up a list in June 1966 describing seventeen incidents in which Shakhbut had 'refused to co-operate or be sensible', to prepare again the case for removing Shakhbut. Among them were his refusal to serve as Chair of the Trucial Council and '[dragging] his heels over forming an administration; and over formulating a budget'.⁶⁵

Finally, on 6 August 1966, British forces moved forward with deposing Shakhbut. A contingent of soldiers, led by Colonel Edward 'Tug' Wilson, took over the local state radio station, removed Shakhbut from Qasr al-Hosn and escorted him to the airport, where he departed the Trucial Coast for Lebanon. His younger brother Zayed, with the endorsement of the family, took up the role

---

⁶¹ Telegram, William Luce (Political Resident, Bahrain) to Foreign Office, 21 May 1965. FO 371/179917. TNA.
⁶² K. N. Barnwell, 'Overthrowing the Shaykhs: The Trucial States at the Intersection of Anti-Imperialism, Arab Nationalism, and Politics, 1952–1966', *Arab Studies Journal* 24, no. 2 (2016): 87–8.
⁶³ *Records of the Emirates*, 1966–71, 116.
⁶⁴ Archie Lamb (Political Agent, Abu Dhabi) to Stewart Crawford (Political Resident, Bahrain), 2 January 1967. *ROE 1966–71*, 19–21.
⁶⁵ *ROE 1966–71*, 91.

of ruler. Zayed had developed a strong working relationship with the British Residents and agents in the previous decades. He had served as the governor of Al Ain and Buraimi since 1946 and had acted as deputy ruler to his brother as well. He actively participated in Trucial Council meetings on behalf of Shakhbut since its inception and was viewed as a strong and effective figure. During his governorship of Al Ain, he had also taken an active role in development, including building the first hospital there and developing lasting public schools in the Buraimi Oasis.

Lamb forecasted a much better working relationship with Abu Dhabi moving forward. In his 1967 report, he noted that Zayed had already gotten off to a strong start in development. In short order, Zayed had begun an 'overly-ambitious' expansion of the Abu Dhabi Defence Force (ADDF), but also had awarded contracts for 'electrification projects in Abu Dhabi and Buraimi, the construction of roads on Abu Dhabi island, in Buraimi and sections of the Abu Dhabi-Buraimi road, a corniche in Abu Dhabi and a second water pipeline between Abu Dhabi and Buraimi'.[66] He also drew up plans for a more fully developed administration, appointing family members to head departments, and working with the Residency to find experts from Sudan and Jordan, hiring police officers, appointing British directors of Health and Education and recruiting lower level administrators from Bahrain. All of this came about by the end of 1966. The rapid growth in Abu Dhabi under Zayed had not been easy. Lamb noted that the months following Zayed's ascension had included a sense of unease and frustration, culminating in a series of strikes in October, November and December. And while oil money was coming in to support Abu Dhabi's growth, tensions were developing with other sheikhs in the Gulf who resented the role Britain had played in removing a fellow ruler.[67]

At the beginning of 1967, then, the British government had rearranged the chess board in the Trucial States and hoped that these moves had set them up for success to protect the emirates from the anticipated moves of Arab nationalist movements as they moved across the peninsula. The rulers would hesitate to make overtures to the Arab League given the forcible removal of Saqr; Zayed's replacement of Shakhbut meant that rapid development would eliminate the criticism Arab states might make against the Trucial rulers as backward relics of

---

[66] Archie Lamb (Political Agent, Abu Dhabi) to Stewart Crawford (Political Resident, Bahrain), 2 January 1967. *ROE 1966–71*, 22.

[67] Archie Lamb (Political Agent, Abu Dhabi) to Stewart Crawford (Political Resident, Bahrain), 2 January 1967. *ROE 1966–71*, 22–4.

British imperial power. The need for this would become increasingly apparent as things elsewhere in the Arabian Peninsula fell apart for the British government.

Crisis in Aden

The Suez crisis had set off a flurry of talk about the significance of development in the Trucial States after 1956. In the 1960s, a new source of anti-British, pro-Nasserist messaging would come to the Gulf by way of South Arabia. With it came greater concern in the Residency that Egypt and other 'radical' states would undermine the British position in the Gulf and would make the Trucial Coast and Gulf even more important as the last vital link to the British Empire east of Suez.

Britain occupied the small peninsula of Aden by force in January of 1839 and it remained under direct control of the Bombay government for the next century. British indirect influence subsequently expanded through the surrounding areas of southwest Arabia through treaty agreements with local rulers.[68] Aden became a free port in 1950 and developed into an important coaling station and commercial centre. For the next century, however, Aden remained largely undeveloped and neglected. Charles Douglas-Home, a journalist and nephew of the former prime minister and career politician Alec Douglas-Home, reflecting on Britain's failed policy in Aden after Britain's military defeat, described 'a poor colonial record' with little to no development in South Arabia.[69] He observed that the '"civilising" mission which normally stands witness to the benefits of British authority' were not in evidence in South Arabia, noting that Britain might have averted disaster had it attracted the tribes out of the hills to 'more amenable territory for economic improvement' and basic services.[70] Douglas-Home's paternalism aside, it is worth noting that his comments about British policy in Aden echo those of Residents and agents regarding the Trucial States.

British control over Aden transferred to the Colonial Office in 1937, when it became a Crown Colony of the empire, around which time Aden grew in significance to Britain's geo-strategic plans. The 1952 nationalization crisis in Iran forced the Anglo-Iranian Oil Company to forfeit its oil refinery in Abadan.

---

[68] Mawby, *British Policy in Aden and the Protectorates, 1955–1967*, 12–13; Z. H. Kour, *The History of Aden, 1839–1872* (London: Frank Cass, 1981), 9–12.
[69] Charles Douglas-Home, 'A Mistaken Policy in Aden: The Case for Union with the Yemen', *The Round Table* 58, no. 229 (1968): 224.
[70] Douglas-Home, 'A Mistaken Policy in Aden', 24.

Little Aden, across a small bay from Aden proper, became the site of the new refinery facility attracting a large migrant labour force for the refinery and the surrounding industries that supported it. British government and military projects provided a second major source of in-migration to Aden. This only intensified further after the Suez crisis, when Britain refocused its Middle East military and communications network from Suez to Aden.[71]

The growth of industries and rapid migration to Aden destabilized what proved to be already tenuous circumstances. New construction in Aden Colony, combined with the growth at the refinery, attracted approximately 20,000 workers. The population of Aden town grew from 51,500 in 1931 to 225,000 in 1963. Workers came from all over the Middle East and the British Empire, but the largest contingent came from Yemen.[72] These changes created divisions between the local populations and migrant labourers in urban areas and a further division between urban populations and the nomadic and agricultural populations outside of Aden. The rapid expansion of the population in Aden and Little Aden created significant unrest. Working conditions in and around the refinery were horrendous and wages were stagnant. Labourers organized no fewer than seventy strikes in 1956 alone as an expression of that frustration. The general dissatisfaction found a voice and a cause to rally around in the person of Nasser, whose 'Voice of the Arabs' radio broadcasts reached even the bedouin in the South Arabian hinterland.

Located to the north of the Aden Protectorates was Yemen. In 1918, Yemen became independent of the Ottoman Empire under the Zayidi Imam, Yahya Hamad al-Din. He ruled until his assassination in 1948 when a rival branch of the family attempted and failed to seize power. Yahya's son Ahmad re-established control following a brief period of instability. Upon his rise to power, Ahmad rounded up as many of the rebels as possible, imprisoning and beheading most of them. From there, he set his sights on expanding Yemen to incorporate the prosperous colony of Aden to the south.

To achieve his goal, Ahmad made an unlikely ally of the new revolutionary Egyptian government. Scholars David Witty and Jesse Ferris have both argued separately that this otherwise improbable move by the Imam was an attempt to silence revolutionary nationalists in Yemen and build on Egyptian military

---

[71] Paul Dresch, *A History of Modern Yemen* (Cambridge: Cambridge University Press, 2001), 77–85; Mawby, *British Policy in Aden and the Protectorates, 1955–1967*, 16–17.

[72] Mawby, *British Policy in Aden and the Protectorates, 1955–1967*, 16–18; Dresch, *A History of Modern Yemen*, 77–85.

expertise.⁷³ In turn, Nasser viewed this as a welcome opportunity to expand his own influence to Arabia, where the British continued in his view to maintain undue imperial power over Arab nations.⁷⁴ In 1954, Egypt and Yemen entered into a defence pact that would provide Egyptian advisors. This relationship allowed Egypt to establish a 'dual-track strategy' in Yemen, appearing to support the government while undermining the Imam through the proliferation of revolutionary ideology and building a military college in Yemen that would serve to support the overthrow of Yemen's government in the future.⁷⁵ Nasser's growing alliance with Yemen made the British government in Aden and southwest Arabia increasingly nervous.

To combat Nasser's and Ahmad's anti-British influence, Britain launched a decade-long series of covert operations across the border into Yemen in an effort to destabilize the Imamate and win the loyalty of some of the Yemeni tribes in the process.⁷⁶ In the early half of the decade, Britain participated in cross-border incursions into Yemen, which Spencer Mawby posits may have been an attempt to deter Ahmad from attempting to expand into Yemen.⁷⁷ In the latter half of the 1950s, though, Britain began planning more concretely to protect its position at Aden. In 1957, William Luce arrived as the newly appointed British Resident at Aden. He began to develop plans for countering the revolutionary threats to Aden. That year, he wrote an assessment of the future of Aden, suggesting the need for a stronger state or federation in southern Arabia to act as a buffer. The possibility of a federation in South Arabia had been considered on and off for several years, but Yemen's 1958 merger with the United Arab Republic (UAR) gave the idea steam.⁷⁸ Over the next year, the Colonial Office and Aden Residency worked to develop a plan for a federation of the western protected states and an eventual merger with Aden.⁷⁹ The new federation officially formed in February 1959. In September 1962, the Aden Legislative Council did vote

---

⁷³ David M. Witty, 'A Regular Army in Counterinsurgency Operations: Egypt in North Yemen, 1962–1967', *Journal of Military History* 65, no. 2 (2001): 401–39; Jesse Ferris, 'The Collapse of the Imamate and Foreign Intervention', *Journal of Arabian Studies* 8, no. 1 (2018): 87–98.
⁷⁴ Owen L. Sirrs, *A History of the Egyptian Intelligence Service: A History of the Mukhabarat, 1910–2009* (New York: Routledge, 2010), 63–83.
⁷⁵ Spencer Mawby, 'The Clandestine Defence of Empire: British Special Operations in Yemen, 1951–1964', *Intelligence and National Security* 13, no. 3 (2002): 107; Sirrs, *History of the Egyptian Intelligence Service*; Ferris, 'Collapse of the Imamate and Foreign Intervention', 97.
⁷⁶ Mawby, 'Clandestine Defence of Empire', 105–30; Mawby, *British Policy in Aden and the Protectorates 1955-67*.
⁷⁷ Mawby, 'Clandestine Defence of Empire', 105–30.
⁷⁸ Mawby, *British Policy in Aden and the Protectorates 1955-67*, 43–7.
⁷⁹ John T. Ducker, 'Historical and Constitutional Background', in *Without Glory in Arabia: The British Retreat from Aden*, ed. Peter Hinchcliffe, John T. Ducker and Maria Holt (London: I.B. Tauris, 2006), 17–21.

to join the federation at Britain's urging, but it had little support from the population, the largest proportion of which comprised Yemenis sympathetic to the ideals of Arab Nationalism and the anti-British rhetoric of Nasser.[80]

In Yemen, Ahmad bin Yahya proved to be an unpopular and paranoid ruler. He employed increasingly oppressive measures to control opposition to his rule – both real and perceived. He faced resistance from Yemeni tribes in the hinterland which resented his attempts to assert his power and often attempted to play British and Yemeni interests off one another to maintain greater autonomy. Yemenis who had become exposed to anti-British and Arab nationalist ideas, either through contact with Egyptian technocrats and military advisors or though work in Aden and beyond, also opposed Ahmad's conservative rule. By the time Nasser and Ahmad's relationship ended in 1961, Yemen had become a hotbed of pent up political frustration.

In September 1962, only a day after Aden voted to join South Arabia, events in Yemen came to a head. Ahmad's son, Muhammad al-Badr, succeeded his father following Ahmad's death. Within a week, a group of young officers forming the Yemeni Free Officers' movement took over the capital city of Sana'a and declared it a Republic. For the next five years, a bloody civil war raged on in Yemen between the Revolutionaries backed by Egypt and the Imam's Royalist allies backed by Saudi Arabia. Almost immediately, Egypt sent 15,000 soldiers to support the Republican forces; three months later, the number of Egyptian troops in Yemen had doubled. Saudi Arabia, from the north, sent financial support and weapons to back al-Badr.

Nasser's revolutionary incursion into Yemen served to amplify British fears that anti-imperialist, revolutionary, Arab nationalist ideology would undermine their control over Aden and South Arabia and threaten Britain's hold on its empire east of Suez. In Yemen, Nasser pursued state-building and modernization to help ensure that Yemen's life as a Republic would serve as an example of the 'Egyptian model' to other states in the region.[81] This included the establishment of the National Liberation Front (NLF) in June 1963, aimed specifically at extending the revolution to South Arabia. A year later, the new organization attacked the nascent federation. Britain, in response, established direct rule over the Federation of South Arabia in 1965. Even as British forces sought to preserve its hold over South Arabia, the situation in and around Aden

---

[80] Smith, 'South Arabia and the Yemeni Revolution', 196–7.
[81] Joshua Rogers, 'Importing the Revolution: Institutional Change and the Egyptian Presence in Yemen 1962-1967', in *Gulfization of the Arab World*, ed. Marc Owen Jones, Ross Porter and Marc Valeri (Berlin: Gerlach, 2018), 113–33.

deteriorated. Egypt's support in the north inspired Republican supporters in and around Aden to act against the British police and Federal forces. In response, the Ministry of Defence reported the need for increased commitments, requiring additional funds and modern equipment.[82]

British policy for the future of South Arabia and Aden had changed dramatically. Instead of moving towards gradual independence, Macmillan and his successor Harold Wilson began to view withdrawal from Aden and South Arabia as the more prudent option. Military failures in Aden joined with a balance-of-payments crisis in the previous year led the Defence and Oversea Policy Committee to speculate about the benefits of withdrawing in 1968 and re-centring British defences on the Persian Gulf.

> If we withdrew from Aden (this is likely to be forced on us anyway) and built up our forces in the Persian Gulf to enable us to continue to meet the Kuwait commitment and to stay in the Gulf until we have prepared the Gulf States and Iran for our withdrawal, the cost in 1969–70 would be higher by £14 Million, i.e., £46 million (saving of £21 million) and there would be capital expenditure before 1970 of £22 million.[83]

If the government could sustain its position in Aden through a withdrawal in 1968, Britain could leave Aden gracefully, cut expenditures and fortify its relationship with Kuwait and the Trucial States. Harold Wilson's advisors began drawing up plans for a 1968 withdrawal from South Arabia.

The withdrawal from Aden would not, however, mean the end of the British presence in the Gulf. Britain would abandon the base Aden only to temporarily increase the forces in the Persian Gulf to two battalions, two ground squadrons and a long-range maritime patrol.[84] This would allow the British government time to stabilize the Gulf and help 'modernize' the rulers of the Trucial States, which the Foreign Office estimated would continue into the mid-1970s at the earliest.[85]

The decision was met with scepticism in parliament. Why would the government incur more expenditure to shift the military forces from Aden to

---

[82] 'Relations with the United Arab Republic': Ministry of Defence brief for Healey, February 1965, DEFE25/190, *BDEEP—East of Suez*, #39.
[83] 'Defence Review': Report to ministers by an Official Committee of the Cabinet Defence and Oversea Policy Committee. 8 November 1965. CAB 130/213. *BDEEP—East of Suez*, #6.
[84] 'The United Kingdom Defence Review': Draft Aide Memoire by HMG for discussion in Washington and Canberra. January 1966. DEFE 13/477. *BDEEP—East of Suez*, #10.
[85] 'Persian Gulf and Iran': Report by Roberts to Brown on his visit to the Persian Gulf and Iran. 21 October to 12 November 1967. 17 November 1967. FCO 8/31. *BDEEP—East of Suez*, #27.

the Persian Gulf if the ultimate goal was to eventually leave the Gulf altogether?[86] Denis Healey responded with Labour's new rationalization:

> The point is to ensure the continued stability of the Gulf until countries in the area are capable of maintaining stability on their own. We do not regard the base in Aden as being necessary for that purpose. But consequent on leaving Aden, we feel it necessary to make a small increase in our forces in the Persian Gulf to maintain our obligations.[87]

Even as the Foreign Office laid plans for a tidy handover and withdrawal from the South Arabian Federation, events spiralled out of control. After announcing in 1966 that Britain would withdraw in 1968, violence in Aden increased. Local security forces in the Federation proved loyal to the NLF based in Yemen. In June 1967, federal police revolted in the area of Sheikh Uthman, just a few miles north of Aden. Nationalists within the police force seized an arms cache, attacked a British truck carrying nineteen soldiers and later managed to take over the armoury. By the end of the day, the NLF controlled the area.[88]

British forces succeeded in reoccupying the area by 5 July. They failed, however, to provide sufficient support to the federal army in the months that followed. Between August and September, the states comprising the federation melted away. The NLF took over eight states by August 28; three days later, they consolidated control over four more.[89] By 13 September, British forces ceded control of Little Aden to the South Arabian Army and withdrew behind their lines in Aden. Command of the Persian Gulf forces transferred to the commander at Bahrain in October. In late November, the federal army in Aden fell to the NLF, and on 29 November, the last British soldier evacuated South Arabia.

Just weeks before the evacuation, British minister of state Goronwy Roberts travelled to the Gulf to meet with all the rulers individually. He sought to assure them of Britain's commitment to stay on despite their withdrawal from Aden. In visits to Kuwait, Bahrain, Qatar and the Trucial Coast, Roberts emphasized three points: that the British would remain in the Gulf 'as long as it is necessary to maintain peace and stability', to encourage continued modernization and to

---

[86] Sato, 'Britain's Decision to Withdraw from the Persian Gulf, 99–117. Backbenchers openly opposed Wilson's plans for the Gulf, and some even shifted from the Labour party to the Liberal party following the withdrawal from the Gulf.
[87] Hansard, Parliamentary Debates, v. 739, oral answers, 402–4. Comment by Mr. Healey in response to Mr. Hooley in the House of Commons.
[88] Jonathan Walker, *Aden Insurgency: The Savage War in Yemen, 1962–67* (Staplehurst, UK: Spellmount, 2005), 240–4.
[89] Julian Paget, *Last Post, Aden, 1964–67* (London: Faber & Faber, 1969), 234.

develop strong cooperation among themselves. The rulers, he said, welcomed his reassurances.

Between 1956 and 1967, the British Residency and the Trucial rulers all faced the reality that Arab nationalism, and Nasserism in particular, had reached the Arabian Peninsula. Bernard Burrows had predicted that the underdevelopment of the Trucial Coast would make the region vulnerable to anti-British forces and had pressed the British government to invest in development projects to modernize the states. As seen in the chapters earlier on, the Foreign Office and Burrows anticipated the expansion of anti-imperialism in the Gulf, and Burrows viewed development as a tool to inoculate the Trucial Coast against its spread.

In the years between the nationalization of the Suez Canal and the British withdrawal from Aden, both British policymakers and the Trucial rulers took Arab nationalism into consideration when making decisions about the states' futures. The British Residency placed an emphasis on expanding infrastructure for future economic growth and encouraged education for the purposes of building state institutions. The meagre resources at their disposal, however, meant that the Residency prioritized major development projects for Dubai and Abu Dhabi, where they expected trade and oil would provide the basis for future stability. This ultimately frustrated the rulers of the smaller states, and particularly Saqr of Sharjah who viewed the rise of Arab nationalism and the offers of aid from the Arab League and Egypt as an opportunity to raise his own profile and that of Sharjah.

Development could be a double-edged sword, though. For Shakhbut, the rapid pace of development the Residency planned for Abu Dhabi threatened the fabric of Abu Dhabi's society and undermined the ruler's sovereignty. The urgency of development also required the introduction of foreign workers, many of whom had been exposed to and supported anti-British, Nasserist and other anti-imperialist ideologies. The British Residency and the Trucial rulers all grappled with the spectre of Arab nationalism and Nasserist, anti-British sentiment as they considered the future of the Trucial Coast. The shadow of Nasser's influence would continue to hang over the Trucial States as the rulers in 1968 looked to a future without Britain.

6

Federation and withdrawal, 1968–1971

Harold Wilson announced publicly in January 1968 that Britain would retreat from its positions East of Suez. This decision alarmed both the rulers of the Trucial Coast and the British officials serving there. Britain's intention to withdraw created the potential for instability in many ways. Great Britain had been the primary protector for the Arab littoral since the 1820s. Britain's very presence served as a deterrent against regional powers' ambitions to dominate the Gulf States and preserved a corner of the Middle East for British interests. The Trucial States lacked the administrative infrastructures of modern nation-states. While they had developed some of the bureaucratic mechanisms of statehood under the Trucial Council and the guidance of British Residents and Political Agents, these were insufficient for the tasks of statehood. In leaving the Persian Gulf, the Foreign Office hoped not to give up Britain's privileged position as ally and advisor to the Trucial States. Rather, the Trucial States would continue to rely on Britain and preserve the economic ties that bound them together. A federation of the Trucial States provided a streamlined way to sustain British influence and would help share the expenses and resources required to keep the inequitably resourced states solvent and sovereign.

For the Trucial rulers, however, British withdrawal presented serious dilemmas. The individual rulers in the Gulf feared the effects of a new political order. Britain's presence had not only secured the rulers' positions but British officials had also mediated disagreements among the rulers, preserved internal security and helped to prevent the infiltration of Nasserists and other Arab nationalists into the Gulf. Britain had also provided important economic opportunities. The military bases at Bahrain and Sharjah had provided important revenues to both of those states. To confess these fears about the British withdrawal publicly, however, would subject the rulers to harsh criticism from anti-imperialists in the Gulf and throughout the Arab world.

The three years between Wilson's announcement and the formal independence of the United Arab Emirates marked a period of extreme uncertainty. For a time, British officials questioned whether a withdrawal would occur. When it became clear that the Conservative government would not be able to reverse Wilson's decision, policymakers and rulers began to consider what the future Gulf would look like and whether neighbouring states would support or disrupt plans for creating a new state. Even in the final weeks, the final shape of the federation remained in doubt. Not until two months after independence did a union of emirates take its ultimate form. In the earliest stages of planning for withdrawal, the shadow of Nasserist and anti-imperialist Arab nationalisms influenced the rulers' reactions to both the Labour and Conservative governments' withdrawal plans. Inter-emirate ambitions as well as those of Saudi Arabia and Iran would prove to be the most significant determinants in the end.

The decision to withdraw

Britain's decision to abandon the Gulf came as a sudden surprise, but the circumstances behind the decision had been building since the Second World War. The costs of war created significant strains on the British domestic economy lasting well into the 1950s and 1960s. The post-war global economy also created significant concerns about sterling reserves, particularly as oil production in the British colonies and protected states helped to buoy sterling. As decolonization movements swept through Africa and the Middle East, British policymakers recalibrated their economic and security goals to match the new international realities.

Oil-producing countries in the British Empire and in the Gulf produced direct income for the British companies extracting oil – but they also provided substantial amounts of money invested in sterling reserves. The oil-producing states in the Gulf invested their enormous profits in the sterling area, a voluntary financial association between Great Britain and many of its primary trading partners. When Great Britain had abandoned the gold standard in 1931 and pegged the pound to sterling, the sterling area became a way for partners to use sterling as a universally convertible currency within the sterling area.[1] The

---

[1] Steven Galpern, *Money, Oil and Empire in the Middle East: Sterling and Post-war Imperialism, 1944–1971* (Cambridge: Cambridge University Press, 2009); Gerold Krozewski, *Money and the End of Empire: British International Economic Policy and the Colonies, 1947–1958* (London: Palgrave Macmillan, 2001), especially 29–58.

oil-producing states in the Gulf invested their enormous profits in the sterling area. A defence review estimated that oil from the Persian Gulf constituted £200 million of British balances for 1965.[2] Nearly all of the sterling from the region came from Kuwait. Iraq had spent almost all of its oil revenues on internal development, and Iran's contributions to the sterling area were severely curtailed following the nationalization crisis. Kuwait's sterling holdings alone were second only to those of Australia. As Abu Dhabi's oil wealth increased, the Foreign Office speculated, and hoped, that Abu Dhabi and the other Trucial States would invest in London.[3]

Crisis after crisis threatened British economic stability in the late 1950s and into the 1960s. The British government became increasingly worried about protecting its interests in the Gulf. Economic instability had plagued Great Britain following the Second World War. The primary economic concern of post-war governments was the balance-of-payments deficit within the sterling area. In the aftermath of the war, the sterling system appeared to work well. Trade within the sterling area in the 1940s constituted approximately half of British trade. The government devalued sterling in 1949 and 1950 in order to strengthen the pound relative to its trade deficits. Sterling reserves subsequently rebounded, but this success was short lived.

Both the Conservative Macmillan government (1957–64) and Wilson's Labour government (1964–70) struggled with the volatile British economy during their tenures in office. The balance-of-payment ratios did not stabilize over time. Trade within the sterling area continued to diminish dramatically. Sterling area members purchased 46.7 per cent of UK exports in 1952; this number fell steadily to only 27.5 per cent in 1968. From 1958 onward, British sterling reserves failed to meet British debts. The government increasingly depended on payments from foreign sterling reserves to make up the difference.[4]

Much of this was the consequence of the pace of decolonization of the British Empire in the 1950s. Following its independence, India redirected substantial sterling reserves to economic development projects, reducing the international sterling pool. As Nigeria, Ghana and Malaya gained independence, Britain

---

[2] 'Long-term Policy in the Persian Gulf': Report by the Defence Review Working Party. 28 September 1967. FCO 49/10. *BDEEP—East of Suez*, #11.
[3] 'Long-Term Policy in the Persian Gulf', note by the Foreign Office for the Defence and Oversea Policy Committee. 18 April 1967. CAB 148/57. TNA.
[4] P. J. Cain and A. G. Hopkins, *British Imperialism: 1688–2015* (New York: Routledge, 2016), 619–44. Alexander Cairncross and Barry Eichengreen, *Sterling in Decline: The Devaluations of 1939, 1949 and 1967* (London: Palgrave Macmillan, 2003); Catherine Schenk, 'Sterling International Monetary Reform and Britain's Applications to Join the European Economic Community in the 1960s,' *Contemporary European History* 11, no. 3 (2002): 345–69.

predicted they would follow suit, drawing down sterling reserves at a rapid pace.[5] In the Middle East, Egypt was also expected to take over control of its more than £128 million for development projects in 1963; Iraq had already spent nearly the entirety of its oil revenue on development, contributing only negligible amounts to the reserves. This, combined with other spending projects throughout the Middle East, led to a cumulative £300 million rundown of sterling after oil-producing countries expended their reserves.[6] In light of these projections, Britain depended on Kuwait's £260 million contribution to fill the gap, as well as contributions from the Trucial States in the future.

Sterling also suffered a crisis of confidence at a time when British imperial power was threatened. Following the British invasion of the Suez in 1956, several member states talked of leaving the sterling area in order to avoid open association with an imperialist power; and, in fact, Sudan did leave in 1957, while Iraq left in 1959 following a nationalist coup in 1958. Open anti-imperial and Arab nationalist groups staged strikes and rallies in the Gulf. The most worrying of these, for the British government, had occurred in Kuwait, where a generation of educated, young Kuwaitis had begun to welcome the aims of Nasser's nationalist agenda.[7]

Kuwait remained in the sterling area and maintained its ties with British advisors following the Suez crisis, despite burgeoning nationalist sentiment. Its loyalty to the sterling area made Britain determined to protect Kuwait from external threats, which might come from the new Iraqi government, especially, which might be able to overthrow the Al Sabahs and annex the sheikhdom. As important to Kuwait's contributions to sterling were, they were not sufficient to stabilize the sterling area as it lurched from crisis to crisis in the 1960s. The British trade deficit rose as sterling reserves dropped. Both the Conservative Macmillan government and Wilson's Labour government concentrated on the sterling area in order to uphold the economic well-being of Great Britain. Over time, however, they both came to view the large British defence role East of Suez as economically impracticable.

When Macmillan took office, his government faced grim economic news. The Treasury commented in a brief to the Colonial Secretary in 1957 that sterling liabilities that year were exceptionally high at 'over £4,000 million' while

---

[5] 'Treasury and Bank of England Report on the Sterling Area': Brief for Lennox-Boyd by A. Emanuel (CO), 19 February 1957. CO 852/1677. *BDEEP—The Conservative Government and the End of Empire, 1957–1964*, #300.
[6] Galpern, *Money, Oil and Empire*, 322.
[7] Ibid., 323.

Great Britain only held reserves of approximately £700 million.[8] Two years later, the Treasury reported that diminishing sterling reserves still posed 'the most notable economic threat ... which could have far graver consequences in the sixties than in the forties'.[9] Macmillan believed the sterling system could stabilize if the government cut expenses. In 1957, defence expenditure constituted 10 per cent of the national budget and seemed the likeliest place to retrench. Macmillan made it his goal to cut it back to only 7 per cent.[10]

Macmillan could not expect to reign in defence expenditures without reducing forces in Europe or East of Suez. Britain had given up large swathes of its empire in the 1950s only to obtain a substantial role-defending Western Europe from communist expansion.[11] Halfway through Macmillan's term, the Treasury warned that Britain's traditional role as an international force was entwined with sterling's well-being:

> Of all the major Powers, the United Kingdom has the most vulnerable economy ... The gold reserves are less than one-third of the sterling liabilities to other countries – precarious backing for an international currency that by its nature must take the strain of political and financial pressures throughout the world.[12]

Despite the warning, Macmillan proved unable to turn the economy around. Defence costs grew on all fronts. Between 1959 and 1964, East of Suez expenditures had nearly doubled from £76 million to £133 million, especially as the crisis in Malaya came to a head. In the Arabian Peninsula, costs began creeping up as the conflict in Yemen expanded. The cabinet estimated that the defence budget for 1965–6 would outstrip its allotment by more than £50 million. Cutting corners in the Department of Defence proved insufficient for reversing the increasing sterling liabilities to reserves ratio.[13] The Conservative government fell in 1964

---

[8] 'Treasury and Bank of England Report on the Sterling Area': Brief for Lennox-Boyd by A. Emanuel (CO), 19 February 1957. CO 852/1677. BDEEP—*The Conservative Government and the End of Empire, 1957–1964*, #300.

[9] 'The Commonwealth, 1960–1970': Draft Cabinet Memorandum by CRO for Future Policy Study Working Group. 30 July 1959. CAB 134/1935. BDEEP—*The Conservative Government and the End of Empire, 1957–1964*, #11.

[10] 'The Implications of Withdrawal from the Middle and Far East': Minutes of a Cabinet (Official) Committee on Defence Meeting, 21 May 1963. CAB 130/190. BDEEP—*The Conservative Government and the End of the Empire, 1957–1964*, #70.

[11] 'Future Defence Policy': Cabinet Defence Committee meeting minutes. 9 February 1963. CAB 131/28. BDEEP—*The Conservative Government and the End of Empire*, #69; Saki Dockrill, *Britain's Retreat from East of Suez: The Choice between Europe and the World?* (New York: Palgrave Macmillan, 2002).

[12] 'Future Policy Study, 1960–1970': Cabinet Memorandum, Report of Officials' Committee (Chairman, Sir N. Brook), 24 February 1960. CAB 131/27, BDEEP—*The Conservative Government and the End of Empire, 1957–1964*, #17.

[13] 'British Strategy in the 1960s': Minutes of Cabinet Defence Committee Meeting, 12 January 1962f. CAB 131/27, BDEEP—*The Conservative Government and the End of Empire, 1957–1964*, #67.

without having made headway in restoring sterling reserves or reducing British liabilities.

Harold Wilson's first priority as prime minister was to review the economic situation. It appeared bleak. The Secretary of the Treasury noted that the government would need to raise taxes, improve industry and trim budgets especially in 'defence and "prestige" projects' to reduce the deficit and prevent the devaluation of the sterling.[14] Britain's dwindling economic power furthered Wilson's reliance on Britain's traditional role as a global military force. He looked to the British naval presence East of Suez as an important tool vis-à-vis the United States, which depended on Britain to support American operations in Vietnam. It also helped cement Britain's relationship with Australia and New Zealand.[15]

Wilson came to office with ambitious goals for Britain's role in international affairs. He wrote to the American president, Lyndon Johnson, with an assessment of the impending economic crisis, stating that the deficit for 1964 could come to £800 million and would continue to rise without extensive budget cuts—but he failed to mention any possibility of reducing defence commitments as part of his economic plan. Instead, he focused on economic growth through reducing imports, increasing exports and speeding up development in under-employed areas of the economy.[16] The following spring, he confided to the US Secretary of State that he had 'a prejudice for the maintenance of the British role East of Suez'.[17] Wilson had no intention of making substantive defence cuts at the risk of losing international influence. He instead hoped to secure financial support from the American government in exchange for continuing on East of Suez.[18] To maintain both an international defence role while preventing an economic collapse, Harold Wilson began trimming the domestic and foreign budgets. Even as he pursued a foreign policy that over-stretched military commitments across the globe, members of Wilson's government began to rebel. Resentment within the Labour government grew, as progress stopped on new housing,

---

[14] Minute by Sir W. Armstrong (Treasury) in preparation for a meeting between Mr. Wilson, Mr. Brown and Mr. Callaghan, 16 October 1964, PREM 13/32. *BDEEP—East of Suez*, #1.
[15] Dockrill, *Britain's Retreat from East of Suez*, 105–17.
[16] Outward telegram from FO to Washington transmitting a message from Harold Wilson to Lyndon Johnson, 23 October 1964. PREM 13/32. *BDEEP—East of Suez* #3.
[17] 'Defence': Record by J. O. Wright of a conversation between Harold Wilson and Dean Rusk, 14 May 1965. PREM 13/1890. *BDEEP—East of Suez*, #4.
[18] Richard Crossman, *Diaries* v. 2 (1978). 'I think [Wilson] has been extremely successful on his visit to Washington in convincing the Americans that Britain is a loyal junior partner ... he has convinced himself at least, that we can get through without devaluation of the pound because we are now built into the American system', 116–17.

hospitals and schools.[19] Wilson demanded cuts from the Foreign Office budget of £100 million in 1966 without any corresponding changes in foreign policy.[20] As the war continued into Wilson's government, so too did increased demands from the military for more money. Members of the military branches began complaining openly – without a substantial reduction in defence commitments, the military would not be able to perform effectively.[21]

By late 1965, Wilson's ministers began to reconsider the British role East of Suez in order to bring foreign policy in line with economic realities. Under the Macmillan government, some members of the Foreign Office and the business community had argued that a military withdrawal from the Gulf in particular could lead to increased stability in British relations with the rulers there. The president of the Board of Trade believed that the British government should eliminate the 'imperialist traditions and associations' in the Gulf and work towards a relationship 'based primarily on a mutually advantageous and straight-forward commercial relationship'.[22] Wilson's own ministers took up this line of reasoning and expanded it, arguing: 'Indeed our presence might even be disadvantageous to our interests by providing an irritant and a focus for Arab nationalist pressures.'[23]

Less than a year later, Wilson and his defence advisors seemed to have taken this advice seriously and began reorganizing defence priorities. In response to the 1965 defence review and subsequent White Paper, the prime minister laid out plans to cut British forces from East of Suez by half and from the Middle East by one-third. This included arrangements for leaving Aden when the Arabian Federation became independent in 1968. It further incorporated an eventual withdrawal from the Gulf, though this was projected to begin in the mid-1970s at the earliest.[24] In fact, the Gulf would become the new base for two battalions,

---

[19] Richard Crossman, *Diaries* v. 2 (1978), 287.
[20] Richard Crossman, *Diaries* v. 2 (1978), 578; Philip Ziegler, *Wilson: The Authorised Life* (London: Weidenfeld & Nicolson, 1993).
[21] 'Defence': Minute by Mayhew to Healey criticizing the Defence Review for its failure so far to recommend cuts in commitments, 6 August 1965. DEFE 13/114, no. 24/1. BDEEP—*East of Suez*, #5.
[22] 'Review of Middle East Policy, Objectives and Strategy': Memorandum by Sir R. Stevens to Sir H. Caccia. 19 July 1963. FO 371/170165. BDEEP—*The Conservative Government and the End of Empire*, #71.
[23] 'Defence Policy': Record of a meeting at 10 Downing Street of ministers, service chiefs and senior officials. 13 November 1965. 130/213, Misc. 17/8. BDEEP—*East of Suez*, #7.
[24] 'The United Kingdom Defence Review': Draft Aide Memoire by HMG for discussion in Washington and Canberra. January 1966. DEFE 13/477. BDEEP—*East of Suez*, #27; 'Persian Gulf and Iran': Report by Roberts to Brown on his visit to the Persian Gulf and Iran. 21 October–12 November 1967. 17 November 1967. FCO 8/31. BDEEP—*East of Suez*, #27.

two ground squadrons and a long-range maritime patrol that would shift from Aden.[25]

The parliament met these recommendations with scepticism and outright hostility. Parliamentary backbenchers openly opposed Wilson's plans for the Gulf, asking why the government would incur more expenditure to shift the military forces from Aden to the Gulf if the ultimate goal was to leave the Gulf altogether?[26] Denis Healey responded with Labour's new rationalization:

> The point is to ensure the continued stability of the Gulf until countries in the area are capable of maintaining stability on their own. We do not regard the base in Aden as being necessary for that purpose. But consequent on leaving Aden, we feel it necessary to make a small increase in our forces in the Persian Gulf to maintain our obligations.[27]

The expense of such an increase continued to be a flashpoint.

Even as the Foreign Office laid plans for a tidy withdrawal and handover to the South Arabian Federation, events there spiralled out of control. Following the 1966 decision to leave, violence in Aden increased. Local security forces in the federation proved loyal to the National Liberation Front based out of Yemen. In June 1967, federal police revolted in an area of Sheikh Uthman, just a few miles north of Aden. The nationalists within the police force seized an arms cache, attacked a British truck carrying nineteen soldiers and later managed to take over the armoury. In the span of a day, the National Liberation Front controlled the area.[28] British forces succeeded in re-occupying the area by July 5 but failed to provide sufficient support to the federal army in the following months. By September 13, the situation disintegrated further. British forces handed control of Little Aden to the South Arabian Army and withdrew behind its lines in Aden. They handed military command of the Gulf forces to the commander at Bahrain in October. By November 29, the last British soldier evacuated South Arabia. In a matter of a few short months, nationalist forces had expelled the British presence which had been there for more than 100 years.

The crisis in Aden had coincided with the nadir of the economic crisis. On 18 November 1967, the Treasury took the steps Harold Wilson had hoped to avoid since coming to office. It devalued sterling from $2.80 to $2.40. The savings

---

[25] 'The United Kingdom Defence Review': Draft Aide Memoire by HMG for discussion in Washington and Canberra. January 1966. DEFE 13/477. *BDEEP—East of Suez*, #10.
[26] Sato, 'Britain's Decision to Withdraw from the Persian Gulf, 1964–68', 99–117.
[27] Hansard, Parliamentary Debates, v. 759, Oral Answers, 402–4. Comment by Mr. Healey in response to Mr. Hooley in the House of Commons.
[28] Walker, *Aden Insurgency*, 240–4.

measures had failed to prevent an economic collapse. An atmosphere of despair took hold of the government in the aftermath.

The devaluation measures meant that the British government would have to make an immediate decision about its defence role. The growing presence of Arab nationalism in the Gulf and the forced withdrawal from Aden convinced the Foreign Office that staying on in the Gulf as a visible imperial power would reduce its influence and jeopardize British interests. Wilson's Cabinet pushed for an earlier withdrawal from the Gulf in an effort to bring expenditure in line with the realities of Britain's economic limitations.[29] The day before his announcement to parliament, Harold Wilson wrote to President Lyndon Johnson. He soberly summed up his hopes for the future of British influence in the international arena:

> If there is any lesson to be learned from the sombre way we have found ourselves obliged to lurch from one defence review to another in recent years, it is that we must now take certain major foreign policy decisions as the pre-requisite of economics in our defence expenditure. Put simply, this only amounts to saying that we have come to terms with our role in the world. And we are confident that if we fully assert our economic strength, we can by realistic priorities strengthen this country's real influence and power for peace in the world.[30]

The days of exerting British will through fire power had drawn to a close. All that was left, then, was to execute a clean withdrawal from the Far East and the Gulf.

Why federation?

The formal move towards a federation of emirates in the Persian Gulf was initiated subsequent to the British government's surprise decision in January 1968 to end its defence role East of Suez no later than December 1971. British officials believed that the best way to protect British interests in the Persian Gulf would be through the establishment of a federation of Trucial States. A federation, ideally, would create a strong government that would engender cooperation among the various rulers, and would allow for the sharing of resources to improve the whole's economic power and defence. As seen in the chapters earlier on, British

---

[29] 'Public Expenditure: Post Devaluation Measures': Cabinet conclusions on withdrawal from East of Suez. 4 January 1968. CAB 128/43. *BDEEP—East of Suez*, #28.
[30] 'Defence Review': Outward FO telegram no. 554 to Washington transmitting the text of Mr. Wilson's reply to Lyndon Johnson. *BDEEP—East of Suez*, #33.

administrators in the Gulf had encouraged cooperation among the rulers of the Trucial sheikhs to facilitate British influence and policy implementation in the previous fifteen years. Even before 1968, British policymakers anticipated that Britain would withdraw from the Gulf eventually and had begun laying the groundwork for the eventuality of future independence.

Federation provided the framework for British policymakers from the outset. Federations were a relatively common aspect of state formation and decolonization in the mid-twentieth century. The Colonial Office had created federations among colonized ethnic, religious and political groupings throughout the Empire in order to form larger states that officials believed would be more economically viable than if they gained independence singly.

Yet, federation as a solution to the perceived problem of unevenly developed and small 'micro states' had not been a successful aspect of decolonization. The Foreign Office knew it. In a briefing for the Cabinet on the possibility of an eventual federation in the Gulf, one Foreign Office official observed that 'for what it's worth, recent British experience elsewhere suggests that political association between reluctant units is an unsatisfactory feature of the decolonisation process'.[31] This was putting the case mildly. Each of the federations organized by the British Colonial Office failed to last long. In 1958, the Colonial Office had established a federation between twenty-four primary islands and a number of smaller islands in the West Indies; the federation collapsed after four years as a result of tensions between the provinces over representation and the division of local and federal powers.[32] Nigeria's federation of the 1950s led to a series of coups in the 1960s, instability and civil war in 1967.[33] The Central African Federation, established in 1953, unravelled ten years later as the constituent parts broke into three independent states.[34] Malaya fared no better, lasting only fifteen years after federation.[35] Closer to home, South Arabia had only just collapsed.

---

[31] 'Long-term Policy in the Persian Gulf': Note by the Foreign Office, April 1967. CAB 148/57. TNA.
[32] Ryan D. Selwyn, *Eric Williams: The Myth and the Man* (Kingston, Jamaica: University of the West Indies Press, 2009); Amanda Sives, 'Dwelling Separately: The Federation of the West Indies and the Challenge of Insularity', in *Defunct Federalisms: Critical Perspectives on Federal Failure*, ed. Emilian Kavalski and Magdalena Zoldos (Farnham, UK: Ashgate Publishing, 2008), 18–30.
[33] Toyin Falola and Matthew Heaton, *A History of Nigeria* (Cambridge: Cambridge University Press, 2008), 137–80; Margery Perham, 'Reflections on the Nigerian Civil War', *International Affairs* 46, no. 2 (1970): 231–46. Perham notes that the federation of Nigeria was engineered with the help of Nigerian leaders but did not have sufficient support following independence to hold it together.
[34] Matthew Hughes, *The Central African Federation, Katanga, and the Congo Crisis, 1958–65*. Salford: European Studies Research Institute, University of Salford, 2003); Rush Weiss, *Sir Garfield and the Making of Zimbabwe* (London: British Academic Press, 1999).
[35] Anthony Reid, *Imperial Alchemy: Nationalism and Political Identity in Southeast Asia* (New York: Cambridge University Press, 2010). David Easter, *Britain and the Confrontation with Indonesia, 1960–1966* (New York: I.B. Tauris, 2004).

Despite these failures, the Foreign Office remained adamant that a federation would be the best route to independence for the Arab Gulf States. The Foreign Secretary contextualized the federal concept in comments for the Overseas Development Committee in 1967, saying:

> Indeed now that the main work of decolonization is complete, the majority of those [remaining] territories are small, scattered islands or 'grains of dust' for which no other solution [except permanent dependence] seems feasible, even if formal colonialism is in some cases replaced by 'free association' or integration. But we have never supposed that the Protected States of the Gulf will fall into this category. They may be small enough to qualify in theory. But they are neither remote enough geographically (cf. the Pacific Islands) nor British enough in character (cf. the smaller West Indies) to qualify in practice.[36]

The Gulf States were too small for independence as they were, but neither did they merit a continuation of their quasi-colonial status under special treaty relations. The sheikhdoms, British officials believed, could not continue individually after British withdrawal. There was little in the way of state structures or infrastructure. What did exist was unevenly distributed between the nine states relative to their wealth. Bahrain, for example, had benefitted from oil revenues following the discovery of oil in the interwar period. Consequently, the government had built and equipped schools, provided primary and vocational education to growing numbers of the population and had begun to establish a sector of the populace capable of filling administrative functions for the state. Abu Dhabi, though, had only been exporting oil since 1966. Until that time, development of administrative offices and public services had been limited in scope. Other emirates, such as Ajman and Ras Al Khaimah, were impoverished and depended almost entirely on financial contributions from Abu Dhabi, Kuwait and Great Britain. They could not afford to establish independent municipal offices and government agencies without support.

For these reasons, the Foreign Office believed a federation of some kind was the only way for the Gulf States to be viable after independence, though they were not hopeful that it would succeed. Among themselves, policymakers frequently expressed doubts about the possibility that any kind of federation could be achieved; and should it be achieved, they believed it would likely fail

---

[36] 'Long-term Policy in the Persian Gulf': Note by the Foreign Office, April 1967. CAB 148/57. TNA.

in the long term. Nevertheless, British officials chose to 'give the impression that we assume it will [work]' in the hopes that the rulers of the Trucial States would continue working towards a union.[37]

In preparation for an eventual withdrawal from the Gulf, the Foreign Office floated several potential models of federation in 1967. These included a 'two-tier system' in which the Northern Trucial States (Dubai and the five smallest emirates) federated and maintained a confederated relationship with Abu Dhabi, Bahrain and Qatar, with each larger territory enjoying greater independence. Alternatively, they considered the possibility that Saudi Arabia might win a territorial dispute with Abu Dhabi, thus leaving Abu Dhabi small and sufficiently weak to be absorbed by Dubai. In another iteration, Bahrain and Qatar might seek a loose confederation with Saudi Arabia for protection. They also imagined a four-state solution whereby Abu Dhabi and Dubai divided the four smaller Trucial States among themselves, and establishing Qatar, Bahrain, greater Abu Dhabi and greater Dubai.[38]

All the careful planning and imaginative configurations developed in the Foreign Office came to naught. Harold Wilson announced Britain's plans to leave only six months after the Foreign Office submitted a summary of possible formulas for the Arab Gulf States. Two Foreign Secretaries, several Political Residents and agents and a special envoy would be required to forge an agreement that would result in the creation of the United Arab Emirates. The path to independence would not follow the path the Foreign Office envisioned. It was by the will of the leaders of the Gulf States as they faced a future without British protection.

The Dubai Agreement, February 1968

In the days following Wilson's announcement, Trucial rulers experienced varying degrees of shock, especially in the smaller states. Several rulers offered to subsidise the British military presence if Wilson would reverse course. The Political Agent at Dubai reported that Sheikh Muhammad bin Hamad of Fujairah might consider forfeiting his sovereignty and allow the British government to rule the emirate as a protectorate. The ruler of Sharjah, Sheikh Khalid III,

---

[37] Minute from D. J. McCarthy (Arabian Department, FO) to R. I. Hallows (Bank of England), 19 December 1968. FCO 8/966. TNA.
[38] 'Long-term Policy in the Persian Gulf': Note by the Foreign Office, 18 April 1967. CAB 148/57. TNA.

expressed dismay at the economic effect withdrawal would have for Sharjah, as the emirate depended on income from the British military installations there.[39] Before long, however, the rulers along the coast recognized the finality of Wilson's decision and the danger of opposing the withdrawal openly. Cairo's Voice of the Arabs had heralded the announcement as an Arab victory that would produce progress towards achieving the regional goals of independence from Western imperialism. When the Conservative government succeeded Wilson, Heath asked whether the rulers would be open to Britain staying on, and the rulers all confessed that there was no turning back – they could not be seen to support the continuation of an imperial relationship.[40] Everyone would need to move forward.

On 18 February 1968, two rulers made strides towards that future. Sheikh Zayed had invited Sheikh Rashid of Dubai to meet to discuss the post-withdrawal future. They converged on al-Samih in Dubai near the Abu Dhabi-Dubai border. There, Muhammad bin Rashid, the regent of Dubai, had selected the meeting point and pitched tents for the two rulers to sit together to discuss a future union.[41] Their meeting concluded with the Dubai Agreement, which affirmed the two leaders' commitment to the creation of a union that would establish inter-emirate cooperation in four matters:

> Shaykh Zayed bin Sultan al-Nahyan, the Ruler of the Emirate of Abu Dhabi, with his brother Shaykh Rashid bin Saeed al-Maktoum, the Ruler of the Emirate of Dubai, in pursuit of their search for the best future for their people, and in order to achieve the aspirations of the people of the region and meet their desires, have satisfactorily agreed to the following, praise God:
>
> The formation of a union comprising the two countries under one flag and entrusted with the following issues:
>
> Foreign affairs;
>
> Defence and security in case of necessity;

---

[39] 'The Future of the Trucial States', D. A. Roberts (Political Agent, Dubai) to A. J. D. Stirling (Arabian Department, FO). 7 February 1968. FO 1016/855. TNA.
[40] 'British Withdrawal from the Persian Gulf, Local View': Minute from D. J. McCarthy to Arthur, Arabian Department. 11 June 1969. FCO 8/979. TNA.
[41] Muhammad bin Rashid al-Maktoum, *My Story* (Dubai: Explorer Publishing, 2019), 79. Bin Rashid al-Maktoum writes with a Romantic nostalgia in describing the meeting:

> I pitched two tents; one for the two Sheikhs to the north, with the doorway oriented so as to welcome a soothing desert breeze – and another to the south for their entourages to stay in. I lit a fire for cooking, while in my heart burned a fire of enthusiasm and excitement for this day, which I knew marked a pivotal moment: one with inevitable repercussions that would shape all our futures.

Services such as health and education;

And Citizenship and immigration.[42]

The accord also supported including the other Trucial States, Bahrain and Qatar to join the union should they wish to. Two weeks later, all seven of the other states accepted the agreement.

This meeting has captured Emirati historical imagination and is celebrated as a significant moment in the origins of the United Arab Emirates. Popular accounts of this meeting describe it as a movement towards unity—two rivals met in the desert and left as co-architects of a future union that would combine the states of the Arab coast into one federated unit that would provide stability, continuity and prosperity for its people. The moment also portends the great role Sheikh Zayed would play as the unifier of the UAE. In this moment, he initiated the process of creating the union, would hold together and lead the union as its president and would reprise the role of unifier as a regional leader during the Iran-Iraq war. In some of the biographies and *festschrifts* in his honor, Sheikh Zayed is described as a 'Man of Union', (*rajul al-ittihad*), 'Man of Unity', (*rajul al-wahda*), and 'Man of Solidarity', (*rajul al-tadhamin*).[43] Most recently, Sheikh Mohammed bin Rashid of Dubai (2006-present) echoed this sentiment, adding that Zayed had 'longed for the Union and dreamed of a single state' from his first days as ruler of Abu Dhabi in 1966.[44]

The optimism and enthusiasm the agreement engendered quickly dissipated under the weight of the numerous problems not addressed in the relatively vague articles of the initial agreement. The internal dynamics of the Trucial States and their links to the major powers in the region stymied federation progress. In late May, the leaders of the nine states met to clarify how they would begin negotiating the details of power sharing between the states, representation and the location of a future capital. The following day, the

---

[42] 'Abu Dhabi and Dubai Union Agreement', 18 February 1968. National Archives of the United Arab Emirates.

[43] See Hamdan Rashid ʿAli al-Darʿaiy, *Zayid: Sirat al-Amjad wa Fakhr al-Ittihad: Qiraʿa fi al-Wathaʾiq al-Britaniya wa Wasaʾil al-ʿIlam al-ʿArabiya wa al-Ajnabiya, 1968-1971* (al-Ayn, UAE: Markaz Zayid lil Turath wa al-Tarikh, 2005), 43–51; *Dawlat al-Imarat al-ʿArabiya al-Muttahida: Khamsa ʿAshira ʿAaman ʿAla Tariq al-Binaʾ wa al-Taqqadum, 1392-1407h. (1971-1986m)* (al-Imarat al-Arabiya al-Muttahida: [n.p., 1986]), 10–15; Andrew Wheatcroft, *With United Strength: H.H. Shaikh Zayid bin Sultan al-Nahyan, the Leader and the Nation* (Abu Dhabi: Emirates Center for Strategic Studies and Research, 2004).

Jane Bristol-Rhys, 'Emirati Historical Narratives', *History and Anthropology* 20, no. 2 (2009): 107–12. Bristol-Rhys isolates four trends in Emiratis' historical narratives as they relate to the British presence in the Trucial States. Two trends specifically address the elevated position that Sheikhs Zayed and Rashid enjoy in Emirati national mythologies on the basis of the Dubai Agreement.

[44] al-Maktoum, *My Story*, 78.

meeting ended without any progress and a public announcement postponing future discussions.

> Between 25 and 26 May 1968, the first meeting of the Supreme Council of the Federation of Arab Emirates was convened in Abu Dhabi. Rulers of the (aforesaid) emirates exchanged consultations about the best methods to implement the Dubai Accord for the realization of the noble objectives stipulated in this accord. From the consultations it transpired that there is a certain divergence regarding such methods. The conferees were of the opinion that this meeting be adjourned, and that another meeting of the Supreme Council be convened in Abu Dhabi on 1 July 1968, so that they can exchange more consultations with the aim of reaching an agreement which should guarantee at the soonest possible time commencement in taking necessary steps for the sound implementation of the Dubai Agreement.[45]

Future negotiations were no easier. From May 1968 until December 1971, it remained unclear whether or not a federation of any of the states would come into existence at all.

The agreement between Dubai and Abu Dhabi had been tentative from the outset. The effort exerted on Zayed's part to gain Rashid's cooperation created suspicion among the other Trucial rulers. To entice Rashid to participate in the agreement, Zayed had ceded approximately ten miles of Abu Dhabi's seabed to Dubai and also paid him £3 million.[46]

Other rulers viewed this with suspicion, believing that Zayed would use Abu Dhabi's oil wealth to buy influence within the federation. Sheikh Ahmad of Qatar complained that he saw the move as a 'first step by Zayed to taking over the whole of the Trucial Coast.'[47] Such complaints would crop up again several times over the next few years. In one instance, Abu Dhabi provided funds and police officers to Sheikh Muhammad of Fujairah for the purpose of training a Fujairah police force. Both Qatar and Dubai commented to the Political Agent at Dubai that the Abu Dhabi officers in Fujairah wore Abu Dhabi uniforms and that this could amount to an effort to eliminate Muhammad through the police force and a takeover of Fujairah.[48]

---

[45] 'Text of Joint Communique Issued by Meeting of the Rulers' council convened on 25–6 May 1968, Abu Dhabi. 26 May 1968. Cited in Taryam, *Establishment of the United Arab Emirates*, 100.

[46] 'Offshore Boundary Agreement Between Abu Dhabi and Dubai, 18 February 1968', https://www.un.org/Depts/los/LEGISLATIONANDTREATIES/PDFFILES/TREATIES/ARE1968OB.PDF (accessed 14 June 2019); 'Draft Report' in 'Tour of the Gulf, 18 April-6 May, 1968', G.11, Papers of Sir William Luce, Special Collections, University of Exeter.

[47] 'Draft Report', in 'Tour of the Gulf, 18 April-6 May, 1968', G.11, Papers of Sir William Luce, Special Collections, University of Exeter.

[48] 'Abu Dhabi and Fujairah', Letter from Julian L. Bullard (Political Agent, Dubai) to M. S. Weir (Political Resident, Bahrain). 3 June 1969. FCO 8/1218. TNA.

Despite his concerns, Sheikh Ahmed signed the accord and agreed to participate in the initial meeting, but his subsequent actions belied his uneasiness. Before the meeting in late May had even taken place, Ahmad seemed to be putting pressure on Sheikh Rashid to slow progress towards implementing the agreement. Things continued to deteriorate when Qatar forwarded several proposals to be included in the meeting's agenda. These included the election of a union president, the establishment of a capital, the creation of a union council and its functions and the discussion and creation of several ministries for the administration of the union.[49] This move on Qatar's part seems to have been an attempt to force the talks to collapse by placing the remaining states in the position of taking the blame for Qatar leaving. This became more apparent as the states' delegates and advisors prepared for the May 25 meeting. The rulers voted to exclude Qatar's proposals for the agenda of the first meeting. Ahmad nevertheless continued to press for the proposals' inclusion and publicly claimed that the move was 'an open violation of the agreement' and '[conflicted] totally with the higher interests of the federation'.[50]

Ahmad's bid for leadership or independence from the federation was not the only source of conflict within the emirates. As already indicated, cooperation between Dubai and Abu Dhabi was only tentative at the outset, and suspicions between the two rulers continued to plague negotiations. Bahrain's Sheikh Isa later intimated to a former Political Resident that he 'felt alienated from the other Trucial rulers and unwelcome in the federation'.[51] The year following the failure of the 25–6 May gathering signalled more disunity than it did progress.

In England, Wilson's announcement had drawn criticism from opponents. Conservative leadership exploited Labour's decision to withdraw and Edward Heath, the leader of the Conservative opposition, campaigned on a platform that included staying on East of Suez. His position added a new element of indecision to the federation talks, at least for a few months.

---

[49] 'Minutes of Meeting of Representatives and Advisers of the Rulers of the Gulf Emirates, Convened in Abu Dhabi on Saturday, 18 May and Sunday, 19 May 1968', cited in Taryam, *Establishment of the United Arab Emirates*, 96–7.

[50] Taryam, *Establishment of the United Arab Emirates*, 98. Taryam, as Balfour-Paul notes, was from Sharjah and participated in the federation discussions. As such, Balfour-Paul says, 'He should know'. Glencairn Balfour-Paul, *The End of Britain's Empire in the Middle East: Britain's Relinquishment of Power in Her Last Three Arab Dependencies* (Cambridge: Cambridge University Press, 1994), 225.

[51] 'Note on Federation', by William Luce, G.15.a. Papers of Sir William Luce, Special Collections, University of Exeter.

Heath toured the Persian Gulf States in April 1969 to discuss a policy reversal with the rulers.[52] Some of the rulers suggested that Britain could postpone the withdrawal, and several indicated that they wanted a continued British military presence. Sheikh Isa of Bahrain told Heath that he welcomed a continued military presence, while Sheikh Khalid Al Qasimi of Sharjah expressed apprehension about Iran's plans to take over the Gulf.[53] Each of the rulers, including Faisal of Saudi Arabia and Sabah in Kuwait, expressed concerns about post-withdrawal stability and defence arrangements. But none of the rulers could support a continuation of Britain's current role in the Gulf.

For each ruler, powerful forces at home and in the broader region made the status quo inoperable after 1971. Even as the rulers hoped for a continued relationship with the British government, they also recognized that the political climate within the emirates and the Middle East had shifted. Support for Arab nationalism had been growing in the Persian Gulf at an increasing rate since Nasser's nationalization of the Suez Canal. The civil war in Yemen brought the Arab nationalist cause to the Arabian Peninsula for the first time in 1962. When war broke out between the monarchy and the republican factions in North Yemen, Nasser had quickly moved to support the republican forces with arms and soldiers. As the conflict spread into British-protected territories in South Arabia and then east into the Sultanate of Oman, the political ideologies informing the rest of the Middle East also made their way to the Gulf coast.

The rulers in the Trucial States by 1969 saw Arab nationalism as a potential threat to the internal stability of their states; but they also recognized that they could not be seen to undermine the goals of Arab nationalism without undermining their own authority and legitimacy as rulers. Khalifah in Bahrain indicated to Heath that he could not support a reversal publicly, while Ahmed assured Heath that he would neither support a reversal nor be willing to house British troops in Qatar. Zayed most adamantly opposed Heath's idea, telling him that 'any offer to extend [British] protection beyond 1971 would meet with sharp rejection' from him. Even the ruler of Sharjah, who was most anxious about the future without Britain, would not be in a position to support Heath's views because it would be unpopular among his subjects.[54] By the time Heath had

---

[52] 'East of Suez': Minute from D. J. McCarthy (Arabian Department, FO) to M. S. Weir (Political Resident, Bahrain). FCO 8/979. TNA.
[53] 'Bahrain and the British Military Withdrawal': Letter from A. J. D. Stirling to Stewart Crawford. April 1969. FCO 8/973. TNA; 'Mr. Heath's Visit': Letter from J. L. Bullard (Political Agent, Dubai) to M. S. Weir (Political Resident, Bahrain). 5 April 1969. FCO 8/973. TNA.
[54] 'British Withdrawal from the Gulf: Local Views': Memorandum by the Arabian Department. 2 May 1969. FCO 8/979. TNA.

arrived to discuss staying on, the rulers had already turned to the promise of independence. When the Conservative government took office in 1970, Heath would become responsible for seeing the withdrawal through.

A federation of nine?

The question of *whether* a federation could occur remained at least as relevant as *what* federation would take place until the last moment. Inter-emirate rivalries persisted within the Trucial States, but Bahrain and Qatar were persistent in their ambivalent participation, which then drew in Saudi and Iranian ambitions. Following the collapse of negotiations in 1968, the Foreign Secretary brought Sir William Luce out of retirement to serve as his special advisor on the Gulf federation. Luce's recent past experiences in Aden as Governor (1956–60) and Political Resident Persian Gulf (1961–6) positioned him to undertake difficult negotiations, as did his strong relationships with the various rulers in the Gulf. Though Luce opposed Wilson's withdrawal, he also understood that reversing course would be an even graver mistake and that a federation would be the only viable path forward. Between 1968 and 1971, Luce made several tours of the Gulf States to gauge and encourage progress. His records provide important insights into the ways Bahrain and Qatar's indecision, pressures from Iran and Saudi Arabia and Britain's own commitment to the nine-state federation complicated local efforts to establish a federation before Britain's withdrawal.

Luce visited unofficially in the spring of 1968 and then in an official capacity again in 1969 and 1970. His notes from that time suggest there were serious resentments between the various rulers but that federation provided the 'best solution' for them in light of Britain's withdrawal.[55] By 1969, he observed that there was a 'considerable head of steam', for a union of the states with all nine rulers, even if the situation was 'complicated'.[56] His initial report supports the idea that the leaders of the Trucial and Gulf states agreed that a nine-state federation could provide the most stable future for all the states involved. Closer readings of his conversations with Ahmad of Qatar and Isa of Bahrain, however, strongly suggest that neither ruler truly ever wanted to join a federation but feared the reactions from Saudi Arabia and Iran too much to state their positions plainly.

---

[55] 'Tour of the Gulf, 18 April–6 May [1968] … Draft Report', G.11, Papers of Sir William Luce Special Collection, University of Exeter.
[56] 'Notes on Federation', G.15.a., Papers of Sir William Luce, Special Collections. University of Exeter.

Sheikh Ahmad identified numerous obstacles to successful federation in his conversations with Luce. In addition to his early wariness over Zayed's aspirations, Qatar's relationship with Bahrain was strained. Britain and Zayed viewed Bahrain's inclusion as a boon to the federation with its educated and skilled population. Sheikh Ahmad, however, raised concerns with Luce and Rashid that Bahrain's skilled and educated workforce would overwhelm those of the other Trucial States and bring 'revolutionary' ideas to the populations.[57] In conversations with Luce and other British policymakers in the Gulf, Ahmad additionally expressed his belief that maintaining a good relationship with Iran was much more important to both him and the ruler of Dubai than appeasing Saudi Arabia which pushed for Bahrain's inclusion.

Sheikh Isa relied on the protection of Britain and Saudi Arabia from Iran, and this compelled him to cooperate in federation talks. The Shah of Iran had revived historic claims to Bahrain (explored further in Chapter 7). Without regional and international support, Isa would be hard pressed to go it alone after British withdrawal. The island would be far too vulnerable without the express protection of Britain and Saudi Arabia, and Bahrain's economy depended in part on trade and Saudi employment.[58] Isa and his deputy ruler Khalifa bin Salman participated actively in federation talks, though they were often circumspect about details regarding resource sharing, particularly those that benefited Qatar.[59] Saudi Arabia, meanwhile, continued to press Bahrain to join the federation in part to temper Abu Dhabi's influence.[60]

The United Nations held a referendum to determine Bahrainis' opinions of Iran's claims to Bahraini sovereignty in April 1970. The subsequent report, presented in May, indicated that an overwhelming majority of Bahrainis supported independence from Iran. This should have eliminated one obstacle to a federation, especially as Iran dropped its claims to Bahrain in response. Khalifa told Luce that Bahrain would continue to participate in talks and make a push for a federation of nine but that the lack of substantive progress combined with continuing tensions with Qatar made it unlikely that Bahrain would persist

---

[57] This idea was repeated in several iterations from both Dubai and Qatar via British policymakers. See, for example, Telegram, Dubai to Bahrain, 15 February 1970. FCO 1016/739; 'Union of Eight', E. F. Henderson to Michael Weir. 12 February 1970. FCO 1016/739. TNA.

[58] 'Record of Conversation in Bahrain on Tuesday 26 January 1971': Papers of Sir William Luce, Special Collections, University of Exeter; 'Record of Conversation in Bahrain on Wednesday 19 May 1971': Papers of Sir William Luce, Special Collections, University of Exeter.

[59] 'Bahrain and the UAE': minute by A. J. D. Stirling, 25 April 1970. FO 1016/739. TNA.

[60] 'Note by HM Ambassador Jedda on a Meeting with Sheikh Khalid of Sharjah on 8 March', W. Morris, 11 March 1970. FO 1016/739. TNA.

much longer.⁶¹ Meanwhile, some of the other rulers' commitment to including Bahrain seemed to wane. The rulers of Dubai and Qatar expressed their own reservations about Bahrain's participation in the union and Zayed suggested that chasing a union of nine when Bahrain and Qatar might not wish to join would only lead to conflict between the two down the road. Instead, he argued, 'The best thing would be to form a Union of those ready to enter it now' and leave the option for other states to join later.⁶²

Union talks broke down in October 1970 when the deputy rulers of the various states met between the 24th and the 27th. At the meeting, representatives from each of the states discussed a draft constitution, the location of a capital and other provisions on representation and veto power of the larger states. The parties reached agreement on the draft constitution, but nothing else. Political agent, C. J. Treadwell wrote to the Resident immediately following the meeting: 'We can now be really certain that the Union of Nine has failed and it can surely only be a matter of time before Bahrain declare themselves free to go their own way.'⁶³ For his part, Treadwell believed the representatives from Abu Dhabi, Dubai and Qatar worked together to exasperate Bahrain until it withdrew and noted that Qatar had come to the meeting 'without any pretence of good faith'.⁶⁴ The deputy ruler of Qatar, however, pointed to Bahrain. Writing to the British Foreign Secretary, Sir Alec Douglas-Home, Khalifah bin Thani stated: 'Agreement was concluded unanimously among the eight Emirates on a number of basic matters with one single Emirate opposing, namely Bahrain. Qatar strove urgently to find a solution by consulting the member Emirates', including Sheikh Zayed.⁶⁵

Once Iran rescinded its claim to Bahrain, the pathway to Bahrain's membership in a future federation of emirates seemed smoothed. But Bahrain's new independent status created a wholly new dilemma. Sheikh Isa seemed more hesitant than ever to join the union. In February 1971, he confessed to Luce that he preferred a 'separate independence' though he was willing to 'make compromises' to ensure the union's success.⁶⁶

---

⁶¹ 'UAE', Telegram, Luce to Weir (Bahrain Residency), 4 August 1970. FO 1016/741. TNA.
⁶² 'Record of Conversation between the King of Saudi Arabia and the Parliamentary Under-Secretary and the Ruler of Abu Dhabi on 29 April 1970 at Abu Dhabi', 11 May 1970. FCO 1016/740. TNA.
⁶³ 'Breakdown of UAE Talks': letter from C. J. Treadwell to M. S. Weir, 27 October 1970. FO 1016/741. TNA.
⁶⁴ Ibid.
⁶⁵ Letter to Sir Alec Douglas-Home from Sheikh Khalifah, Deputy Ruler, Qatar, 8 December 1970. FO 1016/742. TNA.
⁶⁶ 'Record of Conversation in Bahrain on Sunday 7 February 1971', 8 February 1971. G.15.a. Papers of Sir William Luce, Special Collections, University of Exeter.

Luce continued to encourage the rulers to remain open to a union of nine well into 1971. Faisal's continued to press for Bahrain and Qatar to join the union, despite the evidence that neither Isa nor Ahmad wished to pursue it in earnest. Saudi Arabia established a joint mission with the ruler of Kuwait in the wake of the October meeting. This only prolonged half-hearted talks between all of the rulers into the summer of 1971. Talks around regional security in the wake of British withdrawal would finally provide a framework Saudi Arabia could to relinquish its plans for a union of nine. These security arrangements are the subject of the chapter that follows.

7

Security for the UAE

Britain's decision to withdraw from the Gulf left a significant question about the future unanswered. Without Britain's strong military presence to safeguard their territories, who would guarantee the emirates' sovereignty? Initially, British policies that protected British trade routes with India later expanded to protect Britain's economic and defence interests in the Persian Gulf and East of Suez. The Trucial sheikhs were not ready to take up a coordinated defence against external threats. Even with a unified defence agreement, the UAE would not have sufficient populations to build a force capable of defending against or even deterring attacks; furthermore, their indigenous military institutions were new, untested and not yet fully organized. The most obvious Western power capable of taking up the role was the United States, but the American government declared in 1968 that it had no intention of stepping in to take over British commitments.[1]

The surprising solution came in the form of the two regional powers that posed the greatest threat to the Trucial States: Saudi Arabia and Iran. Both states had been at odds with several of the Trucial rulers over territorial disputes, and both the Shah and the Saudi king sought to establish their own states as the unchallenged military and political force in the region. From the outset, the Foreign Office was determined to bring Saudi Arabia and Iran into the negotiation process and obtain their support for the future union. The United States stepped in to use its ties with Saudi Arabia and Iran to smooth the process. With neither the United States nor the United Kingdom willing or able to provide a military presence, they turned to Saudi Arabia and Iran to secure the Gulf. This policy eventually evolved to include military and financial support from Western governments to support the two states as the local guardians and 'twin pillars' of the Persian Gulf.

---

[1] Memorandum of Conversation, 'US/Kuwaiti Relations', 11 December 1968. NSF Country File: Kuwait: Cables and Memos. LBJL.

Such a policy allowed ultimately for the regionalization of responsibility for the Persian Gulf. It also helped to delay some of the potential hazards that a Western military presence would create. As was the case in other aspects of British union building in the Trucial States, Arab nationalism remained in the forefront of the minds of the Trucial sheikhs, and particularly that of Sheikh Zayed. The ruler of Abu Dhabi frequently highlighted the difficulties that Arab nationalism might pose to his sheikhdom and the future of the union whenever conflict between himself and the Foreign Office arose on the question of security. The Foreign Office proposed that local security in the union could be assumed by a reorganized version of the British-formulated and officered Trucial Oman Scouts, but Zayed vehemently opposed the idea. Such a move, he believed, would leave the union open to criticism and attack from nationalists. Instead, he preferred a longer view, which emphasized the need for the emirates' union forces to be established under solely union auspices, thereby eliminating a point of vulnerability and criticism from both outside and within the emirates.

Zayed won the day and on 3 December 1971 the Union Defence Force (UDF) became an independent force separate from that of the Trucial Oman Scouts. The Scouts were eventually absorbed into the UDF in 1976, only after the union had proved its viability. The final arrangement was only possible through the transformation of the Iranian and Saudi Arabian roles in the Gulf, which came about after several years of debate since 1968. Both Iran and Saudi Arabia had to grapple with the problem of nationalism in determining their stances towards the new union. King Faisal in Saudi Arabia had to determine whether giving up his territorial claims to parts of Abu Dhabi outweighed the risk of being seen as a contributor to the failure of the union. For the Shah, he had to consider whether he could risk giving up some of Iran's claims to islands in the Persian Gulf, including Bahrain, in exchange for financial support from Western powers, which he could use to strengthen his own military. In the end, both Saudi Arabia and Iran determined that it was in their best interests to cooperate with one another and support the union.

This chapter examines the evolution of the security policies that underpinned the creation of the United Arab Emirates in 1971. It begins with a review of the British military presence in the Gulf prior to withdrawal and particularly focuses on the creation and jurisdiction of the most important security force in the Trucial States during the time: the Trucial Oman Scouts. There follows a look at the tensions between the Foreign Office, which desired a quick solution for the establishment of a local security force on the one hand, and the local rulers' hesitation to link its security forces directly to a British institution on the other.

The Foreign Office plan consisted of reconstituting the Trucial Oman Scouts as the cornerstone of the new union's defence forces. From the perspectives of the Trucial Sheikhs, and especially that of Sheikh Zayed in Abu Dhabi, such an initiative would undermine the very security the new state sought. It would invite criticism from the very Arab states whose support the union would need if it were going to be viewed as a legitimate, independent, Arab nation. Finally, the chapter traces Iran and Saudi Arabia's shift from rivals for influence in the Gulf to partners to co-guarantors of Gulf stability.

The British military presence in the Arab Gulf

Britain's primary military presence came in the form of the Persian Gulf Squadron (SNOP-G), which formally initiated its patrol of the Gulf in 1821 and maintained a presence there through December 1971. Initially, the squadron focused on patrolling with an eye to protecting British ships and trade, and to enforce the eponymous truces with Gulf leaders. British interests in the security of the Trucial States and the Gulf changed over time, and as they did, so too did the location of the British naval force. The squadron was headquartered initially at Qishm Island before being shifted to Ras al-Jufair at Manama, Bahrain. As long as Britain's chief interests in the Persian Gulf revolved around the stability of its empire in India, the naval squadron served as the main enforcer of British power within the Gulf as well as the chief deterrent to prospective belligerent regional powers.

Two significant changes led to shifts in the way Britain exercised military authority in the Gulf. First, the early discoveries of oil in Kuwait and Bahrain, in 1931 and 1938, and the belief that significant deposits would be found in other emirates created new urgency for the protection of British hegemony in the region, particularly on land. The rise of the airplane as a significant tool of trade and communication between London and British territories East of Suez also served to intensify security concerns on land, where air strips and overnight accommodations required protection.[2]

British officials remained convinced that the security of the Gulf emirates was integral to British economic and geo-strategic interests. Financial contributions from emirati governments paid for the internal infrastructure and social services which the Foreign Office viewed as essential to the Trucial States' security

---

[2] See Stanley-Price, *Imperial Outpost in the Gulf*.

were paid for largely with the royalties they received from their concessionary agreements with the petroleum companies there. Those agreements and payments for exploration were based on the rulers' ability to maintain their legal claims on the territories under exploration. Land-based security accordingly grew in significance in the twentieth century.

Instead of the sea, the borders between the Trucial States, Oman, Saudi Arabia and Abu Dhabi became the flashpoints. As outlined earlier on, in Chapter 4, the Buraimi Oasis became the most significant site of warfare. When the US-backed Saudi Arabia asserted its claims to what the British considered Abu Dhabi's territory, the Foreign Office formed a local ground-based military force in response. As in the other areas of the Trucial Coast under British protection, the origins of the land-based force were modelled after British units that had served in India. The Trucial Oman Levies, created in 1951, drew soldiers from Omani tribes. Local troops, as historian Tancred Bradshaw has pointed out, were cheaper than deploying soldiers from the British Army.[3] Officers came from Jordan's Arab Legion, and the Levies served under a British commander. Though the force began small, with only sixty-five men, it rapidly increased to more than 500 in 1954.[4] In 1955, the Trucial Oman Levies were reorganized as the Trucial Oman Scouts, an all-voluntary army with officers and senior ranking soldiers from the British army. Though largely manned by non-British soldiers, the Scouts remained a largely non-local force. In 1960, the non-British composition of the Trucial Oman Scouts consisted of approximately 600 soldiers from Muscat and Oman; 450 from the Trucial States and 100 of Pakistani, Adeni, Somali and Baluchi origin.[5] The Scouts continued to expand into the 1960s, incorporating as many as five rifle squadrons, a headquarter squadron and various subsidiary troops to operate services such as a small hospital, training schools and transport. The Trucial Oman Scouts numbered approximately 1,400 in total by the mid-1960s and worked frequently in cooperation with Oman's Armed Forces and elements of the British regulars.[6]

The role of the Trucial Oman Scouts shifted to general internal security after the main crises at Buraimi settled down. To prevent outside forces from making incursions from adjacent states, Scouts squadrons were headquartered

---

[3] Bradshaw, 'The Hand of Glubb', 656.
[4] Tom Walcott, 'The Trucial Oman Scouts, 1955 to1971: An Overview', *Asian Affairs* 37, no. 1 (2006): 17–30, 19.
[5] 'Composition of Trucial Oman Scouts': Minute by J. F. Walker. 25 May 1960. FO 370/149048. TNA.
[6] Walcot, 'The Trucial Oman Scouts, 1955–1971', 19–20.

at Sharjah, Manama in Bahrain, at a fort in Buraimi, and eventually another at Mirfa near the Tarif oil field in Abu Dhabi.[7] They also included a coastal patrol, which inspected sea vessels that might carry arms smuggled from Saudi Arabia and Qatar into the Omani frontier. Internally, the force could deploy at times of public unrest, labour unrest and in circumstances where tribal or community strife broke out.

All combined, the Scouts formed the bulk of the military force on land in the Trucial States. It provided internal protection and coordinated with local tribal forces and, eventually, local police forces and defence forces. But it also served as a deterrent to any outside powers – not only because of its size but also because it carried the might of the British Empire behind it.

Local and imperial forces

Britain's presence as a military power and protector created tension within the Trucial States from the beginning. Britain's treaty relations with the local rulers gave Britain extensive rights in the foreign affairs of the Arab Gulf states, but their ability to operate within the Trucial States' territories was limited, at least in theory. They could do so only with the express permission of the local rulers. The Trucial Oman Scouts, though providing a valuable service to the rulers in terms of boundary disputes and general policing efforts, could also provide a point of contention between the Political Resident and the individual rulers, particularly in the past fifteen years of the Special Treaty relationship. By then, the spread of Arab nationalism had emboldened the rulers in their desire to demonstrate sovereignty and independent strength in light of Britain's forthcoming withdrawal. After 1968, the question was What would the future role of the Trucial Oman Scouts be? And how would the rulers manage to police and defend their emirates? The solution would require the Resident to give in to the rulers' demands to build up their own forces and a plan for eliminating the Scouts altogether.

For much of their existence, the Scouts maintained a cordial and cooperative relationship with the rulers. In 1956, the Scouts successfully defended Abu Dhabi's and Oman's claims to Buraimi against Saudi forces. As a local police force, the Scouts were sufficiently welcome in Dubai, leading Sheikh Rashid

---

[7] 'Trucial Oman Scouts: Legal Framework of T.O.S': Minute by the Foreign Office, 8 July 1959. FO 371/140184. TNA.

to offer to finance the expansion of the Scouts' police branch in 1962.[8] Until the mid- to late-1960s, the emirates each had small, and largely inexperienced, local forces. By 1967, Dubai could boast of 300 men, but Sharjah only had 57. Fujairah, Umm Al Quwain and Ajman only first began training small police forces in 1968–9, with support from Abu Dhabi.[9] The Scouts, for most of their existence, served the interests of both the rulers and the Resident.

Things were not always entirely peaceful between the rulers and the Scouts. The Scouts' exercise of power could create difficult and potentially explosive situations between the British Residency and the rulers. At the most basic level, conflicts arose out of questions surrounding the jurisdiction and divisions of labour between the rulers' personal forces and those of the Trucial Oman Scouts. These kinds of questions arose most often in relation to the potential traffic accidents and crime in the Buraimi Oasis but could also arise in more acute criminal instances.[10] In one such incident, the Scouts had arrested an Adeni man accused of murder. Edward Henderson, the Political Agent in Abu Dhabi, determined that the man was likely mentally unstable and unfit to plea and wished to send him to an asylum. This required the cooperation of Sheikh Shakhbut, who guarded the exercise of his sovereignty in these matters carefully.[11] If not handled delicately, though, particularly explosive clashes had the potential to create a rift between a ruler and the British government. During a checkpoint exercise, Scouts stopped a vehicle, removed a passenger and proceeded to hold him at gun point as they searched the vehicle and his person. The passenger turned out to be Sheikh Rashid Al Nuaimi, the ruler of Ajman. Donald Hawley, the agent at Dubai, reflected in a letter to the Resident that such incidents were dangerous for Britain's position in the Gulf:

> I am disturbed that, when our whole position in the Trucial States depends on our treaties with the Rulers, some of the officers are adopting so narrowly military an approach that incidents like this one are even possible It is fortunately unprecedented; this sort of incident, however, especially, if it were to be repeated

[8] Letter from M. Man (Political Resident, Bahrain) to A. R. Walmsley (Arabian Department, FO). 10 March 1962. FO 371/163045. TNA.
[9] 'Trucial States Intelligence Report No. 024', 26 June 1967. FCO 8/901. TNA.; 'Extracts from Mr. L. A. Hicks, Deputy Overseas Police Adviser, Foreign Office/Commonwealth Office's Report of Visit to Bahrain, Qatar and the Trucial States', FO 8/905 TNA; 'Abu Dhabi and Fujairah', Letter from J. L. Bullard (Political Agent, Dubai) to M. S. Weir (Political Resident, Bahrain), 3 June 1969. FCO 8/1218. TNA.
[10] Letter, E. F. Henderson (Dubai, Political Agent) to M. C. Man (Bahrain, Political Resident). 9 April 1960. FO 371/149049. TNA. As it still is today, traffic accidents in the emirates were a regular subject of debate.
[11] Minute, E. F. Henderson (Political Agent, Dubai) to J. A. Ford (Political Residency, Bahrain). 22 November 1960. FO 371/149053. TNA.

in Abu Dhabi, is likely to lead to a shortening of our period of tenure in the Trucial States.[12]

Sincere apologies to Sheikh Rashid from the Scouts' commander and Hawley quickly followed.

The underlying tension that defined the relationship between the rulers and the Scouts became more fraught as Arab nationalism edged into the Gulf, and intensified further once the British announced their withdrawal. A growing awareness in the Trucial States of the political and ideological changes in the larger Arab world since the 1930s shaped political decision making and security decisions. Initially, its influence was subtle and precautionary; by the 1960s, Arab nationalism defined many security decisions, just as it had in diplomacy and development.

Gulf Residents and agents sought to cast the Trucial Oman Scouts as locally administered, rather than imposed from outside. They implored the Foreign Office to support training Arab officers in Britain to this end. As a 'matter of some political importance', Hawley in Dubai pressed for the Arabization and localization of the Scouts, rather than relying on British personnel to lead.[13] Morgan Man, acting as Political Resident, supported this and wrote to the Foreign Office that 'it has all along been our thesis that we should try to build up the [Scouts] as a local force capable of winning the loyalty of the inhabitants of the Trucial States'.[14] As the decade wore on, the perceived need for a reframing of the Scouts intensified among British policymakers. The war in Yemen, and the British defeat at Aden, seemed to confirm the fears that nationalism indeed posed a security threat to the British position in the Trucial States. The forthcoming withdrawal compounded the sense of urgency.

Among themselves, British officials were candid about the complications stemming from the Scouts' British origins and command. Julian Bullard noted from Dubai that a continued military presence through the Trucial Oman Scouts would be 'the only conspicuous British legacy after 150 years as the paramount power in the Trucial States'.[15] Despite this, he and others in the Residency

---

[12] 'Complaint by Ruler of Ajman that he was held up at gunpoint, by a party of TOS, during an exercise on August 24': Minute by D. F. Hawley (Political Agent, Dubai) to G. H. Middleton (Political Resident, Bahrain). 5 September 1960. FO 371/149051. TNA.

[13] Letter from Morgen Man (Political Resident, Bahrain) to R. A. Beaumont (Foreign Office). 28 June 1960. FO 371/149049. TNA.

[14] Letter from Morgen Man (Political Resident, Bahrain) to R. A. Beaumont (Foreign Office). 28 June 1960. FO 371/149049. TNA.

[15] 'British Economic Aid to the Trucial States': Letter from Bullard (Political Agent, Dubai) to Weir (Political Resident, Bahrain). 3 June 1969. FCO 8/1218. TNA.

believed the Scouts would be the best hope for preserving security in the Trucial States and sustaining British influence after British withdrawal.

To study the problem, the Foreign Office sent Major General John Willoughby, a senior British army officer who had served in Aden, to the Trucial Coast to formulate a plan. He completed his report in 1969 with suggestions that, to the Foreign Office, seemed satisfactory. This new formula would fold the Trucial Oman Scouts into a new UDF. Drawing on the original Scouts, the UDF would also include an eighteen-plane air force and twelve patrol boats for a naval branch.[16] To the Foreign Office, this plan provided a quick and efficient solution. It would form a nascent military capable of providing a deterrent to external aggressors and shore up internal policing. It would have a new name and a new form. The problem remained, however, that the Scouts would serve as a core battalion and senior British officers in the Scouts would make up senior personnel in the new force in this new iteration.[17]

The local rulers were concerned about the contradictions the Scouts would present should they be the core of the new federation's defence after 1971. Several of them tried to present alternative possibilities. Sheikh Isa of Bahrain deftly declined the Resident's offer to extend the tenure of the Trucial Oman Scouts. He acknowledged the 'most welcome' support of a British military presence but explained that such an arrangement would be difficult in the face of local and general Arab opinion.[18] So conscious of this were Bahraini rulers that they refused to openly acknowledge security arrangements with both Great Britain and, later, the United States well into the 1980s. It exposed them to criticism from other Arab rulers for their connections with Western powers.[19]

Sheikh Zayed initially viewed the Willoughby Report as entirely unacceptable. The ruler of Abu Dhabi insisted that the Trucial Oman Scouts should not be seen as a core component of the UDF. Doing so, he explained to Agent Bullard, would 'involve the Union force, in its first stages in being too closely associated with British military institutions and that use of TOS facilities could attract political criticism from other Arab countries ... and so compromise the political future of the Union'.[20] Instead, the union itself should create the first battalion

---

[16] Phillip Darby, 'Beyond East of Suez', *International Affairs* 46, no. 4 (1970): 660.
[17] Attachment to 'The Union Defence Force and the TOS': Letter from Stewart Crawford (Political Resident, Bahrain) to Julian Bullard (Political Agent, Dubai). 28 April 1969. FCO 8/983. TNA.
[18] 'Bahrain and the British Military Withdrawal': Letter from A. J. D. Stirling (Political Agent, Bahrain) to Stewart Crawford (Political Resident, Bahrain), n.d. FCO 8/979. TNA.
[19] Anthony Cordesman, *Bahrain, Oman, Qatar, and the UAE: The Challenges of Security* (New York: Perseus, 1997), 38. Anthony Cordesman, *The Gulf and the Search for Strategic Stability* (Boulder, CO: Westview Press, 1986), especially 59–61.
[20] 'Points to be Made Concerning HMG's Attitude towards Union Defence Force and TOS', Stewart Crawford (Political Resident, Bahrain). 28 April 1969. FCO 8/983. TNA.

using only Trucial resources, giving it the outward appearance of being 'wholly independent of Britain'.[21]

Stewart Crawford and the Foreign Office could not endorse Zayed's suggestion. Rather, they would draw personnel from the Scouts, diminish the Scouts' strength and leave the union unprotected at a time when a military force would be necessary to defend the emerging union. Moreover, Crawford contradicted the internal discussions and urged Julian Bullard to refute Zayed's view of the Scouts as a foreign institution. A decade of Arabization, he said, had increased the numbers of non-commissioned and commissioned officers from the Trucial States. The Trucial States had also shared the administrative and financial burden of the Trucial Oman Scouts, and that the Commandant of the Scouts reported to the Trucial Council, which had been chaired by the rulers since 1958. All this, he wrote, made them a 'local force'.[22]

Zayed was not convinced. Arab nationalism continued to hang over the formation of the emirates and was a greater immediate threat to the union than other potential adversaries. If the union did not create a military force, seen as a legitimate 'native growth' at least in the beginning, then the future union would be at risk of being seen as illegitimate in the eyes of other Arab states. In a meeting with the British Secretary of State in May 1969, Zayed again insisted that the union build its first battalion with its own resources.[23] He continued to press this point for several months, proposing that the UDF's first battalion should combine forces from Bahrain, Qatar and Abu Dhabi, in order to demonstrate unity and strength in the formation of the union. Subsequent battalions could then absorb the TOS without attracting criticism from other Arab states.[24] Zayed's concerns extended beyond just the UDF. He pressed Jim Treadwell, the Political Agent at Abu Dhabi at the time, on the issue of Arabizing officers in the Air Force. Reporting back to the Resident, Treadwell indicated that Zayed was

---

[21] 'Points to be Made Concerning HMG's Attitude towards Union Defence Force and TOS', Stewart Crawford (Political Resident, Bahrain). 28 April 1969. FCO 8/983. TNA.
[22] Ibid.
[23] Telegram, Crawford (Political Resident, Bahrain) to FCO. 6 May 1969. FCO 8/983. TNA; Athol Yates, 'Western Expatriates in the UAE Armed Forces, 1964–2015', *Journal of Arabian Studies* 6, no. 2 (2016): 182–200 indicates the importance Zayed stressed on excluding Western expatriates from specific kinds of roles in the Abu Dhabi Defence Force for the same reasons. It was easier to excuse seconded or contracted British officers as temporary than to explain why the commanding officers of a local force were not from Abu Dhabi.
[24] 'Points to be made concerning HMG's Attitude Towards Union Defense Force and TOS', Stewart Crawford (Political Resident, Bahrain) 28 April 1969. FCO 8/983. TNA.

'bothered that his image might become tarnished in Arab eyes if all the Air Force officers were British' and pressed for training Arab pilots.[25]

The lead-up to British withdrawal and the creation of a union generated significant debates over the future of local forces and Scouts. At the heart of it was the question of how other Arab states and the local population would view a British officered force which could provide continued protection. British policymakers acknowledged the inherent contradiction among themselves but focused on the pragmatic need for something to be in place by the end of 1971. They pressed for a superficial re-casting of the Trucial Oman Scouts as a local institution, which could bridge the gap between British withdrawal and the formation of local institutions. This would also have the advantage of preserving British influence in the Gulf through a military presence, for which the British government would not have to pay. The rulers, however, saw danger in this scheme. The union's stability and future success depended on the union and its new institutions being perceived as independent and unfettered by imperial British trappings.

From aggressors to 'twin pillars'

A solution to this dilemma remained elusive until a larger security issue could be resolved. The two dominant regional powers in the Gulf, Saudi Arabia and Iran, each aspired to greater heights of influence and military strength. They also both played important roles in the global security strategies of not only Britain but also the United States. The interests of all parties needed to be met if the future union were to succeed. King Faisal of Saudi Arabia and Muhammad Reza of Iran each made claims to territories the rulers on the Trucial Coast claimed for themselves. And the United States, alarmed at Britain's withdrawal, required a security strategy that would ensure stability, continued oil supply and protection against Soviet influence. The solution that emerged from the negotiations between Britain, the United States, Saudi Arabia and Iran became known as the 'twin pillars' strategy. The two regional rivals became partners in a new arrangement that marked the decline of British power in the Gulf and set the stage for America's ascent to guarantor of regional stability.

---

[25] 'ADDF', C. J. Treadwell (Political Agent, Abu Dhabi) to M. S. Weir (Arabian Department, Foreign Office). 27 September 1969. FCO 8/1242. TNA.

Anglo-American cooperation in the Gulf originated with the realignment of global security during the Cold War. Britain's long history in the Middle East and Gulf made it the obvious Western power to direct and defend security arrangements. In 1955, the Baghdad Pact enshrined this role with the creation of a defensive organization that would respond to and prevent incursions from the Soviet Union into the Gulf and Middle East. The original signatories included Iran, Iraq, Turkey, Pakistan and Great Britain, though Iraq pulled out of the agreement following a military coup in 1959. At that time, the organization became the Central Treaty Organization (CENTO). The defence agreement rested on British forces in Aden, and later in Bahrain and Sharjah. When the Cold War shifted to the Far East and Pacific, the United States and Australia both pressed Britain to maintain its naval presence in the Gulf as a key staging ground for naval operations and patrols in support of CENTO.[26]

The United States had begun expanding its influence in the Gulf through its ties with Saudi Arabia and Iran. Saudi Arabia and the United States had shared a close economic and diplomatic relationship almost since the monarchy's inception. The Saudi state, which was formed in the wake of the First World War, sold oil exploration rights to an American company, which came to be known as the Arabian American Oil Company (ARAMCO). Oil exploration there began in 1933 and oil was discovered in 1938. The American economic and political investment in ARAMCO and the development of the Saudi oil company created extensive links between the two governments in terms of diplomacy, technical and economic advising, and security.[27] Ties between the American government and that of the Shah in Iran had a shorter history but no less significant. The American CIA helped finance and orchestrate the overthrow of nationalist prime minister Mohammed Mosaddeq in 1953 following his nationalization of the Anglo-Iranian Oil Company. This allowed the Shah to return from exile and restore his dynasty to the throne. The United States, in the midst of the Cold War, continued to court Iran in order to maintain a friendly buffer state between the Gulf and the Soviet Union. Following the coup, Dwight Eisenhower and

---

[26] 'Defence Policy: Minutes of a Meeting of Service chiefs and senior Officials at Chequers on Britain's Three Defence Roles'. 21 November 1964. CAB 130/213 MISC 17/1. *BDEEP—East of Suez*, #3; 'British Policy towards South-East Asia': Memorandum by Gordon Walk for Cabinet Defence and Overseas Policy Committee. 19 November 1964, CAB 148/17, OPD(64)10, *BDEEP—East of Suez*, #89.

[27] Robert Vitalis, *America's Kingdom: Mythmaking on the Saudi Oil Frontier* (Stanford, CA: Stanford University Press, 2007); Steven M. Wright, 'US Foreign Policy and the Changed Definition of Gulf Security', in *Reform in the Middle East Oil Monarchies*, ed. Anoushiraven Esteshami and Steven Wright (Reading: Ithaca Press, 2007), 229–46.

succeeding presidents provided considerable economic and military aid as well as technical advisors for development.[28]

The economic crises of the 1960s forced the British government to take a hard look at its military expenditures globally. British defence expenses had grown to more than 10 per cent of the national budget to fulfil its post-war international defence obligations, including CENTO, stationing troops in Europe as part of the North Atlantic Treaty Organization (NATO) and the development of a nuclear weapons programme.[29] The Macmillan government (1957–63) had considered dramatic cuts in British military forces East of Suez, including propositions to reduce British troop numbers to avoid an economic collapse. Succeeding governments, both Conservative and Labour, continued to deliberate over the economic crisis and costs of sustaining a military presence in the Gulf. They raised possibility of cuts with the Americans several times over the next few years but consistently received pushback. The United States would not help shoulder the military burden in the region and Britain, they argued, had the necessary special relationships with local rulers to ensure stability.[30] As sterling reserves continued to fall through 1967, the Labour government took matters into their own hands and announced their plan to withdraw in January 1968. Sir Patrick Dean, the British ambassador to the United States, reported back to the FCO that the Americans had responded with 'astonishment' at the decision to leave an area 'where our economic stake (and incidentally their own), was so large, our political relations with the rulers apparently peaceful and the military costs so relatively modest'.[31] The unthinkable had happened.

A federation of the smaller states appeared to provide the best solution in the minds of many policymakers. Such an arrangement would allow the states to pool resources for development and establish a collective security arrangement. To bring this about would require the cooperation of the Saudi and Iranian governments and a careful balance of their regional ambitions to resolve outstanding conflicts. For Saudi Arabia, the union's formation required the inclusion of both Bahrain and Qatar in order to balance the strength of Zayed's position as an economic power in the union. Iran required recognition of its

---

[28] Nikki R. Keddie, *Modern Iran: Roots and Results of Revolution* (New Haven, CT: Yale University Press, 2003); Mark J. Gasiorowski, *U.S. Foreign Policy and the Shah: Building a Client State in* Iran (Ithaca, NY: Cornell University Press, 1991); William Roger Louis and James A. Bill, eds. *Musaddiq, Iranian Nationalism, and Oil* (New York: I.B. Tauris, 1988).
[29] Drokill, *Britain's Retreat from East of Suez*, 43–75.
[30] Telegram, Cottam (US Ambassador to Kuwait) to Secretary of State, 'Re:EMBTEL 296', 6 January 1964; NSF Country File, Middle East Box #149, Kuwait: Cables and Memos, LBJL.
[31] 'United States Reactions to our Withdrawal from East of Suez': Dispatch from Sir P. Dean (Washington) to Mr. Brown. 4 March 1968, FCO 24/102, no. 319. *BDEEP—East of Suez*, #35.

claims to Bahrain and the Gulf islands, which Sharjah and Ras Al Khaimah held. These two regional powers and the danger they presented for the future union's existence, and for continued British influence after withdrawal, loomed over federation talks. The future of the union depended on gaining recognition and support from both Saudi Arabia and Iran – which was only granted in late 1971.

British policymakers knew before Harold Wilson's announcement in 1968 that future Gulf security arrangements would depend on the cooperation of Saudi Arabia and Iran. Only a year earlier, in a prospective note on Britain's future policy in the Gulf, the Foreign Office acknowledged that no future union could succeed without cooperation from those two powers. Summarizing the potential consequences for a union, the Foreign Office reported to the Cabinet that a future union among the Trucial States, in whatever form, would:

> depend on its chances of success on the Saudis and Iranians developing a minimum understanding both towards ourselves and each other. Saudi Arabia and Iran are the two powers most directly concerned in the future of the Protected States; they are also the two best placed to bring force to bear in the area, the Saudis by virtue of their commanding geographical position and the Iranians through their growing naval supremacy in the Gulf. If they were at loggerheads with each other, local stability would be unlikely to survive our departure. Conversely, if they were to act in concert, or at least with mutual understanding, they could do much to ensure a peaceful transition to whatever new system follows our withdrawal. It will therefore be essential for us to secure Saudi cooperation and at least Iranian acquiescence as our policy evolves; and to bring home to them how important their relations with each other are going to be, for their own interest as well as for ours and our present protégés.[32]

The entire future of the Trucial Coast rested on the cooperation of two rivals for regional supremacy.

The Trucial sheikhs recognized the potential danger of either state becoming too powerful along the Trucial Coast. Just days after Wilson's announcement a British intelligence officer from the Scouts reported back that the rulers had indicated that 'under no circumstances' would they accept Iran in a role as Britain's replacement. Saudi Arabia would be less unacceptable but not desirable.[33] Both the Shah and the King could run roughshod over the sovereignty of the Trucial sheikhs. The United States seemed a more obvious, and ideal, successor to British presence. Despite being approached by rulers from the region, though, the

---

[32] 'Long-Term Policy in the Persian Gulf': Note by the Foreign Office. 18 April 1967. CAB 148/57. TNA.
[33] 'Trucial States Intelligence Report No. 2 of 17 January 1968'. FCO 9/901. TNA.

United States remained steadfast in its view that it could not take on a security role in the Gulf.[34] Harried by the escalating war in Vietnam and its other global security concerns, the Johnson administration had no wish to become directly involved in state formation and security in the Gulf. Instead, they sought to leave that responsibility with the British government.

Because of the United States' influence with Iran and Saudi Arabia, Britain remained in close contact with the American State Department on two major points of regional conflict in the federation plans. Britain and the United States worked in concert over the next several years to secure agreement between Saudi Arabia and Iran. The first component of post-withdrawal security required both countries to accept a federation of the emirates, not only in principle but also in reality. Both the king and the Shah indicated early on that they were amenable to, and even supportive of, the creation of a federation, but both also indicated that their support for a union came with conditions.

Faisal still laid claim to territory that the British and Sheikh Zayed believed belonged to Abu Dhabi and he did not trust Saudi Arabia to honour the disputed boundary lines in eastern Abu Dhabi. The Buraimi dispute was no longer active, but it had not been fully resolved, either. Sheikh Zayed and King Faisal negotiated through British policymakers to little avail. No substantial agreements had come from discussions except to establish a neutral zone near Buraimi that limited Abu Dhabi's ability to drill for oil there. From 1966 onward, the situation remained in a kind of stasis.

Once the British withdrawal became an imminent reality, King Faisal initiated new efforts to resolve the boundary questions. In 1970 he invited Sheikh Zayed to Saudi Arabia to open direct discussions on several issues, including Buraimi. Faisal demanded that the Abu Dhabi Petroleum Company end all drilling near Zarrara, an area within the disputed territories, which Saudi Arabia claimed but which Britain recognized as unquestionably Abu Dhabi's own territory.[35] Those talks ended without the rulers reaching any satisfactory compromise. Faisal continued to press the issue with the British Foreign Office, though. During a meeting with the British ambassador and Under-Secretary for Foreign Affairs, he complained that Zayed was still drilling in the neutral zone. When Ambassador Morris suggested Faisal give up the boundary dispute for the sake

---

[34] US/Kuwaiti Relations, Memorandum of Conversation, Sheikh Sabah al-Salim al-Sabah, Sheikh Sabah al-Ahmed al-Jabir, Abdul Rahman Salem al-Ateeqi, Talat al-Ghoussein, L. B. J., Howard R. Cottam, Parker T. Hart, Harold Saunders, 11 December 1968. NSF Country File, Middle East, Kuwait: Cables and Memos, LBJL.

[35] J. B. Kelly, *Arabia, the Gulf, and the West: A Critical View of the Arabs and Their Oil Policy* (New York: Basic Books, 1980), 75–7.

of regional stability, Faisal threatened to use force to 'recover the occupied areas' if a satisfactory solution could not be reached.[36]

It took another year before Abu Dhabi and Saudi Arabia's rulers agreed to disagree in perpetuity. At the urging of the Foreign Office, Faisal agreed to give up portions of his claims to the areas around Buraimi in exchange for coastal territory that would give the kingdom access to the lower Gulf. Zayed balked.[37] He could not be seen to cede territory just as he was ascending as the most powerful and influential sheikhs in a forthcoming union. Ultimately, Zayed agreed to pause drilling. With this promise secured, Saudi Arabia withdrew demands for an immediate resolution to the boundary dispute, making it possible for the Foreign Office and Trucial States to concern themselves with negotiations over constitutional aspects of the future union.

Bahrain lay at the epicentre of the disagreement between Saudi Arabia and Iran. The Saudis had supported the creation of a federation on the condition that it include both Bahrain and Qatar, thus improving the chances that Riyadh could pull all nine states into the Saudi sphere of influence. Iran, however, remained openly defiant towards the federation and its inclusion of Bahrain. He reasserted historical claims to the islands of Bahrain, which had fluctuated between Persian rule and that of other regional powers since the seventeenth century until 1783 when the Al Khalifah came to power.[38] Bahrain's status as a separate territory was endorsed in 1820 when Britain signed its first treaty with the Al Khalifah. Iran had frequently asserted that Britain's negotiations with theAl Khalifah were illegitimate. Moreover, Bahrain's boundaries approached the median line of the Gulf in an area where Iran and Saudi Arabia each claimed drilling rights.[39] Tensions between the two states climbed following an incident over the boundary line in February 1968. Iran seized an ARAMCO rig flying a Saudi Arabian flag. It took several meetings mediated by American officials to smooth over the crisis and before Iran and Saudi Arabia could negotiate an agreement on the median line.[40]

---

[36] 'Record of Conversation between the King of Saudi Arabia and the Parliamentary Under-Secretary [Luard] at Riyadh on 4 May 1970', 11 May 1970. FCO 1016/740. TNA.
[37] Kelly, *Arabia, the Gulf, and the West*, 85-7.
[38] Roham Alvandi, 'Muhammad Reza Pahlavi and the Bahrain Question, 1968-1970', *British Journal of Middle East Studies* (2010): 159-77. Steven Wright, 'Iran's Relations with Bahrain', in *Security and Bilateral Issues between Iran and Its Arab Neighbours*, ed. by Gawdar Bahgat, Anoushian Ehteshami and Neil Quilliam (London: Palgrave Macmillan, 2016), 61-80.
[39] Telegram, AmConsul Dhahran (Allen) to State Department, 31 January 1968. NSF Country File, Saudi Arabia #155, Saudi Arabia, Cables, vol. 2, 4/67-1/69. LBJL.
[40] Claudia Castiglioni, 'The Relations between Iran and Saudi Arabia in the 1970s', *Confluences en Méditerranée* 97 (2016): 145; Armin Meyer, *Quiet Diplomacy: From Cairo to Tokyo in the Twilight of Imperialism* (Bloomington: IUniverse, 2003), 149-55.

In discussions with British administrators, the Shah maintained through mid-1970 that he would obstruct any attempts of a union to gain membership in the United Nations if Bahrain were included. The US State Department assessed the Shah's commitment to Bahrain as relatively ambiguous. He seemed unlikely to begin a war over Bahrain, but relinquishing his claim at the behest of the British and Americans was simply too difficult for him domestically.[41]

The Abu Musa and Tunbs islands presented a much more tantalizing, and more strategically valuable, prize. The Shah had used Iran's oil wealth in the 1960s to build up its forces and establish itself as the foremost military power in the Gulf. By 1968, Iran's naval power had expanded to allow it to demonstrate significant regional power in the Gulf. To cement that position and protect its primacy in the Gulf, the Shah required the islands of Abu Musa and the Greater and Lesser Tunbs. Abu Musa, the largest of the three islands, lay on the Arab side of the Median line in the Gulf, near Sharjah, and had a population of approximately 800. The Tunbs islands lay just ten miles off the coast of Iran and were home to approximately 150 persons combined.[42] Taken together, the islands form a triangle in the Strait of Hormuz. Control of the islands translates to control of traffic in and out of the Gulf. Ras Al Khaimah and Sharjah both claimed those islands for themselves, and Britain's treaty relations with the Trucial States committed Britain to protect the emirates' territorial integrity. This deterred previous Persian governments from taking charge of the islands (see Map 7.1).

The island dispute was perhaps the most potentially explosive issue in the creation of the federation. Britain viewed the islands as 'intrinsically worthless', but the Arab states with claims to them were unwilling to give them up.[43] To do so would appear as a sign of weakness and could be construed by other states as a sign that Western powers were constructing a federation for their own interests. More pressing, and more concretely, though, Sheikh Saqr of Ras Al Khaimah hoped that an oil discovery on the Tunbs could bring him greater influence among the Trucial States and shift the balance even slightly from Zayed's substantial oil wealth. In 1968, though, the Shah stated that he would withhold his support for the union unless the island disputes were settled.

---

[41] Telegram, Dean Rusk to Amembassy Iran, 'Shah-Secretary June 12 Talk on Persian Gulf', 12 June 1968. NSF Country File, Middle East #137, Iran, Visit of Shah of Iran, 6/11-12-68. LBJL.
[42] Richard A. Mobley, 'The Tunbs and Abu Musa Islands: Britain's Perspective', *Middle East Journal* 57, no. 4 (2003): 628.
[43] Mobley, 'Tunbs and Abu Musa Islands', 627–45.

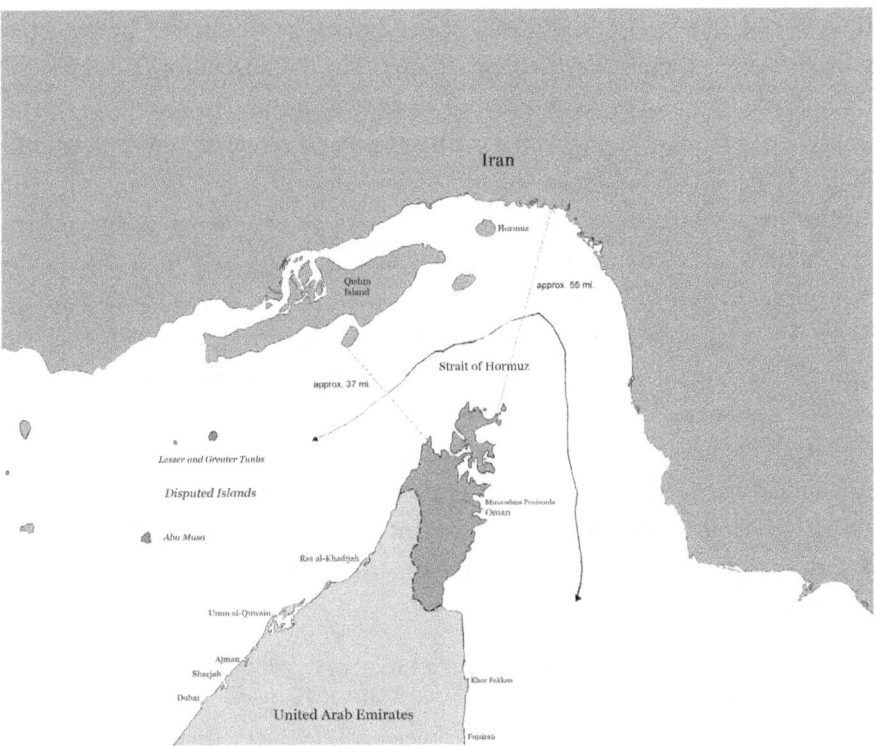

Map 7.1 Map of the Strait of Hormuz.

The Johnson administration, though preferring to leave the details of the new federation to the Foreign Office, was in a strong position to exercise influence over Iran. American-Iranian relations, though rocky in the early 1960s, improved in the late Johnson administration, particularly as Iran benefited from American military aid.[44] Summarizing the visit of Prime Minister Amir Abbas Hoveyda in December 1968, the State Department described the relationship as 'close and cooperative' and judged that they could use this to negotiate some kind of solution if Britain could not.[45] As negotiations wore on, the Shah remained inflexible over the question of the islands. Both Western powers agreed that it would be possible for the Shah to give up claims to Bahrain if he could 'save face' by gaining British support for

---

[44] Andrew L. Johns, 'The Johnson Administration, the Shah of Iran and the Changing Pattern of US-Iranian Relations, 1965–1967: "Tired of Being Treated Like a Schoolboy"', *Journal of Cold War Studies* 9, no. 2 (2007): 64–94.

[45] 'Visit of Amir Abbas Hoveyda, Prime Minister of Iran, 5–6 December 1968, Scope Paper', NSF Country File, Middle East, #138, Iran, Visit of PM Hoveyda of Iran 12/5-6/68. LBJL.

Iran's taking of the Tunbs and Abu Musa islands in exchange.[46] Rather than push directly for a quick settlement, though, the State Department proposed a compromise strategy for the British to present to the Shah and the rulers. In exchange for agreement on the median line, and relinquishing his claim to Bahrain, the Shah would take the mid-Gulf Islands.[47]

The situation remained at a stalemate until finally, in 1971, the British government in conjunction with the American government came to an agreement on how to hand over the islands and end the dispute over Bahrain. The exact details of the arrangement, if there were one, are not available at the time of this writing, due to the sensitive nature of the dispute, which remains a political flash point to this day. However, there are indications in the British and American archives that as the British withdrawal neared, the United States and Britain had accepted as a given that Iran would occupy the islands. In March of 1971, Alec Douglas-Home wrote to the British ambassador at Jeddah. In it, he described a plan suggested to him by the American ambassador to Iran, Douglas MacArthur II. He suggested that

> An Iranian civil presence, perhaps of a technical or developmental kind, should be introduced onto the islands before British military withdrawal (with no more than formal protests from the rulers concerned), in return for withdrawal of Iranian objection of a Union, and generous aid and technical assistance for the rulers concerned from Iran ... The Shah had told [MacArthur] he had assurances from Saudi Arabia, Bahrain, Abu Dhabi and Dubai that they would not ... make trouble over Iranian possession of the islands.[48]

By this time, the United States' administration had changed from Lyndon Johnson to Richard Nixon, and the American government remained just as committed to staying out of the Gulf, though W. Taylor Fain has argued that this had less to do with policy and more to do with the fact that Nixon and Kissinger considered the Gulf a 'backwater'.[49] The State Department and Kissinger also continued to think along the same lines as their predecessors – the United States' influence would be less effective than the British in dealing with most of the

---

[46] Telegram, Meyer to Secretary of State. 15 March 1968. NSF Country File Middle East, #136, Iran Cables vol. 2, 1-66-1/69. LBJL.

[47] 'Persian Gulf', Telegram, Meyer to Secretary of State, 18 May 1968. NSF Country File, Middle East, #136, Iran Cables, vol. 2, 1/66-1/69. LBJL; 'Bahrain', Telegram, Secretary of State to Amembassy Tehran, 2 August 1968. NSF Country File, Middle East, #136, Iran Cables, vol. 2, 1/66-1/69. LBJL.

[48] 'The Gulf Islands and the Union of Arab Emirates': Telegram, Douglas-Home to Morris (Ambassador to Jeddah), 19 March 1971. FCO 8/15554. TNA.

[49] W. Taylor Fain, *American Ascendance and British Retreat in the Persian Gulf Region* (New York: Palgrave Macmillan, 2008), 182.

rulers there.⁵⁰ They were also committed to seeing the British broker a deal that would satisfy the Shah and help stabilise the Gulf in the wake of the withdrawal.

A package solution proved feasible. Iran agreed to a UN-administered plebiscite for Bahrain. Faisal bin Salman al-Saud discusses the origins of this agreement in a footnote, referencing Sir Denis Wright's unpublished memoir. There he notes that while there is some confusion in oral accounts, the archives seem to indicate that the British government proposed this arrangement to the Shah. A popular vote would provide the Shah a way out of sustaining his claim to Bahrain and would neatly resolve the issue.⁵¹ In April 1970, the UN mission submitted its report stating that Bahrainis chose independence over joining Iran. The following year, Bahrain became an independent nation and Britain abrogated its special treaty relations on 14 August 1971.

The islands were all that remained to be settled with Iran. Britain warned the rulers of Sharjah and Ras Al Khaimah that without an agreement between them and Iran before the withdrawal date, they would be on their own to defend their claims. Sharjah relinquished its claims in exchange for an agreement that would allow Sharjah and Umm Al Quwain to receive a sum of money and percentage of profits if oil were discovered. Sharjah did receive regular payments until oil was found in 1972, at which time, Sharjah and Umm Al Quwain received shares of the profits as agreed.⁵² Sheikh Saqr of Ras Al Khaimah, however, continued to hope that he would find oil before the union went into effect, providing him greater influence in the future union, and ensure international support for his continued rule over the islands.

On November 30, only two days before Britain ended its treaties with the Trucial States, Iran occupied the Tunbs and Abu Musa by force. Britain took no action to re-secure the islands, instead leaving Ras Al Khaimah to choose its own course of action. Saqr refused to join the union in protest against Iran's actions and Britain's inaction. He finally accepted membership in the union in February 1972.

For Britain, Iran's seizing of the islands was a small price to pay for Iran's cooperation in the security of the United Arab Emirates and the Persian Gulf. Iran would become one of the two pillars in Nixon's 'twin pillar' strategy from 1971 until the Iranian Revolution in 1978. This strategy was an elaboration on the Nixon Doctrine, expressing the view that the United States would supply

---

⁵⁰ Fain, *American Ascendance and British Retreat*, 187.
⁵¹ Faisal bin Salman al-Saud, *Iran, Saudi Arabia, and the Gulf: Power Politics in Transition* (London: I. B. Tauris, 2003), 146.
⁵² Cordesman, *Gulf and the Search for Strategic Stability*, 417.

regional allies with aid and weapons, rather than troops. This policy, announced in 1969, had encouraged both Saudi Arabia and Iran to participate in a regional security framework of shared influence. In practice, Claudia Castiglioni has argued, the United States viewed Iran as the greater of the two pillars and the only one capable of real potential to secure the Gulf.[53]

Britain's withdrawal proved somewhat incomplete. For several years afterward, British officers would be seconded to the UDF. Britain continued to provide training and advisors for years to come. But most of the security responsibilities of the region had shifted to regional powers. The twin pillars policy was meant to allow the United States and their British allies to meet their foreign policy goals, securing the region and access to oil, with as little involvement as possible. Steve Yetiv has argued that for the first years this seemed promising.[54] The United States relied on Iran as a balance to the threat of Iraq, which was viewed as an extension of Soviet influence that might threaten the Gulf. Iran would provide the enforcement role, while Saudi Arabia would provide the financial and diplomatic support. The seeds for this cooperation had been planted in the Johnson administration, which had courted the Shah, and which had encouraged cooperation between Iran's International Petro Asmari Co (IPAC) and Saudi Arabia's ARAMCO.[55] As the decade wore on, however, the cooperative relationship experienced tension. The United States continued to balance the rival powers against one another, but this grew increasingly difficult as the internal politics of Iran raised significant concerns about the Shah's effectiveness as an ally. The United States had begun supplying Iran with greater quantities of weapons to bolster its role in the Gulf, but the Shah proved impervious to advice in areas of domestic politics and human rights.[56] American concerns proved prescient when in 1979 the Shah was overthrown. The relationship between the United States and the new Iranian government proved unworkable within the year. The responsibility of Gulf security increasingly fell on to the Saudis after 1979, but that government was unable to take on responsibility for the Gulf because it faced its own internal divisions. The Soviet invasion of Afghanistan in December 1979 sealed American resolve to increase its presence in the Gulf.

---

[53] Castiglioni, 'The Relations between Iran and Saudi Arabia in the 1970s', 145–6.
[54] Steve A. Yetiv, *The Absence of Grand Strategy: The United States in the Persian Gulf, 1972-2005* (Baltimore, MD: Johns Hopkins University Press, 2008), 13.
[55] Mohammed Ayoob, 'American Policy toward the Persian Gulf', in *The International Politics in the Persian Gulf*, ed. Mehran Kamrava (New York: Syracuse University Press, 2011), 124–6; Meyer, *Quiet Diplomacy*, 137, 149–58.
[56] Yetiv, *Absence of Grand Strategy*, 36–7.

Through the 1980s, the United States began building up the bases that the British had abandoned only a few short years before.[57]

By that time fears of an Arab nationalist threat to the newly formed union had faded. The Trucial rulers, especially Zayed and Rashid, navigated the decolonization process effectively, balancing Arab opinion with their own interests. Arab losses to Israel in the 1967 War had weakened Nasser's influence, and the disillusionment with pan-Arab ideologies had begun to set in after Nasser's death in 1970. Moreover, the United Arab Emirates demonstrated credible support for the Arab world during the oil embargo following the 1973 Egypt-Israel war.

---

[57] Ayoob, 'American Policy toward the Persian Gulf', 120–43.

Conclusion: Departing from or returning to old patterns

The federation of seven small emirates as the United Arab Emirates has proved surprisingly durable given the pessimism with which British policymakers viewed its formation in 1971. Within two months, the original federation of six had gained its seventh member (Ras Al Khaimah). Nearly two years later, the UAE participated in an international oil embargo which would shake the global economy to its core. The twin pillars security strategy crumbled a few years later when Iranians forced out the Shah and ushered in a new Iranian Republic. The three decades that followed witnessed three regional wars. An Arab Uprising shook most of the Middle East in 2010–12, but the Emirates persisted in relative stability. On 2 December 2021, the UAE celebrated fifty years of independence. Over that time, the UAE has actively worked to build and sustain a high level of involvement in regional diplomacy and to use its oil wealth to build networks of influence in the Arab world.

After federation

The first decade following its founding presented a series of international challenges for the new nation. The Arab-Israeli conflict flared when in October 1973 Egypt and Syria coordinated an attack against Israel. They aimed, in part, to take back the Golan Heights and Sinai Peninsula, which Israel had occupied since 1967. By the end of the conflict, Israel had defeated the Arab forces, but not before both Egypt and Syria had proven in their initial offensive press that Israel could not take its own military power for granted. During the war, the United States airlifted military supplies to Israel and continued shipments for nearly a month after the ceasefire was announced on 25 October.

The members of OAPEC, the UAE among them, responded to US operations supporting Israel with an announcement on 17 October that it would cut oil production by 5 per cent. They also initiated an embargo on oil shipments to the United States and other countries that had supported Israel in the war. The embargo lasted for just five months, but it had lasting impacts on the global economy and on UAE's economy. Prices of crude oil per barrel skyrocketed from $3.38 per barrel in September 1973 to $11.10 per barrel in March 1974; prices floated to approximately $13 per barrel in the next year and remained steady until the end of the decade.[1] The UAE had joined with fellow Arab OPEC countries and sustained their cooperation through the crisis and continued to do so when tested in subsequent oil crises.[2]

The decade closed with another crisis that threatened the security of the Gulf and the UAE, which only rolled over into a decade of volatility. The Iranian people overthrew the Pahlavi dynasty at the end of 1978. The twin pillars strategy collapsed as the new Islamic Republic took shape and rejected cooperation with Saudi Arabia for the purposes of supporting Western global strategies. The revolution and war revived Arab Gulf States' fears of an expansionist Iran, which might reassert its historical claims which had hung over the federation talks between the nine states. On 25 May 1981, the UAE along with Saudi Arabia, Bahrain, Qatar, Kuwait and Oman signed the founding charter of the Gulf Cooperation Council (GCC). The GCC expressed a shared purpose of 'coordination, cooperation and integration between [its members] in all fields', emphasizing economic and cultural ties.[3]

The UAE's participation in both the GCC and OAPEC have bolstered the UAE's profile as an international player in regional and global politics. Its cooperation with Western states has also contributed to its endurance. In 1991

---

[1] Jack L. Harvey, 'The 1973 Oil Crisis: One Generation and Counting', *Federal Reserve Bank of Chicago*, Chicago Fed Letter no. 86, October 1994. https://www.chicagofed.org/publications/chicago-fed-letter/1994/october-86#:~:text=The%20U.S.%20monthly%20average%20import,had%20increased%2023%25%20to%20%243.38 (6 November 2023).

[2] Charles Issawi, in his 1978 article, observed that OAPEC countries were 'tested' three times and demonstrated surprising cohesion during a politically and economically tricky period. He subtly questions the overall success of the embargo; it did not force a new US-Israeli reality, and the embargo accelerated international exploration of alternative sources of oil: Charles Issawi, 'The 1973 Oil Crisis and After', *Journal of Post Keynesian Economics* 1, no. 2 (1978–9): 16–18, 21. Other scholars have recently reconsidered the overall success of the 1973 embargo and argue that the OAPEC states adjusted and met many other goals as they assessed their continued participation and possible outcomes during the crisis and after. Rüdiger Graf, 'Making Use of the "Oil Weapon": Western Industrialized Countries and Arab Petropolitics in 1973–74', *Diplomatic History* 36, no. 1 (2012): 185–208.

[3] The Charter of the Gulf Cooperation Council, issued 25 May 1981. Secretariat General of the Gulf Cooperation Council. https://www.gcc-sg.org.

and 2003, the UAE has extended cooperation to the United States in staging operations against Iraq. In the years since its founding, the GCC has become key to preventing the completion of the mythical 'Shi'i crescent', which Western states and Gulf leaders perceive as a threat to the regional status quo.[4] The UAE's strategic need for US military and diplomatic support combined with the emirates' continued close cultural and political ties with the UK suggest the UAE will remain aligned with most of the other Arab Gulf States in its friendship with the United States, Britain and much of Western Europe.

The UAE, the GCC and Arab solidarity

The UAE has persisted in expanding its political and economic footprint in the Arab world since its founding. Zayed affirmed the Arab orientation of the UAE when he opened the first UAE parliament, or *majlis*, in 1972. The GCC charter also explicitly identified itself as an Arab organization, not a Gulf orientation. The member states' coordination was explicitly in service to the 'sublime objectives of the Arab nation' and 'in conformity with the Charter of the League of Nations'.[5] Peter Hellyer has described the UAE's foreign policy, especially as it relates to the Arab states, as consistent in its approach to maintaining cooperation and conciliation, and that the UAE's foreign policy has persisted in its 'maintenance of solidarity with the Arab world' despite its location on the periphery.[6]

Some of the UAE's most significant contributions to Arab solidarity has been through economic contributions for development and in support of Palestine. As has already been discussed earlier on, the Trucial States maintained links with Palestine from the 1930s onward. During the 1936–9 Arab Revolt, when Palestinians initiated a sustained strike and rebellion against Zionist immigration and British policies, some individuals collected funds to send in support of Palestinians in Dubai and Sharjah, and Niklas Haller points to evidence in the

---

[4] The idea of the 'Shii Crescent' was coined by King Abdullah II of Jordan to describe a demographic and political unity among Shii populations curving from the Gulf, across Iraq and cutting through the Levant. As to whether this threat is real or perceived, there are debates among policymakers and some scholars. *Hardball with Chris Matthews*, 'King Abdullah II of Jordan', NBC News. 7 December 2004; Cinzia Bianco, 'The GCC Monarchies: Perceptions of the Iranian Threat amid Shifting Geopolitics', *The International Spectator* 55, no. 2 (2020): 92–105; Kevin Mazur, 'The "Shia Crescent" and Arab State Legitimacy', *SAIS Review of International Affairs* 29, no. 2 (2009): 21–2; Joseph A. Kechian, 'The Gulf Cooperation Council: Search for Security', *Third World Quarterly* 7, no. 4 (1985): 853–81.

[5] Ibid.

[6] Peter Hellyer, 'The Evolution of UAE Foreign Policy', in *United Arab Emirates: A New Perspective*, ed. Ibrahim Abed and Peter Hellyer (London: Palgrave Macmillan, 2001), 161–78.

British archives indicating that ongoing discussions and sermons related to Palestine circulated, especially in Dubai and Sharjah.[7]

It is difficult to quantify aid sent from the Trucial States and then UAE in support of Palestinian causes, but there is significant evidence that the UAE has been a consistent financial supporter of Palestinian causes and leaders throughout its history.[8] Foreign aid has come both directly from the UAE to Palestinian leaders and indirectly through international organizations such as the World Bank and the Red Crescent. In 1971, the UAE established the Abu Dhabi Fund for Development (now the Official Development Assistance, or ODA), which funnels significant amounts of aid on an annual basis to a variety of countries, including to the Palestinian Territories. Other sources of support include humanitarian aid to the Red Crescent, the United Nations Relief Works Agency for Palestine Refugees in the Middle East (UNRWA), and to the Palestinian National Authority (PA) depending on UAE relations with Palestinian leadership and the nature of the crisis. William Rugh has observed that the UAE provided annual contributions to the PLO until 1991, when Yasser Arafat supported Iraq's invasion of Kuwait. The UAE continued to provide aid and pledged in 1993 to contribute $25 million dollars over five years, but funneled it through the World Bank, rather than directly to the PA.[9] The UAE ranks as the second largest Arab backer of Palestine between 1994 and 2020, having contributed some $2.1 billion dollars over that period.[10] Other aid contributions have been less transparent. For example, unofficial reports indicate the UAE donated $12 million to Gaza victims in 2015 following Israel's 2014 Operation Protective Edge against Hamas.[11]

Additional funds flow from the UAE to humanitarian organizations from individual charitable contributions by emiratis, which is substantial but difficult to quantify. The UAE also contributes to Palestine through several regional and international funds. These include collective contributions made through the GCC's Arab Gulf Programme for Development (AGFUND). Further financial

---

[7] Niklas Haller, 'A Call for Solidarity: Pro-Palestinian Activity in the Trucial States, 1936–1939', *Journal of Arabian Studies* 11, no. 1 (2021): 18–37.
[8] Khalid S. Almezaini, *The UAE and Foreign Policy: Foreign Aid, Identities, and Interests* (New York, 2012) provides valuable insights into the UAE's foreign aid programmes and aims.
[9] William A. Rugh, 'The Foreign Policy of the United Arab Emirates', *Middle East Journal* 50, no. 1 (1996): 65.
[10] Saudi Arabia is the largest contributor having donated $4 billion; UAE contributions total $2.1 billion. Omar Shaban, 'International Aid to the Palestinians: Between Politicization and Development', *Arab Center Washington, D.C.* 4 August 2022. https://arabcenterdc.org/resource/international-aid-to-the-palestinians-between-politicization-and-development/ (accessed 19 July 2023).
[11] 'UAE Money to Gaza Gives Boost to Former Fatah Leader'. *Associated Press*, 17 June 2015.

support comes from the UAE through contributions to OPEC's Fund for International Development (OFID).

Palestinian refugees and the Palestinian Territories are not the only Arab beneficiaries of the UAE's largesse. The UAE allocates approximately 10 per cent of its GDP in foreign assistance to Arab countries, including Arab states of North Africa. Summary statistics for foreign assistance provided via the UAE's embassy website in 2018 indicates the UAE dispersed $6.5 billion dollars to Arab countries through its development programmes and numerous NGOs and charitable foundations.[12] The role of 'soft power' through economic contributions has been a significant part of the UAE's foreign policy since its inception.

The UAE's shifting orientations

There are signs that the UAE's attitudes towards solidarity building with the Arab world has shifted in the past decade or so. While under Sheikh Zayed's leadership (1971–2004) and to a significant degree under the leadership of his son Khalifah after him, the UAE stayed the course: while expanding and diversifying its global relationships, the nation oriented itself first and foremost towards the Arab world. There have been signs, however, that in the later period of Khalifah's rule, and since the presidency of the UAE passed on to Mohammed bin Zayed Al Nahayan (Abu Dhabi), the guiding principles of UAE foreign policy are shifting in new directions.

The Arab Uprisings of 2011 and the subsequent war in Yemen mark one of the first tangible indicators of a departure from the UAE's orientation in the Arab world. The uprisings began in Tunisia in 2010 and quickly spread through much of the Arab world in the following year. Populations across the region began protesting for constitutional reforms, greater political freedoms and the end of authoritarianism. The leaders of Tunisia, Egypt and Yemen were each removed from office, and in Syria the country sank into an extended civil war. In the Gulf, most of the rulers were able to diffuse popular dissatisfaction, but Bahrain faced significant popular unrest. The UAE, along with the other GCC countries, deployed a combined security force to quell the protests in Bahrain.

---

[12] 'Summary of 2018', *Summary Statistics on UAE's Foreign Assistance*. www.mofa.gov.ae https://www.mofa.gov.ae/en/The-Ministry/UAE-International-Development-Cooperation/Summary-Statistics-on-UAE-Foreign-Policy (accessed 19 July 2023). This summary is the most recent available at the time of this writing and includes funds disbursed from the ODA, but also a variety of other NGOs and charities, such as Sharjah Charity Association, Dubai Charity Foundation, Al Maktoum Foundation, Etihad Airways and the General Women's Union.

The UAE then joined a Saudi-led coalition to intervene in Yemen's civil war. From 2015 until its withdrawal from the conflict in 2020, the UAE contributed an estimated 10,000 troops to the conflict. This was the largest – and longest – military engagement in UAE history and a marked departure from its past reliance on diplomacy and aid. These events also represent the UAE government's changing views of how to engage with other Arab States in the region. While the UAE refused to provide aid to Palestine through Yasser Arafat and to the Iraqi government following the 1991 Iraqi invasion of Kuwait, it did continue to make humanitarian and aid contributions to those two countries. And the UAE until 2011 never deployed troops against another Arab country.

The 2020 announcement of the Abraham Accords provides further evidence that the UAE is undergoing a reorientation of its world view through its foreign policy. On 15 September 2020 the UAE and Israel signed onto the accords, formally initiating normalization between the two countries. They were joined by Bahrain, which signed its own bilateral agreement with Israel on the same day. Sudan, Morrocco and Oman followed suit in October and November of the same year. The UAE has engaged in limited discussions and trade with Israel through back channels in the years preceding the Abraham Accords and has been more open than some of the other Arab countries about informal ties with Israel. Until 2020, however, the UAE had maintained its formal position of not normalizing diplomatic relations with Israel in absence of a peace agreement.

The UAE in recent years has also begun to shift its aid contributions towards other regions, including east Africa and Asia. Whether this reflects a change in the UAE's position within Arab world politics generally and is a sign that the UAE seeks to emphasize its Gulf, Islamic or global identities over its Arab identity remains to be seen. It also remains to be seen whether these shifts, which are government led rather than culturally driven, will have a lasting effect on the way emiratis see themselves in relation to the Arab world.

Bibliography

Primary sources

Arabian Gulf Digital Archive (AGDA)
British Documents on the End of Empire (BDEEP)
Buraimi Dispute, 1950–1961 (*Buraimi Dispute*)
Diaries of a Cabinet Minister, 3 volumes (*Diaries*)
Al-Farad'id min Aqwal Zayid
The Gazetteer of the Persian Gulf, Oman and Central Arabia by J. G. Lorimer (*Gazetteer*)
Hansard Parliamentary Debates
Lyndon Baines Johnson Presidential Library (LBJL)
Middle East Centre Archive (MEC)
The National Archive (TNA)
Papers of Sir William Luce, Special Collections, University of Exeter
Qatar Digital Library (QDL)
Records of the Emirates: 1820–1960 (ROE)
Richard Holmes Collection, Middle East Centre Archive, St. Antony's College, Oxford (MEC)
Treaties and Engagements Relating to Arabia and the Persian Gulf, 1600–1960 (*Arabian Treaties*)

Secondary sources

Al-Abed, Ibrahim. 'The Historical Background and Constitutional Basis to the Federation', in *United Arab Emirates: A New Perspective*, edited by Ibrahim Al-Abed and Peter Hellyer, 121–44. London: Trident Press, 2001.
Al-Abed, Ibrahim and Peter Hellyer, eds. *United Arab Emirates: New Perspectives*. London: Trident Press, 2001.
Abu-Lughod, Janet. *Before European Hegemony: The World System, AD 1250–1350*. London: Oxford University Press, 1989.
Agius, Dionisius. *In the Wake of the Dhow: The Arabian Gulf and Oman*. Reading: Ithaca Press, 1999.
Agius, Dionisius. *Seafaring in the Arabian Gulf and Oman: The People of the Dhow*. London: Routledge, 2005.

Ahmadi, Farajollah. 'Communication and the Consolidation of the British Position in the Persian Gulf, 1860s–1914'. *Journal of Persianate Studies* 10, no. 1 (2017): 73–86.
Ajami, Fouad. 'The End of Pan-Arabism', in *Pan-Arabism and Arab Nationalism: The Continuing Debate*, edited by Tawfic E. Farah, 355–73. New York: Routledge, 1987.
Almezaini, Khalid S. *The UAE and Foreign Policy: Foreign Aid, Identities, and Interests*. New York: Routledge, 2012.
Alsharekh, Alanoud, ed. *The Gulf Family: Kinship Policies and Modernity*. London: Saqi Books, 2007.
Alvandi, Roham. 'Muhammad Reza Pahlavi and the Bahrain Question, 1968–1970'. *British Journal of Middle Eastern Studies* 37, no. 2 (2010): 159–77.
Amirell, Stefan Eklöf. *Pirates of Empire: Colonisation and Maritime Violence in Southeast Asia*. Cambridge: Cambridge University Press, 2019.
Anscombe, Frederick F. *The Ottoman Gulf: The Creation of Kuwait, Saudi Arabia, and Qatar*. New York: Columbia University Press, 1997.
Antonius, George. *The Arab Awakening: The Story of the Arab National Movement*. London: J. B. Lippincott, 1939.
Axtell, James. 'Ethnohistory: An Historian's Viewpoint'. *Ethnohistory* 26, no. 1 (1979): 1–13.
Ayoob, Mohammed. 'American Policy toward the Persian Gulf', in *The International Politics in the Persian Gulf*, edited by Mehran Kamrava, 124–43. Syracuse: Syracuse University Press, 2011.
Balfour-Paul, Glencairn. *Bagpipes in Babylon: A Lifetime in the Arab World and Beyond*. London: I.B. Tauris, 2006.
Balfour-Paul, Glencairn. *The End of Empire in the Middle East: Britain's Relinquishment of Power in HCambridgeer Last Three Arab Dependencies*. Cambridge: Cambridge University Press, 1991.
Barendse, R. J. *The End of Britain's Empire in the Middle East: Britain's Relinquishment of Power in Her Last Three Arab Dependencies*. Cambridge: Cambridge University Press, 1994.
Barendse, Rene J. 'Trade and State in the Arabian Seas: A Survey from the Fifteenth to the Eighteenth Century'. *Journal of World History* 11, no. 2 (2000): 173–225.
Barnwell, Kristi N. 'Overthrowing the Shaykhs: The Trucial States at the Intersection of Anti-imperialism, Arab Nationalism, and Politics, 1952–1966'. *Arab Studies Journal* 24, no. 2 (2016): 72–95.
Batatu, Hanna. *The Old Social Classes and the Revolutionary Movements of Iraq: A Study of Iraq's Old Landed and Commercial Classes and of Its Communists, Ba'thists and Free Officers*. Princeton, NJ: Princeton University Press, 1978.
Bayly, Christopher A. *Imperial Meridian: The British Empire and the World 1780–1830*. New York: Routledge, 1989.
Benjamin, Walter. 'Theses on the Philosophy of History', in *Illuminations: Essays and Reflections from One of the Twentieth Century's Most Original Cultural Critics*, edited by Hannah Arendt, 253–64. New York: Schoken Books, 1968.

Bentley, G. W. 'The Development of the Air Route in the Persian Gulf'. *Journal of the Royal Central Asian Society* 20, no. 2 (1933): 173–89.

Bianco, Cinzia. 'The GCC Monarchies: Perceptions of the Iranian Threat amid Shifting Geopolitics'. *The International Spectator* 55, no. 2 (2020): 92–105.

Bishara, Fahad. 'Circulation and Capitalism in a Maritime Bazaar: Notes from a Pearl Merchant's Chest'. *Law and History Review* 40, no. 3 (2022): 491–3.

Bishara, Fahad. 'The Many Voyages of *Fateh Al-Khayr*: Unfurling the Gulf in the Age of Oceanic History'. *International Journal of Middle East Studies* 52, no. 3 (2020): 397–412.

Bishara, Fahad. *A Sea of Debt: Law and Economic Life in the Western Indian Ocean, 1780–1950*. Cambridge: Cambridge University Press, 2017.

Bishara, Fahad, Bernard Haykel, Steffen Hertog, Clive Holes and James Onley. 'The Economic Transformation of the Gulf', in *The Emergence of the Gulf States*, edited by J. E. Peterson, 187–222. London: Bloomsbury Publishing, 2016.

Blyth, Robert. *The Empire of the Raj: India, Eastern Africa, and the Middle East, 1858–1947*. London: Palgrave Macmillan, 2003.

Bradshaw, Tancred. 'The Dead Hand of the Treasury: The Economic and Social Development of the Trucial States, 1948–1960'. *Middle Eastern Studies* 50, no. 2 (2014): 326–42.

Bradshaw, Tancred. 'The Hand of Glubb: The Origins of the Trucial Oman Scouts, 1948–1956'. *Middle Eastern Studies* 53, no. 4 (2017): 656–72.

Bristol-Rhys, Jane. 'Emirati Historical Narratives', *History and Anthropology* 20, no. 2 (2009): 107–12.

Bristol-Rhys, Jane. *Emirati Women: Generations of Change*. London: C. Hurst Publishers, 2010.

Burrows, Bernard. *Diplomat in a Changing World*. Spennymoor: The Memoir Club, 2001.

Burrows, Bernard. *Footnotes in the Sand: The Gulf in Transition, 1953–1958*. Norwich: Michael Russell Publishing, 1990.

Butt, Gerald. 'Oil and Gas in the UAE', in *United Arab Emirates: A New Perspective*, edited by Ibrahim Abed and Peter Hellyer, 231–48. London: Trident Press, 2001.

Cain, Peter J., and Antony G. Hopkins. *British Imperialism: 1688–2015*, 3rd edn. New York: Routledge, 2016.

Cairncross, Alexander, and Barry Eichengreen. *Sterling in Decline: The Devaluations of 1939, 1949 and 1967*. London: Palgrave Macmillan, 2003.

Campbell, Gwyn. *Abolition and Its Aftermath in Indian Ocean Africa and Asia*. New York: Routledge, 2005.

Campbell, Gwyn, ed. *Bondage and the Environment in the Indian Ocean World*. London: Palgrave Macmillan, 2018.

Carter, Robert. 'The Prehistory and History of Pearling in the Persian Gulf'. *Journal of the Economic and Social History of the Orient* 48, no. 2 (2005): 139–208.

Casey, Michael S. *The History of Kuwait*. Westport, CT: Greenwood Press, 2007.

Castiglioni, Claudia. 'The Relations between Iran and Saudi Arabia in the 1970s'. *Confluences en Méditerranée* 97, no. 2 (2016): 143–53.

Ceylan, Ebubekir. *The Ottoman Origins of Modern Iraq: Political Reform, Modernization, and Development in the Nineteenth-Century Middle East*. London: I.B. Tauris, 2011.

Chaiklin, Martha, Philip Gooding and Gwyn Campbell, eds. *Animal Trade Histories in the Indian Ocean World*. London: Palgrave Macmillan, 2020.

Cleveland, William. *The Making of an Arab Nationalist: Ottomanism and Arabism in the Life and Thought of Sati' al-Husri*. Princeton, NJ: Princeton University Press, 1972.

Cole, Juan. *Colonialism and Revolution in the Middle East: Social and Cultural Origins of Egypt's 'Urabi Movement*. Princeton, NJ: Princeton University Press, 1993.

Collins, Michael. 'A Technocratic Vision of Empire: Lord Montagu and the Origins of British Air Power'. *Journal of Imperial and Commonwealth History* 45, no. 4 (2017): 652–67.

Cordesman, Anthony. *Bahrain, Oman, Qatar, and the UAE: The Challenges of Security*. New York: Routledge, 1997.

Cordesman, Anthony. *The Gulf and the Search for Strategic Stability: Saudi Arabia the Military Balance in the Gulf and Trends in the Arab-Israeli Military Balance*. Boulder, CO: Westview Press, 1984.

Couvreur, P. 'Charles de Visscher and International Justice'. *European Journal of International Law* 11, no. 4 (2000): 905–38.

Cox, Percy. 'Some Excursions in Oman'. *The Geographical Journal* 66, no. 3 (1925): 193–221.

Crystal, Jill. *Kuwait: The Transformation of an Oil State*. New York: Routledge, 1992.

Darby, Phillip. 'Beyond East of Suez'. *International Affairs* 42, no. 4 (1970): 655–69.

Davidson, Christopher. *Abu Dhabi: Oil and Beyond*. London: Oxford University Press, 2009.

Davidson, Christopher. *Dubai: The Vulnerability of Success*. London: Oxford University Press, 2008.

Davies, Charles. *The Blood-Red Arab Flag: An Investigation Into Qasimi Piracy, 1797–1820*. Exeter: University of Exter Press, 1997.

Dawisha, Adeed. *Arab Nationalism in the Twentieth Century: From Triumph to Despair*, 2nd edn. Princeton, NJ: Princeton University Press, 2016.

Devlin, John F. 'The Baath Party: Rise and Metamorphosis'. *The American Historical Review* 96, no. 5 (1991): 1396–407.

Dokrill, Saki. *Britain's Retreat from East of Suez: The Choice between Europe and the World?* Houndmills: Palgrave Macmillan, 2002.

Douglas-Home, Charles. 'A Mistaken Policy in Aden: The Case for Union with the Yemen'. *The Round Table* 58, no. 229 (1968): 221–7.

Dresch, Paul. *A History of Modern Yemen*. Cambridge: Cambridge University Press, 2001.

Ducker, John T. 'Historical and Constitutional Background', in *Without Glory in Arabia: The British Retreat from Aden*, edited by Peter Hinchcliffe, John T. Ducker and Maria Holt, 8–59. London: I.B. Tauris, 2006.

Eames, Edwin, and Parmata Sara, eds. *District Administration in India*. New Delhi: Vikas Publishing House, 1988.

Easter, David. *Britain and the Confrontation with Indonesia, 1960–1966*. London: I.B. Tauris, 2004.

Ehteshami, Anoushiravan et al., eds. *Security and Bilateral Issues between Iran and Its Arab Neighbours*. London: Palgrave Macmillan, 2016.

Ehteshami, Anoushiravan, and Steven Wright, eds. *Reform in the Middle East Oil Monarchies*. Reading: Ithaca Press, 2008.

Al-Fahim, Mohammed. *Rags to Riches: A Story of Abu Dhabi*. London, 1995.

Fain, W. Taylor. *American Ascendance and British Retreat in the Persian Gulf Region*. New York: Palgrave Macmillan, 2008.

Falola, Toyin, and Ann Genova. *The Politics of the Global Oil Industry: An Introduction*. Westport, CT: Greenwood Publishing Group, 2005.

Falola, Toyin, and Matthew Heaton. *A History of Nigeria*. Cambridge: Cambridge University Press, 2008.

Farah, Tawfic E., ed. *Pan-Arabism and Arab Nationalism: The Continuing Debate*. New York: Routledge, 1987.

Ferris, Jesse. 'The Collapse of the Imamate and Foreign Intervention'. *Journal of Arabian Studies* 8, no. 1 (2018): 87–98.

Fowle, Trenchard Craven William. *Travels in the Middle East: Being Impressions by the Way in Turkish Arabia, Syria, and Persia*. New York: E. P. Dutton, 1916.

Fuccaro, Nelida. *Histories of City and State in the Persian Gulf: Manama since 1800*. Cambridge: Cambridge University Press, 2009.

Galpern, Steven. *Money, Oil and Empire in the Middle East: Sterling and Post-War Imperialism, 1944–1971*. Cambridge: Cambridge University Press, 2009.

Gasiorowski, Mark J. *U.S. Foreign Policy and the Shah: Building a Client State in Iran*. Ithaca, NY: Cornell University Press, 1991.

Gordon, Joel. *Nasser's Blessed Movement: Egypt's Free Officers and the July Revolution*. Oxford: Oxford University Press, 1992.

Graf, Rüdiger. 'Making Use of the "Oil Weapon": Western Industrialized Countries and Arab Petropolitics in 1973–74'. *Diplomatic History* 36, no. 1 (2012): 185–208.

Grant, William. *Zambia Then and Now: Colonial Rulers and Their African Successors*. Hoboken, NJ: Wiley Publishing, 2009.

Al-Gurg, Easa Saleh. *The Wells of Memory: An Autobiography*. London: John Murray, 1998.

Haller, Niklas. 'A Call for Solidarity: Pro-Palestinian Activity in the Trucial States, 1936–1939'. *Journal of Arabian Studies* 11, no. 1 (2021): 18–37.

Haller, Niklas. 'Selective Recognition as an Imperial Instrument: Britain and the Trucial States, 1820–1952'. *Journal of Arabian Studies* 8, no. 2 (2018): 275–97.

Halliday, Fred. 'Labour Migration in the Middle East'. *MERIP Reports* 59 (1977): 3–17.

Hamdan, Rashid ᶜAli al-Darᶜaiy. *Zayed: Sirat al-Amjad wa Fakhr al-Ittihad: Qiraᶜa fi al-Watha'iq al-Britaniya wa Wasa'il al-ᶜIlam al-ᶜArabiya wa al-Ajnabiya, 1968–1971*. Al Ain, 2005.

Al-Hamdani, Ali Hasan. *Dawlat al-Amirat al-ᶜArabiyya: Nisha'ituha wa Tatawuruha*. Kuwait: Maktaba al-Maᶜala, 1986.

Al-Hammadi, Muna M. *Britain and the Administration of the Trucial States, 1947–1965*. Abu Dhabi: Emirates Center for Strategic Studies and Research, 2013.

Hannig, Hugh. 'Britain East of Suez Facts and Figures'. *International Affairs* 42, no. 4 (1966): 253–60.

Harvey, Jack L. 'The 1973 Oil Crisis: One Generation and Counting'. *Federal Reserve Bank of Chicago*. October 1994.

Hay, Rupert. 'The Impact of the Oil Industry on the Persian Gulf Shaykhdoms'. *Middle East Journal* 9, no. 4 (1955): 361–72.

Hay, Rupert. *The Persian Gulf States*. Washington, DC: The Middle East Institute, 1959.

Heard-Bey, Frauke. *From Trucial States to United Arab Emirates: A Society in Transition*. Dubai: Motivate Publishing, 2004.

Hellyer, Peter. 'The Evolution of UAE Foreign Policy', in *United Arab Emirates: A new Perspective*, edited by Ibrahim Abed and Peter Hellyer, 161–17. London: Palgrave Macmillan, 2001.

Henderson, Edward. *This Strange Eventful History: Memoirs of Earlier Days in the UAE and Oman*. London: Quartet Books, 1988.

Hightower, Victoria Penizer. 'Pearling and Political Power in the Trucial States, 1850–1930: Debts, Taxes, and Politics'. *Journal of Arabian Studies* 3, no. 2 (2013): 215–31.

Hightower, Victoria Penizer. 'Pearls and the Southern Persian/Arabian Gulf: A Lesson in Sustainability'. *Environmental History* 18, no. 1 (2013): 44–59.

Hinchcliffe, Peter, John T. Ducker and Maria Holt. *Without Glory in Arabia: The British Retreat from Aden*. London: I.B. Tauris, 2006.

Hopper, Matthew S. *Slaves of One Master: Globalization and Slavery in Arabia in the Age of Empire*. New Haven, CT: Yale University Press, 2015.

Hughes, Matthew. 'The Central African Federation, Katanga, and the Congo Crisis, 1958–65'. *European Studies Research Institute, University of Salford: Working Papers in Military and International History*, no. 2, 2003.

Hunt, Roland. *The District Officer in India, 1930–1947*. London: Scholar Press, 1980.

Issawi, Charles. 'The 1973 Oil Crisis and After'. *Journal of Post Kenesian Economics* 1, no. 2 (1978–9): 3–26.

Johns, Andrew L. 'The Johnson Administration, the Shah of Iran and the Changing Pattern of US-Iranian Relations, 1965–1967: "Tired of Being Treated Like a Schoolboy"'. *Journal of Cold War Studies* 9, no. 2 (2007): 64–94.

Jones, Marc Owen, Ross Porter and Marc Valeri, eds. *Gulfization of the Arab World*. Berlin: Gerlach Press, 2018.

Jones, Stephanie. 'British India Steamers and the Trade of the Persian Gulf, 1862–1914'. *The Great Circle* 7, no. 1 (1985): 23–44.

Kamrava, Mehran, ed. *The International Politics of the Persian Gulf*. Syracuse: Syracuse University Press, 2011.

Kavalski, Emilian, and Magdalena Zoldos, eds. *Defunct Federalisms: Critical Perspectives on Federal Failure*. New York: Routledge, 2008.

Kazim, Aqil. *United Arab Emirates: A Socio-Discursive Transformation in the Arab Gulf*. Dubai: Gulf Book Centre, 2000.

Kechian, Joseph A. 'The Gulf Cooperation Council: Search for Security'. *Third World Quarterly* 7, no. 4 (1985): 853–81.

Keddie, Nikki R. *Modern Iran: Roots and Results of Revolution*. New Haven, CT: Yale University Press, 2003.

Kelly, John B. *Arabia, the Gulf and the West: A Critical View of the Arabs and Their Oil Policy*. New York: Weidenfield & Nicholson, 1980.

Kelly, John B. *Britain and the Persian Gulf, 1795–1880*. Oxford: Oxford University Press, 1968.

Kelly, John B. *Eastern Arabian Frontiers*. New York: Basic Books, 1964.

Kerr, Malcolm. *The Arab Cold War: Gamal 'Abd al-Nasir and His Rivals, 1958–1970*, 3rd edn. Oxford: Oxford University Press, 1971.

Khalili, Laleh. *Sinews of War and Trade: Shipping and Capitalism in the Arabian Peninsula*. New York: Verso Books, 2020.

Khour, Zaka H. *The History of Aden, 1839–1872*. London: Frank Cass, 1981.

Krozewski, Gerold. *Money and the End of Empire: British International Economic Policy and the Colonies, 1947–1958*. London: Palgrave Macmillan, 2001.

Kyle, Keith. *Suez: Britain's End of Empire in the Middle East*, reprint edn. New York: I.B. Tauris, 2011.

Lorimer, John G. *Gazetteer of the Persian Gulf: Oman and Central Arabia*. Calcutta: Superintendent Government Printing, 1908–15.

Louis, Williamm Roger. 'The British Withdrawal from the Gulf, 1967–71'. *Journal of Imperial and Commonwealth History* 31, no. 1 (2003): 83–108.

Louis, William. Roger. *The Ends of British Imperialism: The Scramble for Empire, Suez and Decolonization*. New York: I.B. Tauris, 2005.

Louis, William Roger, and James A. Bill, eds. *Musaddiq, Iranian Nationalism, and Oil*. New York: I.B. Tauris, 1988.

Maclean, Matthew. 'Spatial Transformations and the Emergence of "The National": Infrastructures and the Formation of the United Arab Emirates, 1950–1980'. PhD diss., New York University, 2017.

Maitra, Jayanti, and Afra al-Hajji. *Qasr al Hosn: The History of the Rulers of Abu Dhabi, 1793–1966*. Abu Dhabi: The Centre for Documentation and Research, 2004.

Al-Maktoum, Mohammed bin Rashid. *My Story*. Dubai: Explorer Group, 2019.

Matthee, Rudi. 'Boom and Bust: The Port of Basra in the Sixteenth and Seventeenth Centuries', in *The Persian Gulf in History*, edited by Lawrence Potter, 105–28. London: Macmillan, 2009.

Matthews, Chris. 'King Abdullah II of Jordan', in *Hardball with Chris Matthews. NBC News*, 7 December 2004.

Mawby, Spencer. *British Policy in Aden and the Protectorates, 1955–1967: Last Outpost of a Middle East Empire*. London: Routledge, 2005.

Mawby, Spencer. 'The Clandestine Defence of Empire: British Special Operation in Yemen, 1951–1964'. *Intelligence and National Security* 17, no. 3 (2002): 105–30.

Mawby, Spencer. *The Transformation and Decline of the British Empire: Decolonisation after the First World War*. New York: Bloomsbury Academic, 2015.

May, Samantha. 'Political Piety: The Politicization of Zakat'. *Middle East Critique* 22, no. 2 (2013): 149–64.

Mazur, Kevin. 'The "Shia Crescent" and Arab State Legitimacy'. *SAIS Review of International Affairs* 29, no. 2 (2009): 21–2.

McNamara, Robert. *Britain, Nasser and the Balance of Power in the Middle East, 1952–1967: From the Egyptian Revolution to the Six-Day War*. London: Frank Cass, 2003.

Meirs, Suzanne. 'Slavery and the Slave Trade in Saudi Arabia and the Arab States of the Persian Gulf, 1921–1963', in *Abolition and Its Aftermath in Indian Ocean Africa and Asia*, edited by Gwyn Campbell, 120–36. New York: Routledge, 2005.

Meyer, Armin. *Quiet Diplomacy: From Cairo to Toyko in the Twilight of Imperialism*. Bloomington: iUniverse, 2003.

Mirzai, Behnaz A. 'The 1848 Abolitionist Farmaan: A Step towards Ending the Slave Trade in Iran', in *Abolition and Its Aftermath in Indian Ocean Africa and Asia*, edited by Gwyn Campbell, 94–102. New York: Routledge, 2005.

Mobley, Richard A. 'The Tunbs and Abu Musa Islands: Britain's Perspective'. *Middle East Journal* 57, no. 4 (2003): 627–45.

Morton, Michael Quentin. *Buraimi: The Struggle for Power, Influence, and Oil in Arabia*. New York: I.B. Tauris, 2013.

Morton, Michael Quentin. 'Calypso in the Arabian Gulf: Jacques Cousteau's Undersea Survey of 1954'. *Liwa* 7, no. 13 (2015): 3–28.

Morton, Michael Quentin. *Keepers of the Golden Shore: A History of the United Arab Emirates*. London: Reaktion Books, 2016.

Morton, Michael Quentin. 'Narrowing the Gulf: Anglo-American Relations and Arabian Oil, 1928–1974'. *Liwa* 3, no. 6 (2011): 39–54.

Mueller, Chelsi. 'The Persian Gulf, 1919–39: Changes, Challenges, and Transitions', *Journal of Arabian Studies* 8, no. 2 (2018): 259–74.

Mufti, Malik. *Sovereign Creations: Pan-Arabism and Political Order*. Ithaca: Cornell University Press, 1996.

Nafaa, Hassan. 'Arab Nationalism: A response to Ajami's Thesis on the "End of Pan-Arabism"', in *Pan-Arabism and Arab Nationalism: The Continuing Debate*, edited by Tawfic E. Farah, 133–51. New York: Routledge, 1987.

Nakhleh, Emile. *Bahrain: Political Development in a Modernizing Society*, 2nd edn. New York: Lexington Books, 2011.

Nakib, Farah. *Kuwait Transformed: A History of Oil and Urban Life*. Stanford: Stanford University Press, 2016.

Onley, James. *The Arabian Frontier of the British Raj: Merchants, Rulers, and the British in the Nineteenth-Century Gulf*. Oxford: Oxford University Press, 2008.

Onley, James. 'Transnational Merchant Families in the Nineteenth- and Twentieth-Century Gulf', in *The Gulf Family: Kinship Policies and Modernity*, edited by Alanoud Alsharekh, 37–56. London: Saqi Books, 2007.

Onley, James. 'Transnational Merchants in the Nineteenth-Century Gulf: The Case of the Safar Family', in *Transnational Connections and the Arab Gulf*, edited by Madawi al-Rasheed, 37–56. New York, Routledge, 2004.

Paget, Julian. *Last Post, Aden, 1964–67*. London: Faber & Faber, 1969.

Perham, Margery. 'Reflections on the Nigerian Civil War'. *International Affairs* 47, no. 2 (1970): 231–46.

Petersen, John E. 'Britain and the Gulf', in *The Persian Gulf in History*, edited by Lawrence Potter, 277–94. London: Palgrave Macmillan, 2009.

Petersen, John E. 'Sovereignty and Boundaries in the Gulf States: Settling the Peripheries', in *The International Politics of the Persian Gulf*, edited by Mehran Kamrava, 21–49. Syracuse: Syracuse University Press, 2011.

Petersen, Tore T. 'Anglo-American Rivalry in the Middle East: The Struggle for the Buraimi Oasis, 1952–1957'. *The International History Review* 14, no. 1 (1992): 71–91.

Petersen, Tore T. *The Middle East between Great Powers: Anglo-American Conflict and Cooperation, 1952–7*. London: Palgrave Macmillan, 2000.

Potter, Lawrence G., ed. *The Persian Gulf in History*. London: Palgrave Macmillan, 2009.

Potts, Daniel T. 'The Archaeology and Early History of the Persian Gulf', in *The Persian Gulf in History*, edited by Lawrence G. Potter, 27–56. London: Palgrave Macmillan, 2009.

Power, Timothy, Nasser al-Jahwari, Peter Sheehan and Kristian Strutt. 'First Preliminary Report on the Buraimi Oasis Landscape Archaeology Project'. *Proceedings of the Seminar for Arabian Studies* 45 (2015): 233–53.

Power, Timothy, and Peter Sheehan. 'The Origin and Development of the Oasis Landscape of al-'Ain (UAE)'. *Proceedings of the Seminar for Arabian Studies* 42 (2012): 291–308.

Al Qasimi, Sultan ibn Muhammad. *Sard al-That*. Sharjah: Al Qasimi Publications, 2009.

Rabi, Uzi. 'Oil Politics and Tribal Rulers in Eastern Arabia: The Reign of Shakhbut (1928–1966)'. *British Journal of Middle Eastern Studies* 33, no. 1 (2006): 37–50.

Al-Rasheed, Madawi. *A History of Saudi Arabia*. Cambridge: Cambridge University Press, 2011.

Reid, Anthony. *Imperial Alchemy: Nationalism and Political Identity in Southeast Asia*. New York: Cambridge University Press, 2010.

Reilly, Benjamin J. 'A Well-Intentioned Failure: British Anti-slavery Measures and the Arabian Peninsula, 1820–1940'. *Journal of Arabian Studies* 5, no. 2 (2015): 91–115.

Rogan, Eugene. *The Fall of the Ottomans: The Great War in the Middle East.* New York: Basic Books, 2015.

Rogers, Joshua. 'Importing the Revolution: Institutional Change and the Egyptian Presence in Yemen, 1962–1967', in *Gulfization of the Arab World*, edited by Marc Owen Jones, Ross Porter and Marc Valeri, 113–33. Berlin, 2018.

Rugh, William A. 'The Foreign Policy of the United Arab Emirates'. *Middle East Journal* 50, no. 1 (1996): 57–70.

Said-Zahlan, Rosemarie. *Origins of the United Arab Emirates: A Political and Social History of the Trucial States*. New York: Routledge, 1978.

Satia, Priya. *Spies in Arabia: The Great War and the Cultural Foundations of Britain's Covert Empire in the Middle East*. New York: Oxford University Press, 2008.

Sato, Shohei. *Britain and the Formation of the Gulf States: Embers of Empire*. Manchester: Manchester University Press, 2016.

Sato, Shohei. 'Britain's Decision to Withdraw from the Persian Gulf, 1964–68: A Pattern and a Puzzle'. *Journal of Imperial and Commonwealth History* 37, no. 1 (2009): 99–117.

Al-Saud, Faisal bin Salman. *Iran, Saudi Arabia, and the Gulf: Power Politics in Transition*. London: I.B. Tauris, 2003.

Schenk, Catherine. 'Sterling International Monetary Reform and Britain's Applications to Join the European Economic Community in the 1960s', *Contemporary European History* xi, no. 3 (2002): 345–69.

Schofield, Richard, ed. *Territorial Foundations of the Gulf States*, 94–108. New York: Routledge, 1994.

Scott, James C. *Against the Grain: A Deep History of the Earliest States*. New Haven, CT: Yale University Press, 2017.

Scott, James C. *The Art of Not Being Governed: An Anarchist History of Upland Southeast Asia*. New Haven, CT: Yale University Press, 2009.

Selwyn, Ryan D. *Eric Williams: The Myth and the Man*. Kingston, Jamaica: University of the West Indies Press, 2009.

Shaban, Omar. 'International Aid to the Palestinians: Between Politicization and Development'. *Arab Center Washington, D.C.*, 4 August 2022.

El Shakry, Omnia, ed. *Understanding and Teaching the Modern Middle East*. Madison, WI: University of Wisconsin Press, 2020.

Simon, Reeva Spector. 'The View from Baghdad', in *The Creation of Iraq: 1914–1921*, edited by Reeva Spector Simon and Eleanor H. Tejirian, 36–49. New York: Columbia University Press, 2004.

Simon, Reeva Spector, and Eleanor H. Tejirian, eds. *The Creation of Iraq: 1914–1921*. New York: Columbia University Press, 2004.

Sirrs, Owen L. *A History of the Egyptian Intelligence Service: A History of the Mukhabarat, 1910–2009*. New York: Routledge, 2010.

Sives, Amanda. 'Dwelling Separately: The Federation of the West Indies and the Challenge of Insularity', in *Defunct Federalisms: Critical Perspectives on Federal Failure*, edited by Emilian Kavalski and Magdalena Zoldos, 18–30. Farnham, UK: Ashgate Publishing, 2008.

Smith, Simon C. 'The Anglo-American "Special Relationship" and the Middle East, 1945–1973'. *Asian Affairs* 45, no. 3 (2014): 425–48.

Smith, Simon C. *Britain's Revival and Fall in the Gulf: Kuwait, Bahrain, Qatar, and the Trucial States, 1950–71*. New York: Routledge, 2004.

Smith, Simon C. *Ending Empire in the Middle East: Britain, the United States and Post-war Decolonization, 1945–1973*. New York: Routledge, 2012.

Smith, Simon C. 'South Arabia and the Yemeni Revolution'. *International Diplomacy and Colonial Retreat* 28, no. 3 (2000): 193–208.

Stanley-Price, Nicholas. *Imperial Outpost in the Gulf: The Airfield at Sharjah, 1932–1952*. Brighton, UK: Book Guild Publishing, 2012.

Stoler, Ann Laura. *Along the Archival Grain: Epistemic Anxieties and Colonial Common Sense*. Princeton, NJ: Princeton University Press, 2010.

Taryam, Abdullah O. *The Establishment of the United Arab Emirates*. London: Croom and Helm, 1987.

Thesiger, Wilfred. 'Desert Borderlands of Oman', *The Geographical Journal* 116, nos. 4–6 (1950): 137–68.

Townsend, Peter. *Proconsul to the Middle East: Sir Percy Cox and the End of Empire*. London: I.B. Tauris, 2010.

Troeller, Gary. *The Birth of Saudi Arabia: Britain and the Rise of the House of Sa'ud*. London: Routledge, 2013 (a reprint edition of a 1976 version).

Ulrichson, Kristian Coates. *The First World War in the Middle East*. London: C. Hurst, 2014.

Vitalis, Robert. *America's Kingdom: Mythmaking on the Saudi Oil Frontier*. Stanford, CA: Stanford University Press, 2007.

Von Bismarck, Helene. *British Policy in the Persian Gulf, 1961–1968: Conceptions of Informal Empire*. London: Palgrave Macmillan, 2013.

Walcot, Colonel Tom. 'The Trucial Oman Scouts, 1955 to 1971: An Overview'. *Asian Affairs* 37, no. 1 (2006): 17–30.

Walker, Jonathan. *Aden Insurgency: The Savage War in Yemen, 1962–67*. Staplehurst, UK: Spellmount, 2005.

Walker, Julian. 'Practical Problems of Boundary Delimitation in Arabia: The Case of the United Arab Emirates', in *Territorial Foundations of the Gulf States*, edited by Richard Schofield, 109–17. New York: Routledge, 1994.

Walker, Julian. *Tyro on the Trucial Coast*. Durham, UK: The Memoir Club, 1991.

Webster, Anthony. *Twilight of the East India Company: The Evolution of Anglo-Asian Commerce and Politics, 1790–1860*. London: Boydell & Brewer, 2009.

Wein, Peter. 'Preface: Relocating Arab Nationalism'. *International Journal of Middle East Studies* 43, no. 2 (2011): 203–4.

Weiss, Rush. *Sir Garfield and the Making of Zimbabwe*. London: British Academic Press, 1999.

Wheatcroft, Andrew. *With United Strength: H.H. Shaikh Zayid bin Sultan al-Nahyan, the Leader and the Nation*. Abu Dhabi: Emirates Center for Strategic Studies and Research, 2004.

Wilkinson, John Craven. *Arabia's Frontiers: The Story of Britain's Boundary Drawing in the Desert*. New York: St. Martin's Press, 1991.

Wilkinson, John Craven. 'Britain's Rôle in Boundary Drawing in Arabia: A Synopsis', in *Territorial Foundations of the Gulf States*, edited by Richard Schofield, 94–108. New York: St. Martin's Press, 1994.

Witty, David M. 'A Regular Army in Counterinsurgency Operations: Egypt in North Yemen, 1962–1967'. *The Journal of Military History* 55, no. 2 (2001): 401–39.

Wright, Steven M. 'Iran's Relations with Bahrain', in *Security and Bilateral Issues between Iran and its Arab Neighbours*, edited by Anoushiravan Ehteshami et al., 61–80. London: Palgrave Macmillan, 2016.

Wright, Steven M. 'US Foreign Policy and the Changed Definition of Gulf Security', in *Reform in the Middle East Oil Monarchies*, edited by Anoushiraven Esteshami and Steven Wright, 229–46. Reading: Ithaca Press, 2008.

Yates, Athol. *The Evolution of the Armed Forces of the United Arab Emirates*. Warwick: Helion, 2020.

Yergin, Daniel. *The Prize: The Epic Quest for Oil, Money and Power*. New York: Free Press, 2008.

Yetiv, Steve A. *The Absence of Grand Strategy: The United States in the Persian Gulf, 1972–2005*. Baltimore, MD: Johns Hopkins University Press, 2008.

Zdanowski, Jerzy. 'The Manumission Movement in the Gulf in the First Half of the Twentieth Century'. *Middle Eastern Studies* 47, no. 6 (2011): 863–83.

Ziegler, Philip. *Wilson: The Authorised Life*. London: Weidenfeld & Nicolson, 1993.

Index

Abbas I (Safavid Shah) 16
Abdullah al-Salem (neighbourhood in Kuwait City) 110
Abdullah bin Julawi (Al Saud) 77, 83
Abdullah bin Rashid (Al Mualla) 19
Abdullah Salim 88
Abraham Accords 180
Abu Dhabi Defence Force 123
Abu Dhabi Fund for Development 178
Abu Dhabi Marine Areas, Ltd. (ADMA) 122
Abu Dhabi Petroleum Company 166
Abu Musa 168, 170
Aden 25, 53, 113, 116, 137–9, 156, 158–60, 163
    Aden Legislative Council 126
    Aden Protectorate Levies 93, 120, 125
    Aden/Yemen civil war 104
    crisis in 124–30
Africa 3, 13, 34, 63, 75, 103, 132, 179, 180
Ain al-Dhawahir 76. *See also* Al Ain
air-route to India 36–40
Al Ain. *See* United Arab Emirates
Alexandria 105
Allied Powers 25
Anglo-Arabian Treaty 76 n.12
Anglo-Iranian Oil Company (AIOC) 41, 124, 163
Anglo-Persian Oil Company (APOC) 41–3
Anglo-Trucial 24
anti-imperialism 2, 10, 103, 105, 130
Arab Gulf 2 n.2, 9, 51, 54, 57, 107, 141, 142, 155–7, 177
Arabian American Oil Company (ARAMCO) 72, 80, 96–7, 163, 167, 172
Arabian Coast 14, 15, 19, 33–4, 38, 66
Arabian Federation 137
Arabian Peninsula 4, 13, 15, 18, 27, 41, 97, 130
Arabian Sea 13 n.2, 18

Arab-Israeli war (1967) 6
Arab League 56, 116, 117–18, 123
Arab nationalism, 1956–1967 103–30
    Baathism 5
    crisis in Aden 124–30
    foreign influence 113–24
    the Gulf 104–9
    Nasserism 5, 6, 103–5, 116
    nationalism 113–24
    pan-Arabism 5–6
    reactive development 109–13
    Suez crisis 104–9 (*see also* Suez)
Arab Palestinians 47
Arab Revolt (1936–9) 177
Arab Revolt (June 1916) 26
Arab solidarity 177–9
Arab Uprisings of 2011 179
Arafat, Yasser 180
Arbitration Agreement 99
Arthur, Geoffrey 58
Asia 3, 13, 23, 180
Australia 42, 133, 136, 163
Awamir (Al Amri) tribe 18
Azzam, Dr. Abdul Rahman 99

Baghdad 22, 25, 25 n.33, 47
Baghdad Pact 163
Bahrain 4, 6, 12, 15, 17–20, 22–3, 37, 43–8, 52–4, 57, 67, 76, 85, 107, 109–10, 115, 119–21, 123, 138, 142, 144, 147, 149–51, 154–5, 157, 160, 164–5, 167–8, 170–1
Balfour Declaration 27
Balfour-Paul, Glencairn 58, 119–20
Bandar Abbas 14, 16–17, 24
Bani Kaab 87–8, 92
Bani Qitab 75, 77
Bani Yas (tribal confederation) 17–18, 75, 87
Batinah Coast 13, 74–5
Belgrave, Charles 46, 110
Biscoe, Hugh 39

Black Sea 25
Blue Line (Saudi Boundary dispute) 66, 80
Board of Trade 137
Bombay Government 19–20, 124
Bombay Marine 17
Bombay Office 24
borders, drawing 65–70
Boustead, Hugh 58
British Air Force 38
British/Egyptian war 104
British Empire 2, 4, 9, 11, 21, 29, 37, 40, 51, 53, 104, 124–5, 132–3
British Labour Ministry 108
British Locust Control Squad 59
British Mandates 27
British Residency 30, 43–4, 46, 52–7, 67, 89, 105, 122, 130, 158
British Royal Navy 105
Bullard, Julian 58, 159–61
Bullard, Sir Reader 98–9
Buraimi 18, 30, 33, 45, 63, 68
Buraimi Dispute 71–101, 166
Buraimi Oasis 11, 69, 71–101. *See also* Hamasa, under Oman
  arbitration 96–101
  arrival and blockade 82–9
  confrontation 96–101
  denouement 96–101
  poverty in 89–95
  precursors 78–82
  villages at 73–8
Burrows, Bernard 56–8, 61, 65, 68, 90–7, 99, 107–8, 112, 116, 130
Bushehr 17, 20, 24–5
  Residency 17, 53, 110

Central African Federation 140
Central Treaty Organization (CENTO) 163, 164
Cold War 163
Colonial Office 24 n.29, 52, 54–5, 124, 126, 140
Compagnie Française des Indes Orientales 16
Concession Syndicate 42
Conservative Macmillan 133–5, 137, 164
cooperation 62–5
Cox, Percy (Acting Political Resident, Persian Gulf) 26, 74, 74 n.7, 74 n.9, 77 n.15, 78

Acting Political Resident 25
  expedition in Abu Dhabi 113
  Political Agent and consul in Oman 25
Craig, James 58
Crawford, Stewart 58, 161
Crossman, Richard 136 n.18
Ctesiphon 25
Curzon, George (Viceroy of India) 24–5

Damascus 27, 101
D'Arcy, William Knox 42
D'Arcy Concession 42
Das Island, Persian Gulf 13
Dean, Sir Patrick 164
Dhafrah 83, 85
Dhak 86
Dhawhir (Dhahiri) tribe 18
Dibba 39
dispute 46, 65, 68
  between the Al Nahayan and Al Bu Shamis 76
  at Buraimi 71–101, 166
  diplomatic side of 81
  internal 30
  between the sheikhdoms 20
  succession and fratricide 30
  territorial/boundary 67, 142, 153, 157, 166–8, 170
  tribal 44
Douglas-Home, Alec 124, 150, 170
Douglas-Home, Charles 124
Dubai, United Arab Emirates
  Dubai Agreement, February 1968 142–8
  Dubai Creek 68, 91, 95
Dutch East India Company (VOC) 16

East India Company (EIC) 4, 16–17, 19–21
  Charter Act of 1833 23
  diplomatic and military arms of 24
  role in India 23
economic crises 36, 136, 138, 164
economic decline 2, 29, 33–6
Eden, Anthony 57, 98
Egypt 5, 26, 26 n.36, 48, 103–9, 115–16, 121, 124–8, 130, 134, 175, 179
  Cairo 26, 38, 47, 101, 107, 110, 143
Egyptian Republic 106
Egypt-Israel war (1973) 173, 175

Eid al-Adha 71
Eisenhower, Dwight 163–4
Emir of Hasa 83
Empty Quarter 66, 67. *See also* Rub al-Khali
England 37, 41, 95, 146
  London 10, 23–5, 37–8, 85–6, 133, 155
Europe 14, 16, 41, 135, 164
  declaration of war in June 1914 25
  encroachment in 22
  expansion of 15–21
Exclusive Agreement of 1892 42

Al-Fahidi fort 68
Fain, W. Taylor 170
Faisal bin Turki Al Said (Sultan of Muscat and Oman) 25, 75
Al Bu Falasah of Dubai 17
Far East 139, 163
  Britain's air route to India and the 29
Faisal of Saudi Arabia 147, 154, 162, 166, 167. *See also* Al Saud
federation of the Trucial States 131–51, 175–7
  Britain's decision to abandon the Gulf 132–9
  Dubai Agreement, February 1968 142–8
  role of 139–42
  Union of Nine 148–51
first Saudi emirate 22, 75
First World War 15, 25, 27, 37, 41, 42, 65, 78, 105, 163. *See also* Second World War
Foreign Office 51, 52–7, 86, 90, 131, 137, 141
Fowle, Trenchard 44, 47, 48, 78
France 2, 42
Frere, Sir Henry Bargle 37
Fujairah 13, 39, 44 n.38, 60, 67–9, 112, 118, 119, 145, 158

Gazetteer 18 n.10, 32–3, 35, 68
General Maritime Treaty of 1820 19
General Strike 1936 47
Geneva 98–9
Georges-Picot, François 27
Ghana 133–4
Golan Heights 175

Great Britain 2, 4, 26 n.36, 33, 36, 42, 80, 88–92, 94, 98, 100, 105, 127–8, 131–43, 147, 149, 166, 168, 171
  administration on the Trucial Coast 23–7
  affairs concerned with India 51
  control over the Gulf and Arab 27
  decision to abandon the Gulf 55, 100, 132–9, 153, 172 (*see also* East of Suez)
  declaring Egypt independent 106
  diplomatic and military intervention 106
  entrée to oil exploration and extraction 42
  failed policy in Aden 124
  geo-strategic plans 124
  imperial twilight 71
  India Office 7
  invasion of the Suez 134
  landing at the Shatt al-Arab 26
  military presence in the Arab Gulf 155–7
  1928 Red Line agreement 43
  occupying small peninsula of Aden 124
  presence in the Gulf 21, 27, 54
  primacy in the Gulf 53
  protectorate over the Trucial Coast 100
  role in Palestine 47
  sea power 16
  search for oil in the Middle East 41
  trade and political power 17
the Gulf 2 n.2, 3, 42
  air-route to India through 36–40
  Arab nationalism 104–9
  expansion of 15–21
  map of 14
  Persian 13, 16, 18 n.10, 19, 21, 24, 25, 29, 33, 55, 62, 103, 123, 128, 138, 139–40
Gulf Cooperation Council (GCC) 176–9
  Arab Gulf Programme for Development (AGFUND) 178
Gulf Residency Office 17
al-Gurgh, Easa Salah 117, 120

Al Hajar 73
Hamasa. *See* Buraimi Dispute; Oman
al-Hamdani, Ali Hasan 21

Hamza Line (Saudi Boundary dispute) 43, 79–80, 85. *See also* Red Line (Saudi Boundary dispute)
Hasa 18, 22, 23, 77, 83
Hashemite monarchy 115
al-Hashimi, Husayn bin Ali (Grand Sherif of the Hijaz) 26–7, 26 n.36
Hawley, Donald 58, 109, 158–9
Hay, Rupert 53, 56, 57, 58, 59 n.14
Healey, Denis 129, 138
Heath, Edward 146–7
Hijaz 23, 26, 27
Hormuz, Straits of 15–16
Hoveyda, Amir Abbas 19

Ibb 66–7
ikramiyah 88 n.54
imperial forces 157–62
imperialism
  British 55, 116
  colonization and 41
  Western 5
India 4, 13, 15, 18, 23, 26, 33, 133
  Bombay 25, 35
  Calcutta 22
  Khozikode (Calicut) 14
Indian Army 25
Indian Empire 36
Indian Ocean 2, 3–7, 15–16, 21
Indian Uprising of 1857 24
India Office 7, 21, 24, 24 n.29, 26–7, 52–7
India Steam Navigation Company 37
International Petro Asmari Co (IPAC) 172
Iran 12–13, 56, 122, 132, 148–50, 153–5, 162–72, 176
  Abadan 124
  anti-British sentiment in 27
  1952 nationalization crisis in 124
Iraq 11, 16, 22, 23, 42, 48, 78, 103, 105, 133–4, 144, 163, 172
  Basra 14, 16–17, 22, 24–5, 33, 37–8
  Kirkuk 25
Iraq Petroleum Company (IPC) 43, 78

Jabal Hafit 73, 74
Jeddah 80, 88, 94
Joasem (Joasemi). *See* Al Qawasim

Johnson, Lyndon 136, 139, 169, 170
Jordan 103, 105, 121, 123
Juffair 53

al-Kaabi, Obaid bin Juma 92, 99
Kelly, J. B. 4
Kendall, Bryan 117–18
Kerr, Malcolm 5
Al Khalifah (ruling family of Bahrain) 4, 167
  Abdullah bin Ahmed 19
  Isa bin Salman 147–51, 160
  Khalifah bin Salman 149
  Suleiman bin Ahmed 19
al-Khandaq 75
Khor al-Udayd 79, 80, 100
Kitchener, Herbert 26 n.36
Kung 16
Kut 25
Kuwait 14, 43, 44, 47, 57, 109, 110
Kuwait Oil Company 44

Lamb, Albert (Archie) 58, 122–3
Lawrence, T. E. 26–7
League of Nations 27
Little Aden 125, 129, 138
Liwa 18, 63, 77, 78, 81, 84, 85, 93
local forces 157–62
Longrigg, Stephen 44–5
Lorimer, J. G. 18 n.10, 34, 35 n.10, 36, 68, 76 n.12
Luce, Sir William 8, 58, 116, 118, 122, 126, 148, 149, 151

MacArthur, Douglas, II 170
majlis 1, 46–7, 177
Makins, Sir Roger 56, 90
Makran 74
Al Maktoum (Ruling family of Dubai)
  Maktoum bin Butti (founder of the Al Maktoum) 17
  Mohammed bin Rashid 143, 143 n.41, 144–6
  Rashid bin Said 121, 143
  Said bin Maktoum 44, 46, 67–8
al-Maktoum Hospital 112
Malaya 133–4, 140
Man, Morgan 159

Manama, Bahrain 4, 108, 110, 155–6
Manasir (Mansouri) tribe 18, 83, 85
Mandates, French 27
Mandatory Palestine 47
Maqta 82
Masaid 93
Mazari (Mazrui) tribe 18
McMahon, Sir Henry 26
Mediterranean 25
mercantile
  companies 16
  empires 15
  mission 24
  networks 18
Mesopotamia 26, 37
Middle East 1, 2, 3–7, 26, 27, 41, 43, 56, 103, 125, 163
Middleton, George 58, 121
Midhat Pasha 22–3
Mikimoto, Kokichi 36
Ministry of Defence 128
Mossadeg, Mohammed 27, 163
Mosul 25
Mozambique 14
Mozzafar al-Din (Persian Shah) 42
Al Mualla, Abdullah bin Rashid 19
Muhammad al-Badr (son of Ahmed bin Yahya) 127
Muhammad bin Hamad. *See* Al Sharqi, Muhammad bin Hamad
Muhammad ibn Abd al-Wahhab 22
Muhammad Ibn Mansour (Saudi official) 88–9
Al Murrah 79, 83
Musandam Peninsula 39
Muscat 14, 16, 63, 85. *See also* Oman; Sultanate of Muscat and Oman
Mutatas mutandas 48
al-Muwaijih 78 n.17

Nady al-Ahaly al-Watany (Club for the National Peoples) 114
Nady al-Bahri (the Marine Club) 114
Nady al-Itihaad (the Union Club) 114
Al Nahyan (ruling family of Abu Dhabi) 76, 78, 122
  Hamdan bin Zayed 30, 76, 77
  Hazza bin Sultan 30, 80, 81, 84, 99
  Khalifah bin Zayed 30

Mohammed bin Zayed 179
  Saqr bin Zayed 30, 31, 74 n.9, 77
  Shakhbut (I) bin Diyab 19
  Shakhbut (II) bin Sultan 6, 30, 31, 40, 44, 59, 61, 67, 77, 109, 111–12, 116, 118, 122
  Sultan (II) bin Zayed 30, 31, 84
  Tahnoun bin Zayed 20, 30, 31, 76, 77
  Zayed (I) bin Khalifah (Zayed the Great) 30, 31, 74, 76, 82, 87, 95, 109, 144, 145, 150, 154, 155, 166, 179
  Zayed (II) bin Sultan 1, 100, 122–3, 143
Naimi (Nuaimi) 75, 76
Nasser, Gamal Abdul 103, 106–7, 126–7, 173
nationalism, Arab 113–24
National Legislative Council 45
National Liberation Front (NLF) 127, 138
Nigeria 133–4, 140
Nile River 106
Nixon, Richard 98, 170
Nixon Doctrine 171
North Atlantic Treaty Organization (NATO) 164
Al Nuaimi (ruling family of Ajman) 84, 86
  Rashid bin Humaid (III) 109, 112, 143, 157, 158–60
  Saqr bin Sultan 87, 90, 93, 98

oil concessions 40–9, 78
oil exploration 163
oil producing state 132–3
oil production 113 n.27
Oman 11, 13, 17–20, 65, 71, 74, 75, 81, 85, 87, 89, 156
  Hamasa 71, 73–5, 84–7, 89–90, 92, 94, 98–100 (*see also* Buraimi Dispute; Buraimi Oasis)
Omani Coast 14, 17, 76, 82
Omani Empire 14
Sultanate of Muscat and 55 n.4, 56 n.5, 60 n.18, 60 n.20, 62 n.28–9, 67 n.44
Omani Yarubids 73
OPEC's Fund for International Development (OFID) 179
Operation Bonaparte 99

Organization of Arab Petroleum Exporting Countries (OAPEC) 176, 176 n.2
al-Otaishan, Turki bin Abdullah (emir of Ras Tanura) 71, 86, 87, 88, 90, 93, 98. *See also* Buraimi Dispute
Ottoman Empire 2, 5, 22, 25, 26, 85, 125
defeat of the Al Saud in 1818 by 22
Ottomans 16, 21–3, 26 n.36, 76–8
Tanzimat 6
Overseas Development Committee 141

Pahlavi dynasty (Iran) 176
Muhammad Reza 162
Reza 38
Palestine 6, 15, 26, 27, 47, 48, 177–8, 180
Palestinian National Authority (PNA) 178
pearl diving/pearling 17, 34
boat/ships/vessels 35, 63, 74
collapse of 29, 33, 77, 89
communities 18
cultured pearl 36
enslaved labour(ers) 34, 63–4, 74–5
fisheries 36
fleet 30, 45
Great Dive 34
industry 29, 35, 36, 36 n.13, 89
Nakhuda 34, 35 n.10
operations 3
seasons 17, 20
trade 74
truces 19
Perpetual Treaty (1853) 20–1
Persia 3, 15, 18, 22, 38, 41, 42, 63
Persian Gulf Squadron (SNOP-G) 155
Petroleum Concessions Ltd. 43–4
Pirie-Gordon, Christopher (C. M.) 58, 61, 66, 92
Political Agents 25, 46, 58, 61–2, 65–8, 74–5, 81, 94, 108–9, 118, 120–2, 145, 150
Political Residency 69, 86, 116
Political Residents 10, 20–1, 24–6, 29, 39, 42, 48–9, 51–3, 57, 58, 78, 83, 87, 90, 103, 108, 112, 121, 142, 146, 148, 157
Portugal (Portuguese Empire)
collapse of trade 15
position in the Gulf 15
Protectorate Treaties of 1892 21

Al Qasimi 18
Al Qasimi (of Kalba)
Hamad bin Said 60
Said bin Hamad 40
Al Qasimi (ruling family of Ras Al Khaimah)
Hassan bin Rahma 19
Humaid bin Abdullah 31, 32
Ibrahim bin Sultan 32
Salim bin Sultan 31, 32
Saqr bin Muhammad 32, 60, 61, 67, 115–17, 168, 171
Saqr bin Sultan bin Salim (attempted ruler of Kalba) 60
Sultan bin Salim 31, 60
Al Qasimi (ruling family of Sharjah)
Khalid (bin Mohammad III) 142–3, 147
Khalid bin Ahmed 32
Khalid bin Sultan 32
Saqr bin Khalid 31–2
Saqr bin Sultan 60–1, 68, 118, 119, 130
Sultan bin Muhammad 108
Sultan bin Saqr (I) 19, 20
Sultan bin Saqr (III) 32, 39–40, 60
Qasr al-Hosn 120, 122
Qatar 6, 8, 12, 17, 18, 22, 23, 30, 35, 44, 65–6, 79–81, 100, 108, 110, 129, 142, 144–6, 148–51, 161, 164, 167, 176
Doha 81, 108, 119
Qatif 23, 34
Qawasim (Sharjah) 18, 19. *See also* Al Qasimi
Qishm Island 18, 24
Qubaisat 18, 97

Ras al-Jufair at Manama, Bahrain 155
Rashid bin Humaid 19, 118, 121
Rashid ibn Hamad of Hamasa 86
reactive development 109–13
Red Crescent 178
Red Line (Saudi Boundary dispute) 43, 79–80, 85. *See also* Hamza Line (Saudi Boundary dispute)
Red Sea 16, 18
Riyadh Line (Saudi Boundary dispute) 80
Roberts, David 58

Roberts, Goronwy 129
Rockefeller, J. D. 41
Rothschilds of England 41
Royal Air Force 39, 87
Royal Dutch Petroleum Company 41
Royal Navy 37
Rub al-Khali 66, 79, 80
Rumaithat 18
Russia 2, 22
Ruweihah, battle at 67
Ryan Line (Saudi Boundary dispute) 85

Al Sabah (ruling family of Kuwait) 134
Al Sabah, Ahmad al-Jabir 47
Safavid Empire 15, 16
al-Samih 143
Al Saud (ruling family of Saudi Arabia) 22, 77, 83
   Abdulaziz bin Abdul Rahman ('Ibn Saud') 9, 83, 84, 96
   Abdulaziz bin Muhammad 82
   Abdullah bin Faisal bin Turki 75
   Abdullah bin Julawi 77, 83
   Faisal bin Abdulaziz 85, 100, 118
   Faisal bin Turki (emir of Nejd) 23
   Saudi Arabia 11–12, 13–15, 21–3, 34, 43, 60, 64–6, 68, 70, 75, 79–80, 84–6, 89–91, 100, 107, 118, 127, 142, 148–9, 153–6, 162–3, 165–7, 170, 172, 176, 178 n.10
Saudi Boundary dispute
   Blue Line 66
   Hamza/Red Line 43, 79–80, 85
   Riyadh Line 80
   Ryan Line 85
   Violet Line 66, 85
Saudi Frontiers 78
Scottish Rifles 25
Second World War 44, 48, 67, 74, 110. *See also* First World War
security 153–73
   British military presence in the Arab Gulf 155–7
   local and imperial forces 157–62
   'twin pillars' strategy 162–73
Al Bu Shamis 76, 84, 86
Al Sharqi, Muhammad bin Hamad (ruler of Fujairah) 60, 67–8, 118, 142
Shatt al-Arab 25, 26

Sheikh Uthman 129, 138
'Shell' Oil Company. *See* Royal Dutch Petroleum Company
Shihuh (Al Shehhi) 39
Sinai Desert 106
Sinai Peninsula 175
slavery 75, 100
   domestic 59, 63–4
   enslaved people 63–4, 74–5
   enslavers 63, 75
   maritime slave trade 63
   unfree labour 3
Sloop of War, Coote (ship) 20
Somali Coast 25
South Arabia 66, 124–9, 138, 140, 147
South Arabian Federation 129, 138
South Asia 13
Standard Oil Company (SOCAL) 41, 43, 44
Standstill Agreement 88
sterling area 132–4
Stobart, Patrick 80
Strait of Hormuz, map of 169
al-Subarah 75
Sudan 123
Suez
   Canal 37, 105–6, 130, 147
   Canal Company 105–6
   crisis 4, 104–9
Sultanate 13
Sultan of Oman 75, 76
Sykes, Mark 27
Syria 23, 27, 103, 105, 121
   Greater Syria 5

Tanzimat 22
Al Thani, Khalifah bin Hamad 150
Al Thani, Ahmad (bin Ali) 145–6, 148–9
Thesiger, Wilfred 78, 78 n.17
Thompson, Thomas (Captain) 19, 24
Thwaites, Otto 93
Townsend, John 25, 74 n.7
Treadwell, C. J. 58, 150, 161
Treaty of Jeddah (1927) 27
Tripp, J. P. (Peter) 55, 58, 61, 62, 65, 115
Trucial Coast 2–4, 8, 17, 20, 21–3, 24, 33, 39, 41, 44
   Britain's air route to India and the Far East 29

population growth in 114
presence of British administration on the 23-7
Trucial Oman Levies (TOL) 71-2, 87-8, 92, 94, 98, 99, 156
Trucial Oman Scouts (TOS) 108, 154, 160, 161
Trucial sheikhs 20-1, 32, 39, 76, 140, 153-5, 165
Trucial States 2, 6, 7, 9, 15, 21-2, 23, 33, 40, 43, 44, 51, 52, 56, 110
  Council 52, 57-65, 67, 94, 115, 117, 122, 123, 131, 161
  Development Office 117-18
  map of internal boundaries of 69
Tunbs Islands 168, 170
Turkish Petroleum Company (TPC) 43
'twin pillars' strategy 162-73

Union Defence Force (UDF) 154
Union of Nine 148-51
United Arab Emirates (UAE) 32, 51-2, 65, 100, 177-9
  Abu Dhabi 1, 8, 13, 17, 18, 18 n.10, 21, 29-31, 34-6, 40, 42-4, 46, 62, 67, 69, 71, 73-4, 76-90, 92-3, 95-7, 100, 109-14, 116, 118-23, 130, 133, 141-4-146, 149-50, 154-9, 166-7, 178
  Ajman 13, 21, 31, 42, 44, 44 n.38, 59, 118, 119, 141, 158
  Al Ain 1, 33, 73, 76, 78 n.17, 87, 95, 99, 110-11, 123
  Dubai 6, 13, 17, 21, 30, 35, 37, 40, 42, 44, 46, 47, 60, 62-4, 67-9, 76-7, 86, 90-1, 95, 107-9, 112-13, 115, 117-19, 122, 130, 157-9, 170, 177-8
  Kalba 31, 40, 44, 67

Khor Fakkan 31
Ras Al Khaimah 13, 18, 19, 21, 29, 31, 33, 38, 42, 59, 60, 67, 109, 114, 115, 117, 119, 141
Sharjah 10, 13, 21, 29, 30, 31, 33, 42, 44, 58 n.13, 60, 85, 113
shifting orientations 179-80
Umm Al Quwain 13, 21, 31, 42, 44, 44 n.38, 59, 68, 118, 119, 158
United Arab Republic (UAR) 126
United Nations 100, 149, 168, 178
United Nations Relief Works Agency for Palestine Refugees (UNRWA) 178
United States 12, 41-2, 78, 81, 97, 106, 136, 153, 160, 162-6, 170-3, 175-7
US State Department 168

Violet Line (Saudi Boundary dispute) 66, 85
Voice of the Arabs 107, 125, 143

Walker, Julian 58, 66
Weightman, Hugh 46
Weir, Michael 58, 59, 64
Willoughby, John 160
Wilson, David (Captain) 20
Wilson, Edward 'Tug' 122
Wilson, Harold 12, 128, 131, 133, 136, 138, 139, 143, 165
Witty, David 125
Worsnop, E. R. 58
Wright, Sir Denis 171

Yasin, Yusuf 98
Yemen 104, 107, 114, 120, 125-7, 129, 135, 138, 147, 159, 179-80

zakat 83-4, 88 n.54, 89
Zanzibar 14

www.ingramcontent.com/pod-product-compliance
Lightning Source LLC
Chambersburg PA
CBHW052116300426
44116CB00010B/1687